THE FIELD HOSPITAL THAT NEVER WAS

Diary of Lt. Col. Karl D. Macmillan's, MD, 96th Field Hospital in China-India-Burma Theater 1945, WWII

Ruth Clifford Engs, Editor

ISBN: 978-1-63490-456-8

Printed on acid-free paper.

Published by Magic Farm, Bloomington, IN
magicfarmimprint@gmail.com

Library of Congress Cataloguing in Publication Data

The Field Hospital that never was: Diary of Lt. Col. Karl D. Macmillan's, MD, 96th Field Hospital in China-India-Burma Theater 1945, WWII / edited by Ruth Clifford Engs
  xvii 257 p. ill. 23 cm
    Includes bibliographical references and index.
1. World War II. 2. HISTORY—Military—World War II. 3. World War, 1939-1945 —Personal narratives, American. 4. World War II—biographies. United States. 5. Army—Medical personnel—Biography. 6. Medical personnel—United States- Correspondence. 7. United States. Army Medical Corps—Biography. 8. Physicians—personal narratives. 9. World War, 1939-1945--China. 10. World War, 1939-1945—Burma. 11. World War, 1939-1945—India. I. Engs, Ruth C. (Ruth Clifford), editor

Library of Congress Control Number: 2015939863

2015

First Edition

Dedication

This book is dedicated to the members of the 96th Field Hospital who served in the WWII China-Burma-Indian (CBI) Theater, 1945, and their descendants.

Table of Contents

Foreword

While volumes have been written of the Second World War, the China-Burma-India (CBI) Theater is often referred to as the "Forgotten War." Officially opened in March of 1942, the Allies fought not only the Japanese but unrelenting mountainous jungle terrain and often intolerable weather conditions in their effort to establish and maintain a supply line through Burma (now Myanmar) to China. Eventually and at great human cost the Japanese were pushed out of Burma in late 1944 and a continuous flow of supplies and equipment made its way over the Burma and Ledo Roads.

The U.S. Army's 96th Field Hospital organized in October 1944 under the command of Lt Col Karl D. MacMillan, MC (Medical Corps) an ophthalmologist, began an epic thirteen month journey from Camp Barkeley, Texas travelling by ship and rail and ultimately driving in a convoy the entire length of that critical supply route arriving in Shanghai, China two months after the war's end.

In any military operation, leadership challenges ebb and flow inversely to the intensity of the unit's engagement. While focused on pre-deployment training or later during the execution of the mission, an organization will display good cohesiveness and a sense of purpose minimizing personnel issues. However, when those best laid plans begin to unravel and the goals are not so obvious, morale suffers and leadership is put to the test.

Every bit a community on the move, the 96th not only had to contend with terrain, weather and bands of Chinese bandits, but unsanitary environmental conditions, malaria carrying mosquitoes and with young soldiers, the ever present threat of accidental injury and sexually transmitted diseases (STD's). Reaching far beyond his training as an ophthalmologist and the typical responsibilities of a commanding officer, Colonel MacMillan assumed the role of "public health officer" to ensure such basics as functional latrines, safe water and clean food preparation as well as effective personal hygiene and preventive health educational programs were part of the plan of the day.

Colonel MacMillan's diary, written in a style reflecting his attention to detail and interest in anthropology, photography, geography and other scientific disciplines captures the essence of both the physical difficulty of the journey and his daily leadership challenges as the 96th Field Hospital's carefully formulated and eagerly anticipated mission to establish a field hospital near Kunming, China begins to fall by the muddy roadside while its ranks are depleted in providing relief personnel to war-weary units along the route. The commander himself eventually accepts the painful reality and like most soldiers his private thoughts turned evermore toward home and family. A captivating collection of personal impressions and observations, the diary provides a unique insight into the man and the many challenges he faced.

Howard F. Rundell, Jr.
Captain USN (Ret)

Preface

Background Information

For a number of years when I visited my maternal uncle, Karl D. MacMillan, I often suggested that he write his memoirs of World War II and his experiences as an ophthalmologist and Commanding Officer of the 96th Field Hospital in the China-Burma-India (CBI) Theater. He told stories about going up, and then down, 24 switch backs on a steep Chinese road because his convoy took the wrong turn. Other tales concerned Chinese bandits, poor sanitation, and diseases among the troops. Another story was the "flip of the coin" with a friend and colleague. This was to see who would receive a pair of Chinese cloisonné vases offered them by a Chinese friend. They didn't want to split the pair, so they tossed a coin and he won.

A few of years before his death in 1994, when I visited him and again asked him about writing his war diary, he said, "Wait here," and went into his study. I heard him rummaging around and he soon came back with a packet wrapped in large yellowed brown paper. He handed the bundle to me and said, "You write it, as you are the author and historian in the family."

I opened the packet and found a carbon copy of 171 type-written pages of a daily diary he had written during 1945. He had sent this material to his parents in Pittsburgh, PA in the form of hand-written letters. The letters had been typed with a carbon copy by his mother, Mary Louise. Unfortunately, the original letters are not available. Of course, without the original correspondence, errors could have crept in during the first transcription process from handwriting to typewriter. I digitized the diary into MSWord from this carbon copy. Errors could also have occurred during this keyboarding process. A scan of the first page is found on the page previous to page 1. Due to wartime censorship, he was not allowed to mention the ship's name (*USS General W. A. Mann*) in his early correspondence. Sailing dates were not allowed thus the hand written notes on the bottom of the first page in the scan. In several cases dates and days in the diary sometimes did not match the 1945 calendar; these are noted with a [*sic, actual date*].

Although a few historical diaries and publications of the CBI Theater have been written, most have been from the 1942-1944 period. In 1945 the tides of war turned against the Japanese although the United States military and its allies were preparing to invade the Japanese home islands in the fall of 1945. However, the Japanese surrendered September 2, 1945 after American forces had dropped an atomic bomb both on Hiroshima and Nagasaki. Macmillan's field hospital had likely been sent to China in anticipation of this invasion and the hundreds of thousands potential war related casualties.

The journal is from the last year of the war and little military action was seen along his route of travel. The mission of the field hospital was to take care of the sick and wounded. However, he notes public health and sanitation issues and is forced to become a "public health officer" by demanding measures to prevent diseases among the personnel with whom he traveled.

The diary begins with MacMillan's deployment across the Pacific on February 7, 1945 and his experiences on this troopship to India. It continues with travel by train and then vehicle convoy through Burma and into China over the treacherous Ledo-Burma Road. The journal describes him leading his convoy through mud, monsoons, sweltering heat, and the battle against disease, unsanitary conditions, and local bandits. It details additional travels to some other towns and cities as well as flying "over the Hump."

In the latter part of the journal, he discusses his frustration and the confusion as to where the 96th Field Hospital was even to be located. Repeatedly his men and materiel were taken and assigned to other units which frustrated him greatly. He considered his unit the "kicked around field hospital." The journal ends as MacMillan is waiting for the liberty ship *USS Hocking*, November 13, 1945, in Shanghai to take him back to United States.

Macmillan was an intellectual who had a wide variety of interests and was knowledgeable about many subjects. He was an amateur physical anthropologist and was able to describe facial features of various tribal groups and populations encountered in his trip across Northern India and over the Ledo Road. He was also an amateur geologist and took interest in the terrain across the route. Some levity in the book comes from his detailed descriptions of meals eaten at restaurants, while on convoy, in addition to shopping for exotic East Asian goods.

He was an amateur photographer but photos of his ventures in the CBI have not been located. A snapshot of him in uniform found among family photographs is on the book's cover. MacMillan's only child, Donald A. MacMillan, has kindly given permission to publish the correspondence which forms the diary. Other images, illustrations and maps are used by permission or have been taken from public domain sources.

Editorial information and caveats

The journal has been arbitrarily divided into ten chapters at natural break points, e.g. leaving Assam, India to travel over the Ledo-Burma Road to Wanting, China on the way to Kunming, China.

To give the historical significance of something mentioned in his diary, I have added information in *italics* as part of the body of the manuscript or as endnotes. The complete reference, including United States Governmental and public domain websites when available are found in the Bibliography. Further Reading is also included.

I have done little editing of the diary. MacMillan uses upper case for towns and rivers and upper case and underline for the day of the week. These conventions have been kept. Any item not clear on the original transcription, typed from hand-written correspondence to his parents, or which I could not verify by a reference source, I have placed a [*?*].

When I found military abbreviations or items that were not clear, I put an explanation or clarification in brackets and *italicized* it the first time it was encountered. These abbreviations are also located in Appendix A.

MacMillan generally uses the last name and most of the time the ranks of individuals, not only in the 96th Field Hospital, but also those he meets in his travels. A list of all persons he has encountered and the unit they were assigned to is found in Appendix B. Appendix C includes all units he encountered.

Within his diary, if an individual is mentioned who had been reprimanded by MacMillan or had done something illegal, such as getting into a knife fight, a pseudonym replaces the actual name. The pseudonyms, generally begin in successive order from the first to the last chapter, and were formed as follows: *XXX1, XXX2, XXX3,* etc. If *XXX1*, for example, had been mentioned in an uncompromising light in a previous chapter, the same pseudonym is used again.

The spellings of towns in the CBI Theater were sometimes changed in the post-World War II era. The names of towns as he has written them and their modern transliterations, the first time they appear, are put in brackets and *italicized*. The spelling of names of individuals MacMillan met in his travels is often different. This was likely due to the difficulty of reading the original hand-written letters. If there are inconsistencies, these are noted in the list of individuals in Appendix B and also in the body of the diary.

Throughout the diary there are inconsistencies in the writing of terms. For example, "General Quarters" is sometimes spelled out and sometimes abbreviated as "Gen. Quarters." Times are sometimes written in 24 hour time such as 1300 and in other cases 1:30. Field hospital is sometimes written "Field Hospital" and sometimes "F. H." To keep the flavor of the work, these inconsistencies have been left as written. For typesetting needs, "-" have been turned into "— ." In addition, the World War II era abbreviations for rank are kept as written by MacMillan such as Lt. Col. which is now abbreviated as LTC. Appendix D contains a biographical time line of MacMillan.

The reader needs to be aware that some terms acceptable and in common use during the World War II era, are generally not used today or are considered offensive. Some examples include: "Colored boys" (African-American enlisted personnel), "Holy Roller" (evangelical religious), "Chinks" (Chinese) and "Japs" (Imperial Japanese military personnel).

Purpose of the book

In researching secondary sources of the CBI Theater, I found it to be an almost forgotten theater of the war. Supplies were often short and it was not considered as important in the war against Imperial Japan as the Pacific Theater. The 96th Field Hospital, which was sent to the CBI Theater late in the war, was never fully established inasmuch as the war had ended by the time the convoy had arrived at its destination and was unneeded. The military literature and websites for hospitals in the CBI are almost silent about the 96th Field Hospital; it has essentially become lost to history. Thus, the purpose of this book is to give light to the personal diary of an Army Reserve Physician who responded to the call for duty to his country and to bring some recognition to the 96th Field Hospital in the CBI Theater.

When I received the diary, I was at the peak of my academic career. Therefore, I put his packet on the top shelf of "to do projects" to work on at a later time in my life. That time has now come.

Ruth Clifford Engs

April 2015

Acknowledgment

I would like to thank the staff of several Indiana University (Bloomington) library departments. Librarians in the Government Publication division were very helpful in locating maps and finding public domain references. The library's Digital Laboratory personnel assisted in scanning images as did Bradley Cook, Curator of Photographs, Office of University Archives & Records Management. Copyright Program librarian, Nazareth A. Pantaloni, III, was most helpful in verifying public domain images. I would like to thank Jian Liu, head librarian, School of Public Health, Indiana University, Bloomington, who clarified modern transliteration of Chinese place names and also reviewed the manuscript and made needed comments.

Captain Howard Rundell (USNR, Ret.) read the manuscript, and in particular Chapter 1, concerning naval operations on a troopship. I appreciate his comments that clarified many items and also for writing the Foreword. I also would like to thank LTC Raymond A. Hrinko, History Department, US Military Academy, West Point, NY for permission to use a map held by his department and Marc E. Levitt, National Naval Aviation Museum, Pensacola, FL for the photograph of a P-40 aircraft.

I am indebted to Donald A. MacMillan, only child of Karl Macmillan, for permission to publish the correspondence which forms the diary.

Finally, this book could not have been written without the patience, understanding and space given to me by my husband, Jeffrey Franz, for that exciting, but lonely, task of researching and writing many academic books and articles over the past three decades.

Prolog

John W. Mountcastle, former Chief of Military History of the United States, suggests that, "World War II was the largest and most violent armed conflict in the history of mankind." However, the fifty [*now 70 years*] that now separates us from that conflict has exacted its toll on our collective knowledge. While World War II continues to absorb the interest of military scholars and historians, as well as its veterans, a generation of Americans has grown to maturity largely unaware of the political, social, and military implications of a war that, more than any other, united us as a people with a common purpose." [1]

Part of that war was the China-Burma-India (CBI) Theater. During the war, the primary concern of American military leaders in China and northern Burma was the development of an effective Chinese fighting force and to keep them in the war against Japan. However, overwhelming problems of disease and malnutrition among the millions in the China-Burma-India Theater along with internal conflict within China made this a difficult mission to accomplish. [2]

The CBI Theater command realized that sanitation and environmental conditions were deplorable. In order to keep American and Chinese troops healthy, mobile units such as field hospitals, in addition to treating war casualties needed to pay attention to public health measures—called sanitation at that time—as part of the Army Medical Service mission. [3]

Throughout MacMillan's diary, he mentions preventive measures to keep his, and nearby units, healthy. The troops took daily doses of Atabrine and used mosquito nets or "bars" to prevent malaria infections. Plague, cholera, and typhoid fever were endemic throughout the area, thus the medical unit gave immunizations against these diseases to the troops and Chinese military personnel who worked with them. Sexually transmitted diseases were rampant among local women and the American troops with whom they consorted.

Education on how to prevent these diseases and treatment with sulfonamides were introduced. [4]

Tropical diseases including scrub typhus, schistosomiasis, cholera, and amebic dysentery, never seen by most of the American Army physicians, affected most units in the theater. These diseases were often difficult to prevent or treat. Waste disposal, personal hygiene and sanitation was lacking among the local populations leading to serious diarrheal diseases.[5] Drinking water had to be boiled and it was an ongoing struggle to find and maintain clean latrines, reduce disease carrying insects, and to prevent vehicle accidents on the rough Ledo-Burma, Burma, and other roads. These were the conditions encountered by Macmillan and the 96th field hospital in the CBI as they traveled to establish their hospital in China.

ENDNOTE

---

[1] John W. Mountcastle in *Central Burma. The US Army Campaign of World War II,* ed. George L. MacGarrigle (U.S. Army Center of Military History, 1996), 1-2.

[2] *Ibid.*; Kirk T. Mosley and Darrell G. McPherson, "Chapter XVII: China-Burma-India Theater," in *Army Medical Service. Preventive Medicine in World War II* (Office of the Surgeon General, Department of the Army, 1976), 633.

[3] *Ibid.*; Mary Ellen Condon-Roll, and Albert E. Cowdrey. *The Medical Department: Medical Service in the War against Japan* (Center of Military History, United States Army, 1998), 45-46.

[4] *Ibid.*

[5] *Ibid.*

TUESDAY, FEBRUARY 7, 1945

All men had chalk numbers on their helmets, taken from passenger list. The morning on which we were to embark was clear and sunshiny, with the usual morning haze. The morning was spent cleaning and policing the area around our barracks and orderly rooms, and in cleaning up our quarters. A preliminary inspection at 11:00 revealed the usual things left behind, such as paper, empty hair tonic bottles, etc.

The remaining men who were on details, such as K. P., etc. had returned. Pads were rolled, and the equipment put outside.

The Officers, as usual, were the last to finish up, but all were present at 1330 at the orderly room. Lt. Cole, the inspecting Officer came at 1400, found a few things out of order, including a large box of 3 pairs of civilian, low quarter shoes in it. The Lord knows where they came from. The box wasn't there when I inspected the place at 1100. He was quite satisfied and was generous enough to say that he found our area to be perfect, anyhow, there weren't bushels of stuff to be cated out, as had been the case with our rival organization.

At 1430, the men were fallen in, the Roll called. I made a little speech, starting out with "This is it!", which produced a laugh.

"The "This is it" stems in part from a Regulation "must" film, TROOP SHIP, in which one character gets panic stricken on the General Quarters alarm, and jumps out of his bunk to run away saying, "This is it!"

Left Camp Barkeley, Texas, on (date, time) to San Francisco.

96ª Field Hospital — Lt. Col. Karl D. MacMillan
O 262311

Chapter 1: Across the Pacific to India: On the USS General W. A. Mann

The diary begins with the assembly of the unit getting ready to board a ship to India. The field hospital, along with other units, such as the 95th Field Hospital, left Camp Barkeley *for Camp Anza, CA, January 27, 1945, a staging area for pre-deployment across the Pacific.*[1]

During World War II, Camp Barkeley, *Texas, was a large United States Army training installation located eleven miles southwest of Abilene. The base had several training missions including the Medical Administrative Officer Candidate School that had been established in May 1942.*

At Camp Barkeley, *the 96th Field Hospital was established October 6, 1944. Lt. Col. Karl D. MacMillan was assigned to Camp Barkeley, on December 11, 1944, for medical administrator training. He was made commanding officer of the 96th Field Hospital.*

TUESDAY, FEBRUARY 7[*sic, actually 6th*] 1945

All men had chalk numbers on their helmets, taken from passenger list. The morning on which we were to embark was clear and sunshiny, with the usual morning haze. The morning was spent cleaning and policing the area around the barracks and orderly rooms, and in cleaning up our quarters. A preliminary inspection at 11:00 revealed the usual things left behind, such as paper, empty hair tonic bottles, etc.

The remaining men who were on details, such as K. P.[*Kitchen Patrol*], etc. had returned. Pads were rolled, and the equipment put outside.

The Officers, as usual, were the last to finish up, but all were present at 1330 at the orderly room. Lt. Cole, the inspecting Officer came at 1400, found a few things out of order, including a large box of three pairs of civilian, low quarter shoes in it. The Lord knows where they came from. The box wasn't there when I inspected the place at 1100. He was quite satisfied and was generous enough to say that he found our area to be perfect, anyhow, there weren't bushels of stuff to be carried out, as had been the case with our rival organization.

> *This rival organization was likely the 95th Field Hospital. Both traveled and interacted at convoy camps in the C-B-I theater, over the Ledo Road, in China and finally in Shanghai and home.*

At 1430, the men were fallen in, the roll called. I made a little speech, starting out with "This is it!" which produced a laugh.

The "This is it" stems in part from a regulation "must" film, TROOP SHIP, in which one character gets panic stricken at the General Quarters alarm, and jumps out of his bunk to run away saying, "This is it!"

Due to roll call, and forming on the street, instead of the Co. [*company*] Street, which was blocked by a truck and a ditch just dug, we started out late.

The nurses were taken by truck to the assembly area, and Sgt. Brojac, who had a severe reaction from his last inoculation, was taken to the train by a staff Corp. along with his equipment. We arrived at the assembly area, were joined by the nurses, and marched off, with the rest of the shipment, to the train which was awaiting us.

We filed to our cars without a hitch and were off at 1505. We sat in Maritime coaches—excursion type cars, with two and three seat benches, and were soon off to LA.

The journey from LA to the POB [*Planned Operating Base*] was marked by our engine hitting a truck loaded with cylinders of roofing paper. The train was proceeding slowly, then it came to a grinding stop. No one thought much of it, until someone looked out of the window and shouted, "We hit a truck!" Sure enough the truck was on its side, and the load spilled on both sides of the truck. We were delayed half an hour while the train backed a few feet to clear the truck. It was righted and pushed off the track, not greatly damage. The flatlands near the coast were dotted with isolated forests of oil derricks. There certainly is a lot of oil here.

Soon the train pulled to the dock area and was batted at the pier house. We had caught a glimpse of our ship just before we pulled in. We detrained in our car groups. The Red Cross handed out its coffee and sandwiches—we ate sparingly—if we had known then, that we were to get no supper we would have eaten a lot more.

Soon the men went aboard, Car F, first, then two, etc., calling out their first name and initial when their last name was read off the passenger list. Last aboard, over another gangplank, went the officers, followed by the nurses. Each nurse, as she went up the gang plank, was met by cheers from the O & M (and Naval personnel) lined up along the ships rails. Lamber and I followed. They gave us a slight cheer with lots of boos. Didn't like us too close to the nurses, I guess. Oh, yes, just before all our men were aboard and I was standing with the O & M [*Officers and Men*], a Naval Doctor came up to me and introduced himself as Dr. Carnsworth [*Cornwath in rest of diary*], Sr., Ship*'s* surgeon and asked me if I was Sr. Medical Officer of the troops. That rather set me back, as I had given it no thought at all. I said, "I suppose I must be. I don't know of anyone who outranks me." I just hadn't thought of that before. He must have gotten my name from the passenger list. He wanted me to see him later that evening and talk things over.

Well, there went any thought of a lazy voyage. Now I was saddled with the health and illnesses and sea sicknesses of the 5000 troops aboard. Some job. Once aboard, I was shown to my state room, 102, where I found my Val-pac [*duffle bag*], which had preceded me. Most of the bunks were taken. I got a lower one, about 6 inches off the floor and started to make myself at home.

We soon discovered that we were too late for supper, so we reconciled ourselves to that fact, and the fact that we would only have two meals a day.

At 2000 Lt. Col. McNair, the ship transportation officer, called a meeting of all the cabin passengers. What a group, not enough chairs and seats for all of us. Army officers, nurses, some Naval Med. O. who were passengers, ARC [*American Red Cross*] men and girls, OSS [*Office of Strategic Services*] men and civilian girls, all traveling together. After this meeting, I went to see Dr. Cornwath in sick bay, which is a nice, clean, place. He told me what was needed, telling me that there was a fore and aft battle dressing station, where sick call was to be held and giving me numerous instructions, as well as a list of O and EM, who needed additional shots, syphilis treatment and treatment for pediculosis [*lice*] as well.

WEDNESDAY, FEBRUARY 8 [*sic, actually 7th*], 1945

The next morning we were still in dock. I had Capt. Hogan working on a duty O. D. [*Officer of the Day*] roster, saw Dr. Cornwath again and met Capt. Lenert, a MO [*Medical Officer*] familiar with insects and their control, who was to be Sanitary watch officer.

At about 1100, while talking to Col. McNair in his cabin, noticed that we were gradually getting underway and had a couple of tugs pushing us. Soon we were out in the harbor and soon under our own steam. We steamed W for quite a while, paralleling that section of the Cal. [*California*] coast and later towed [*sic; turned*] 180° right back to the harbor for a while, and then set out in a SW direction. We noticed that at this time that the gun crews of the pompoms and 5" guns were getting ready for action.

> *These guns universally known as the "pom-poms" due to the sound it made where fired, the QF-2 pounder or "quick firing" gun, was a 40-millimeter (1.6 in) anti-aircraft auto cannon. It was primarily used by the British but also on some US Naval ships.[2]*

Soon an airplane with a tow target appeared, and soon the flak began. It was really ear shattering. It was quite lively for a while and the shooting was quite accurate. The tracers looked like red-hot ping pong balls, sailing through the air with a white trail of smoke behind them. Later we were sent below deck at which time they fired the 5" guns. They really made a great noise and gave us quite a thrill. All that evening we watched the coast and the 10 Islands fadeout. "Old Baldy" of the San Bernardino range showed its whitehead over the low-flying mist for miles.

Later in the day I went below deck to see how the troops were getting along. Some were not quite so good — in fact, quite a lot were seasick, despite the perfect sea, the heads [*toilets*] were really in a mess.

The ship was darkened, no passenger allowed out on deck, and all lights but the battle lights—dim, red bulbs—were extinguished by a master switch. That evening we had a song-fest in the lounge. Everyone singing and Lorenz playing the piano.

THURSDAY, FEBRUARY 8, 1945

It was rather cool this morning and overcast. The field jacket felt good out on deck. The dispensary system, two men in each battle dressing station, with 12 EM in each one, taking turns—4 hours on, 20 hours off—was being prepared to start working the next day. Capt. Lenert and his sanitary watch were getting ready to take care of any insects on board.

Some men are still quite ill; the sea is smooth, with a fair number of white-caps evident.

At 1330 we had the first of our daily "Gen. Quarters," and "abandon ship" drills. We had to dress in pistol belt and canteen full of water, life belt and helmet liner near our stations. My station #7 was near a wooden chain ladder for climbing overboard. The nurses are to go into the lifeboats if the need arose.

At 1400 we put the clock back to 1300—that means 15° longitude west of L.A. No one now thinks that we are to go by means of the Panama Canal. We are all agreed that it looks as if we were to go around Australia.

Japanese Forces and areas occupied, February 1, 1945 included the Marshal and Caroline Islands, the Philippines, and the South China Sea. This made skirting south of Hawaii islands and going around Australia to India imperative.

This morning we saw a small Navy tug towing an oil barge and a couple of what appeared to be inland canal boats along the course. It didn't take us long to pass them at our 20 knot speed. Many EM, some of the O and N [*Officers and Nurses*] are still ill. It really is hot in the troop berthing areas.

FRIDAY, FEBRUARY 9, 1945

It is quite definitely warmer today, no field jackets needed on deck this morning. Still nice weather, some blue sky, mostly low clouds.

The dispensaries are running well and my scheduled meetings with Code Commanders appeared in the D.I.B. [*Directory Information Base*] for meeting on Saturday 1100 and shots on Sunday 0930. We are all getting sunburned now and all but the seasick have a healthy glow. Our routine of two meals daily isn't hurting us a bit. I could get on the three meals daily, ship detail list, as Sr. Med. O. of troops but find two meals enough. Of course, we really eat as much in these two meals as we would in an ordinary three.

Our course still seems to be SW by W (240° azimuth) as well as our pocket compasses can tell aboard ship. Very inaccurate, to say the least.

The female passengers are getting quite a rush, as is to be expected with five or six O to each one of them. Some of those that wouldn't be looked [*at*] twice while ashore, are quite popular now. It will probably get worse the farther we are from the U.S.A.

There is talk of all the troops going into cotton clothes the next day. Well, it's too warm in wool for comfort now.

SATURDAY, FEBRUARY 10, 1945

Sure enough—order today to get into cottons. We are wearing fatigues and have to dress in cotton with necktie for evening meal. The weather on deck is perfect. Hot, yet a cooling breeze, just right. Had a meeting with Code Commanders about inoculation and other medical details. Capt. McAuliffe is to be in charge. Rather cloudy weather with occasional misty squalls. The clocks were set back another hour again today, at 1400, showing we had crossed another 15° longitude. Hot in cabin, no need for blankets now.

SUNDAY, FEBRUARY 11, 1945

A clearer day than yesterday. Saw numerous flying fish today, small ones, appearing about four or five feet long. Gave shots to most of the remaining men, including *XXX1*, a religious fanatic—a recent convert to some Holy Roller sect, who didn't believe in shots. Well he took them. Five of the Lt. Col.'s were invited to the Captain's cabin for lunch today and had a nice time. Guess I'll be in the next batch to go.

Brummett figured at noon today that we were at 18° N. about 100-150 miles S. E. of Hawaii. It's really getting hot. Nearly everyone is looking sunburned. It looks funny to see people with pieces of paper over their noses to protect them from burns.

This evening was one of the most enjoyable yet. A beautiful blue sea, a few cumulus clouds and a nice steady trade wind. The temperature on deck was just perfect. Just a reminiscence [*sic*] of the heat, with a cooling breeze, not cold, just at the right temperature. We stood, it seemed for hours on deck, until we were ordered below for "Darkened Ship." After we were down in the cabin, the officers there organize the "Fraternal Order of Fuddy-Duddies." [*FOF*]. $1 dues and a $1 bill with emblems and signatures. The money in dues and fines [*are*] to go for a party when we land at our destination. It's, of course, a screwball organization, and will probably take in half of the Officers and Nurses and others among the cabin passengers. After this meeting, Lamber and I went to Dr. Cornwath's at his invitation, to spend a few hours talking and sipping a Coca-Cola and ice, nothing else. It was good. Cokes are not available here. Crew buys them by the case. Guess they can buy them from ship store, too.

MONDAY, FEBRUARY 12, 1945

A really hot day. Certainly didn't need any covers today. We passed a ship to port this morning, a fairly large Liberty ship, about 7 miles away.

Heard that one of the EM aboard had slipped on one of the ladders and had cracked his spine. Too bad. Those stairs are really steep and dangerous. About 1100 was told that I was one of the 5 Lt. Cols invited to the Captain's cabin for lunch We went there at noon and met Capt. Maguire, full Captain, USNR, a medium-size man, very nice host. The six of us were seated at a round table and served by two colored mess boys. We had roast beef, mashed potatoes, cauliflower, milk, coffee and ice cream. Very enjoyable.

After lunch we went on the navigating bridge and looked around. General Quarters were sounded, meaning that all passengers go to their berths below deck and crew members assume their post and man the Flak guns. They fired a few of them, as they do every day, at a balloon released from deck. They didn't hit it, but some bullets got mighty close.

We watched a drill during which they change from manual operating to gyrocompass operation, to hand operation of the steering mechanism in the stern. This is done so as to be able to steer the ship if the navigation room is put out of action.

After this, we returned to our part of the ship and initiated the new members [*into FOF*]. The deck was so hot that it even felt hot through my shoe soles, which are fairly thick.

Attended another Chinese class this evening. The words just don't seem to stick to my mind at all. Just don't make any impression at all. Maybe it's too hot to study, or something.

The clock was set back another hour. We must be averaging about 7 1/2° daily, as the time has been changed every other day during the trip.

XXX2 is still looking unhappy. He was issued a Kapok life jacket, a thing that fits like a big, fat vest with a collar. It is as hot as the devil and about as bulky as a bushel basket. He wants one of the inflatable kind, that are a lot less bulky and are worn around the waist like a big, fat belt. I kid him whenever I see him lugging his Kapok jacket around, and call it his "Old Man of the Sea." He is very unhappy and is looking around for the other kind and will steal one if necessary, so he says, and leave his Kapok jacket in trade.

It's really hot tonight, getting harder all the time. "Darkened ship" came early and we were not able to enjoy the evening breeze as we had anticipated.

TUESDAY, FEBRUARY 13, 1945

It has really been hot today. Our cabin was uncomfortable even this morning. Later in the day it just kept getting worse and was really bad at noon when our ventilator stops working. The temperature and humidity were both extreme. Earlier this morning I did some washing. It didn't take much exertion to make the sweat roll. To guard against salt depletion, I had salt tablets placed in the fore and aft battle dressing stations and in the Officers lounge, as well as in the galley, bakery and at the four mess lines for the EM.

Everyone is now sunburned and everyone has a sweaty face. Many have their fatigue clothes and uniform wet in patches. The ocean has been a clear blue with lots of whitecaps, all heading in our general direction. The white sea horses of the Vikings.

We initiated some more members of the FOF at 1430 today. The decks were so hot they could hardly sit on them.

Forgot to go to the Chinese class today. It isn't too hard, except that one word may mean 4 different things depending on the inflection of the word.

It was really hot today so hot and humid, that I felt it myself. We started to put out salt tablets, which are a great help. We certainly are drinking lots of water. For a while our ventilation system was off, which made our compartment a Turkish bath.

This evening the deck wasn't so good, as it was raining. The rain has helped cool things a lot. Lamber and I went up to Dr. Cornwath's cabin and had a nice iced Coca-Cola there. Even there it was hot. It's nearly too hot to sleep, but we managed to, all the same.

WEDNESDAY, FEBRUARY 14

Ash Wednesday and St. Valentine's Day. Didn't send Babbie [*his wife, is called Babs or Babbie*] a Valentine for the first time in years. Tried to get one at Camp Anza, but they didn't have any. Today was rainy. Went on deck between squalls and it was very enjoyable, cooled off some since the rains started. Brummet had figured that we should be crossing the equator close to noon today. Wonder how close his calculations were. So far no news of it. Understand we will get certificates as shell backs [*person who has crossed the equator*] issued to us when we arrived at our port. Hope to get a nice one to hang up in my office on return. They really have some dandies. Saw a ship (Liberty freighter) at about 0900 and just before twilight this evening, both heading back home. Our clocks were set back again today at 1400. That's a 4th time since our journey. Approximately 60° since we left LA.

Had our FOF initiation again today and Chinese class. Well, if I study the d—words, maybe I can learn them. Still is hot and sultry today, not quite as bad as the day before. Through fussing with Captain Bronson. TC [*transit coordinator*] had myself, and Hogan and the actively participating Medical Officers put on the ship detail list for the extras that these people get. I got a $5 fountain pen for $3 today. I may need it if this one gives out. Today was sweltering hot again. We certainly drink a lot of water. Lights out early, due to change of time, and little time to enjoy evening cool.

After "darkened ship," a number of us sat in the darkened lounge, lit dimly by the red battle lights only, and played "Geography." One person names a geographical spot, such as a country, and the next person must name one starting with the last letter of the first name. Lt.

Col. McNair was with us and he was good. A lowland Scotsman, born in Karachi, India, I believe.

THURSDAY, FEBRUARY 15, 1945

For centuries in many navies, initiation rites for crossing the Equator, International Date Line, Arctic Circle, or other lines have been traditional. The uninitiated sailor, or traveler, is considered a "pollywog." When the equator is crossed, the pollywog is summoned to King Neptune's court by Davy Jones. Other characters include Queen Amphitrite, a man dressed in drag, or a policeman, bears and mermaids, various antics by the shellbacks—initiated crew members—are imposed upon the pollywogs. These include activities such as shaving the head, paddling, dunking the person into water and other activities.

The new shellback gets a certificate which is often cherished by the sailor or traveler as they tend to be colorful and artistically rendered with colorful drawings of mermaids, King Neptune and sea creatures.[3]

Crossed the equator all right, by best information at about 0100 this morning. We're all shellbacks now, but weren't duly initiated, which doesn't make me feel bad, as it can be rough. Understand we will get certificates later on as proof. Hope I get a nice one that I can get framed and hung in the (future) waiting room or office.

Today dawned clear and warm. A soft breeze from the south and a sparkle on the sea. 7 B-17's [*Flying Fortress bombers*] passed us, heading N. W. at not too high an altitude. Saw a few gulls, not identical with the ones we're accustomed to. They didn't stay with the ship.

It got real hot again, today. The water has been rationed, so that soft water for washing and shaving purposes is on only a few hours a day. The scuttle-butts [*drinking water in containers with taps*] are going all the time and people are using their salt tablets, too. Bet I drink gallons daily. This morning, got my hair cropped short, about a 1/2" long. Looks like a shoe brush, I guess. Not too bad, although people are tempted to run their hands over my new haircut.

Quite a day to day. (1) we crossed the equator, (2) went back on standard time, losing another hour again and (3) crossed the international date line early this evening.

$$180°$$
$$\_\_\_|\_\_\_\_0000$$
$$|$$

We really are in the Orient and Antipodes now. The old ocean still looks the same and it's just as hot as ever. This evening had a nice entertainment in the lounge, mostly talent from EM, especially good was a Negro quartet.

Ed O'Neill is raising a beard now, he really will look like Mephistopheles. He's funny the way he cusses the women aboard. Don't have any use for them at all. Brummett seems to be fairly close with his nautical figures, and said we were just about 40 miles E of 180° at local noon.

Having a lot of ringworm on board, most of it, I believe brought on board by the men themselves and blossoming out due to the heat and humidity. I sunned my own tootsies today as a therapeutic measure.

Hear that there will be no Friday the 16th in our lives. It seems funny to lose a whole day.

SATURDAY, FEBRUARY 17, 1945

That's right, Saturday follows Thursday the 15th this week, Friday just got lost in the shuffle. It's funny to think of, but Friday, Feb. 16 has just not existed in my life, I never experienced it at all, just jumped over it completely, making this February one of 27 days for all aboard.

We passed the equator and the 180th meridian within 24 hours. Last night was hot and sweltering. Today dawned nice and clear, then clouded up and we have been driving through the rain and squalls most of the day. While it is hot aboard, there is quite a good breeze outside and it is nice, cool on deck.

This is the ship's inspection day, and everyone is busy in final preparations for this. Had our Chinese class this morning. Maybe I'll learn something about it yet. Who knows? Also had a large initiation into the FODs today. Had the mimeographed ringworm sheets out today, and will have to get after the barber's sanitary rules.

We ran into a squall after supper and it looked as if we might be headed for a touch of weather. They were singing, "It was sad, sad, sad when the big ship went down, and the men and women all drowned." Hillbilly, ballad type, for which words can be easily improvised.

SUNDAY, FEBRUARY 18, 1945

The day dawned clear and beautiful. The sea was barely marked by waves and no whitecaps were visible anywhere. I sat up on the upper deck for several hours in the sun and cool breeze and it certainly was a pleasure. By noon we were S. far enough to be 4° S. of the sun. First time I'd ever seen the sun to the North. Later in the day the moon was visible, which was much higher than I had ever seen it before. We were W. of the Fiji and due N. of New Zealand and E. of the New Hebrides. The course all day was due S. as well as we could tell from our Army compasses.

The weather was fine all day except for a few squalls later in the evening.

MONDAY, FEBRUARY 19, 1945

The sea was very smooth today. The weather generally cooler, although quite hot at noon. Capt. Brummett says that his navigation was off a lot. He had us going over New Caledonia today. As a matter of fact, I learned later that we had just gone around the tip of it, and so he wasn't so far off.

TUESDAY, FEBRUARY 20, 1945

Another beautiful day. Pleasantly hot, and quite cool after supper, really too cool on the windward part. We saw some marine substance that was in long irregular bands across the sea's surface. Wonder if it was plankton? Also saw a number of birds, swallow-like, of a sooty brown color, which were skimming the surface and paying no attention to the ship at all.

WEDNESDAY, FEBRUARY 21, 1945

It's definitely cooler now, last night was good one for sleeping and it was quite cool this morning. The same 5 of us had dinner with Capt. Maguire again. He had ham, creamed corn, sweet potatoes, iced tea, coffee and ice cream. During "General Quarters," he had the ship turn a complete circle for us. He had his National-Geographical map on some cloth and on rollers, as I expect to do later on with my own. Discovered that Maury, for whom the highway through that beautiful pass in Virginia is named, was the originator of collecting wind, temperature, and current data from log books.

It got hot again this evening about 5:00 p.m., the ship started to pitch. We found out that we were hitting swells, some 10' from trough to top and enough to make the ship roll. Way off to the W. there were thick masses of black clouds, as if there were a big storm between us and Australia. Quite cool by evening.

THURSDAY, FEBRUARY 22, 1945

We arose early today and went up on deck. Sure enough to the N. of us off the starboard side we saw land. Some bluffs and a lot of lower land, stretching out quite a distance to the W. The Lt. Col.'s were allowed up on the signal bridge and we had a good view. There were quite a lot of clouds, all fairly high. Many black clouds to the S. In the distance off bow, starboard, we could see a lighthouse. We soon changed course and headed toward it. The pilot boat was sighted in the distance and our pilot flag was run up. The pilot ship came close and soon the pilot was in a small low boat, being rowed to us. He boarded and we soon were off. The entrance to the bay was very narrow and well-fortified on both sides. It's about 40 miles up the bay to Melbourne, which is quite a large city, (1,300,000). It has a small ship yard and lots of dock area. The first line was put ashore at 1032. We had an anchorage pool, $60.00, as usual I contributed. No Army personnel was allowed ashore. Really would like to put foot ashore another continent at that. Could see the spires and business buildings to the NE of our pier.

After supper the cold S. wind was blowing again, in from the sea. After dark, we were allowed out on deck for the first time since we sailed. We enjoyed it, although it was cold. There were thick black clouds to the W., lighted at times by streaks of lightning. Old Orion was to the N. Hard to become accustomed to, and a 3/4 moon was to the N. too. Toward the S. was the Southern Cross, not too much to look at but my first glimpse of it: something like a kite headed toward the earth.

SATURDAY, FEBRUARY 24, 1945

A nice clear day, warm, due to a lack of wind in the morning, but getting cold in the evening when the S. wind started up again. This morning Read [*Reed*] and Workizer and I accompanied the ship's engineer. We climbed up inside the fore funnel and looked out over the harbor. The stack is mainly false. After that we went all over the boiler and engine rooms. That certainly is a complicated assortment of machinery. We saw the shafts, water stills, etc.

The bay was pretty this evening. A brisk S. wind. Lots of cumulus clouds and about 100 little sailing boats, like seagulls, all over the harbor. A few star type, mainly triangles and British dinghies. Reminded me of Sydney [*Nova Scotia*] and Dave's [*His brother-in-law, David McCurdy*] sail boat, summer of '37. The evening was cool and cloudy, not much like summer at all.

SUNDAY, FEBRUARY 25, 1945

Early this morning, the ship's automobiles were slung aboard and the rat-shields taken off the hawsers [*a thick rope for mooring a boat*]. At about 1100 the pilot came aboard and soon after two tugs appeared. Before noon the lines were cast off and we were on our way again, the shorter, but I expect, the hotter leg of our sea journey. Still cold and pretty much overcast. Our course was S. W. after we passed Cape [*?*] our course turned W. again.

MONDAY, FEBRUARY 26, 1945

Back to our routine again of ship life. Cold weather, partly overcast, and greasy looking swells part of the time. We were amused by a letter posted on our lounge bulletin board, to Mr. Anthony, the troubleshooter, which purported to be from a very young and very lovelorn shavedtail [*2nd Lt.*], about his troubles with his ladylove. Everyone laughed at this. (Inman, pulled it off, however.)

17

TUESDAY, FEBRUARY 27, 1945

In waters where enemy submarines might be lurking, it was common for ships to zigzag in an effort to prevent torpedoes from hitting them. The War Instructions United States Navy 1944, states that, "When practicable, known submarine waters are avoided. Also effort is made to avoid passing through, or in close proximity to the same waters traversed in the preceding twenty-four hours...When cruising, the officer in tactical command normally orders his command to zigzag in accordance with a prescribed plan, whenever there is a probability of encountering enemy submarines." [4]

Cool this morning and in the shade this evening, beautiful this day however. Ocean blue and sparkling. Saw a school of porpoises at noon. Have been followed all day by about 20 albatrosses. White bodies, brown wings with white under surfaces. One brown one among them. We have been zig-zagging all day. Guess this area must be considered fairly dangerous. Understand the Jap subs got some ships in this region not long ago.

The ship was likely in the Indian Ocean skirting south of Ceylon (Sri Lanka) an island off the southern tip of India to travel to Bombay on the western side of India. On Tuesday February 6, 1945 in the Indian Ocean off Western Australia a Japanese submarine attacked the American Liberty Ship, Peter Silvester, en route from Melbourne, Australia to Colombo, Ceylon. This was to be the last attack by a Japanese submarine in Australian waters and the Indian Ocean, but, of course, this was not known at this time. [5]

WEDNESDAY, FEBRUARY 28, 1945

The last day of our shortest month. Only 27 days. Still cold and blustery. Waves quite high. The roughest day yet. We had an escort airplane with us most of the day. A boom alongside the ship was torn off. Tonight, in "Passion Park," there was an orchestra of EM. Played popular songs, not too bad.

THURSDAY, MARCH 1, 1945

Another month. Slightly warmer today, very much smoother. The storm threat is evidently gone. Tonight a number of us, many Lt. Col's were invited to the ship's Officers Lounge. We didn't know what to expect, as we heard we were to be initiated into a ship's Officers society. So, at 1900, we went up expecting the worst.

When we enter the lounge, it was filled by ship's officers and we had to stand in a row. I noticed a large holy-stone on a table and figured correctly as it turned out, that it had something to do with the forthcoming initiation. Soon Captain Maguire came in and told us that we were to be initiated into the "Ancient Order of Splicing the Mainbrace." He read the rules and then placed a red ribbon around our necks at the end of which was a little corkscrew. Our order, with signs and countersigned is another of the elbow-bending group. We were all given a very nice mimeographed and duly signed paper, showing that we were members. We had to take on an oath, with our hands on the holy stone, before this.

After the meeting, we had coffee (instead of the liquid used by the organization) and we sat around a while telling stories. A very pleasant evening.

FRIDAY, MARCH 2, 1945

We are definitely entering the tropical zone now. We are heading N. W. by W. and the days are getting warmer. The air outside is nice and cool in the breeze, hot where it is confined and the sun is getting hotter.

SATURDAY, MARCH 3, 1945

Still warmer than before. Guess I'll have to take off my undershirt pretty soon. Bought 1/2 dozen Navy T shirts about a week ago and am wearing them now. This evening 6 of us challenged the Navy to a deck tennis game. It was a farce. The Navy Officers came out wearing boxing helmets; Kate Sweeney and Bell were referees and umpires. Their decisions really were something. More time was spent arguing then playing, of course, and often we couldn't play for laughing. In one play, one of our men threw the grommet to Lt. Col. Eliot, who was watching from the superstructure deck and threw it down on the opponents deck. We claimed that our point also. Later on someone threw in the extra grommets and the game broke up with the air full of them. The victors, Navy, received a cabbage head, with nose, mouth, teeth, eyes, eyebrows, etc. as a prize. The losers, us, received an egg with a sad face painted on it. A good game.

That evening, showed the Sgts. our map and we sweltered out an orchestra session in the "passion pit."

SUNDAY, MARCH 4, 1945

Another nice day, hot and clear. We went to church this morning. Rev. Scholz of the 95th [*Field Hospital*] held a nice service. Later on, our cabin presented Capt. Maguire with his honorary membership in the FOF, up in his quarters.

MONDAY, MARCH 5, 1945

It's really hot now, as we are near to crossing the equator. We were presented with our shellback certificates today. By mistake, Lamber and I were given two each of the large ones. I can have one of them hang up in my office area waiting room sometime in the dim, distant future, nicely framed. As usual, we had a nice, cool evening, with a good breeze.

TUESDAY, MARCH 6, 1945

It's 4 weeks today that we came aboard the good ship Gen.W.A. Mann. It's been a most interesting month too. We truly have been on the longest boat ride possible, and are actually closer to home now then we were a week ago.

The General W. A. Mann, *was a P 2-type troopship built by the Federal Shipbuilding and Drydock Company of Kearny, New Jersey, in 1942-43. She was named in honor of Major General William Abram Mann, USA, who served in the Sioux Indian, Spanish-American, and First World Wars. On October 13, 1943, the ship was commissioned and commanded by then Comdr., and later Capt. Paul S. Maguire, USNR. He was commander from November 16, 1943 to June 23, 1945. The ship transported troops to and from combat areas in the European, Mediterranean, and Asians theaters. After serving in both the Korea and Vietnam conflicts, on December 1, 1965, she was decommissioned; on April 10, 1987 she was sold for scrap for $1,050,050.[6]*

Capt. Maguire had us Lt. Col.'s up to the signal bridge during General Quarters today. We watched them shoot at a balloon with their 20 mm guns. Good shooting, but no hit. If it had been an airplane, it would have been down, I'm sure. They then fired a number of star shells from two of the 5" guns. It's a type of illuminating shell, which eventually releases off bright flares and a parachute.

At 3:15 this evening, Gen. Quarters was rung. This is the first real one we have had. The rest all were practice ones at 1:30. We didn't know what to expect. The crew rushed about, on their way to their stations. We had heard rumors that we were to pick up our escort today, a couple of limey corvettes [*small, maneuverable, lightly armed warship*] in all probability. Still and all, it might be a Jap sub or surface craft, one never can tell. Soon we had "Secure General Quarters," and we went out on deck and sure enough saw a small war ship, either a cruiser or corvette coming to us. She is to be our escort to port, I guess.

Our amateur navigators have us recrossing the equator to the Northern hemisphere again today, on or about noon.

WEDNESDAY, MARCH 7, 1945

Our escort is still with us this morning, first on one side, in front and then on the other. Have to get busy on the final report. Have Capt. Lennert working on his sanitary report and Nowell on a graph. Have scheduled a meeting tomorrow on our inspection before debarking. This evening was clear and there was a cool, nearly cold breeze.

THURSDAY, MARCH 8, 1945

Working on the report this morning. Meeting at close of "General Quarters" and "Abandon Ship" drill. Assigned MO to every compartment. Had DOs [*duty officers*] and MACs [*Medical Administrative Corps*] collect all the U.S. currency from EM. Hogan collected from O. We are to get Indian money instead.

Our escort left us this evening. Guess we must be in safe waters now. Saw a sailing vessel this morning and a freighter later on in the day. This evening there was an amateur show, all-male cast, who put on some skits. It certainly was hot and crowded in there.

FRIDAY, MARCH 9, 1945

It's getting hotter, as we are getting closer to Bombay [*Mumbai, on west coast of India*]. All the Lt. Col.'s were invited up to Capt. Maguire's for lunch today. Had a nice meal of cold cuts. He showed us charts of Bombay and its harbors and told us we were to dock in the morning.

US troops aboard a transport waiting to go ashore in an Indian Port
From: Kenneth E, Hunter, *United States Army in World War II. Pictorial Record. The War against Japan* (Office of the Chief of Military History, Department of the Army, 1952), p. 416

SATURDAY, MARCH 10, 1945

At sunrise we were outside the harbor and entered as soon as it was light and safe enough. There was a lot of shipping in the harbor, mainly freighters and two smaller type hospital ships as well. We saw a hermaphrodite brig, a rarity these days and lots of lateen rigged chows. The harbor was misty, as is usual in the morning.

Didn't get much opportunity to see much of the place, and the boarding party came on with the pilot, and there were a number of meetings to attend. So many, in fact, that I had no breakfast that day. Meeting of code CO as well as Sr. Med. O. Later had coffee and ice cream in ship's party with Cmd. Snow.

Signed partial pay for $100 (33OR)[*Indian Rupee*]. Some of the troops and O got off at about 1630 and went to Bombay. I left with Cmd. Snow and some others at 1915 and drove to the Taj Mahal Hotel in the ship's station wagon. Near this hotel is a sea gate the "Gate to India," used for official occasions. The drinks in the hotel were poor, but some FOF officials had some bottles of Scotch, so I had a few drinks anyhow. Met some of the nurses there later and escorted them back to the ship at 2300. They were still busy unloading the hatches at that time.

This chapter from diary pages 1-21

ENDNOTES

[1] Gettis, Erin. *City of Riverside: Camp Anza/Arlanza 2006–2007*, (Planning Commission, City of Riverside, Ca, 2007); James M. Myers, "Camp Barkeley," *Handbook of Texas Online* (Texas State Historical Association, n.d.), 2010.

[2] See: Buford Rowland and William B. Boyd. *U.S. Navy Bureau of Ordnance in World War II* (Department of the Navy, 1953),17.

[3] Harry Miller Lydenberg. *Crossing the Line: Tales of the Ceremony during Four Centuries* (New York Public Library, 1957).

[4] The Navy Department Library, "Chapter 7. Action against Submarines, Aircraft, Mines, Chemicals," in *War Instructions United States Navy 1944. Section I. Antisubmarine Measure* (United States Navy, 1944), 29.

[5] Robert J. Cressman, "Chapter 7: 1945," in *The Official Chronology of the U.S. Navy in World War II* (Naval Institute Press, 2000).

[6] "USS General A. Mann (AP-112)." *Wikipedia* (2015); "General W. A. Mann." *Dictionary of American Naval Fighting Ships* (Dept. of the Navy, n.d.).

Chapter 2: From Bombay to Chabua, India: Railroad and Truck Convoy

The Japanese until early August 1944 had control of most of Burma [See Map 1]. By early fall they had been pushed south out of their northern zones of occupation. However, based upon the tenacity of Japanese fighters on Guadalcanal and other Pacific islands, a potential long and protracted bloody campaign was considered likely for the proposed invasion of the Japanese home islands planned for in the autumn of 1945. Thus medical care was considered crucial for both Chinese and American military personnel in addition to refugees as the allies continued to push the Japanese military out of Burma and China.[1]

In March and April, 1945, the 96th Field Hospital traveled by train through what is now Bangladesh to Siliguri, West Bengal, India. They then traveled about 540 miles (871 Km) by vehicles through the Brahmaputra River valley to Chabua near Dibrugarh, Assam, India [See Maps 1 & 2].

SUNDAY, MARCH 11, 1945

We are to debark at 1100. Signed the reports of the Med. Serv. and packed. Quite a job and what a weight before I was through. Could hardly carry my Val-Pac. We got off at 1130 and waited around to 1300 in the shed at the pier and then our whole train marched to the Victoria terminal. The majority of the O and all the nurses rode in trucks.

The train had about 18 passenger cars, I, II and III class and about 6 small freight cars in which our baggage and TAT equipment was placed. The Officer's car was up front; another end was an officer's car, troop type, and a I class coach for the nurses. Right back

27

of this was the part of the train composed of the baggage or freight cars. BOMBAY [*now Mumbai*] is on an island and is a large city. We rode a number of miles and then crossed the marshes and water over a causeway. Near the coast were eroded hills and mountains and we soon were starting up hill slowly. Rice paddies were the main feature of the landscape, which was flat or undulating, well adapted to such type of agricultural.

Much to my surprise, I found that the central provinces of INDIA were on a flat plateau, up to 1000 feet above sea level and punctuated by eroded hills and ranges. The flat plains reminded me very much of parts of Texas, except that they were slightly more wooded. The hills often reminded me of those of Pa., being of somewhat the same type of erosion and similarly wooded. Even the trees didn't look too dissimilar. The country is parched, though, there are numerous tanks and waterholes and the sluggish, shallow streams usually contain some water. The tributaries all seem to be dry and were used as roads. There are numerous cattle, water buffalo and goats all over the place as well as a few sheep and horses. We saw a few camels and a small group of monkeys to. We rode all day and night of Monday 12th, Tuesday 13th, Wednesday 14th and arrived at our staging area about mid-morning, Thursday 15th. We had ridden for several hours through the suburbs of CALCUTTA [*now Kolkata*].

We put in a tent area at the S. end of camp, near the hospital, 18th F. H. We found the latrines filthy and in bad condition. They were on one side of our area and the wash stands and showers were on the other side. A poor arrangement.

The latrines were in native-type buildings. Wood supporting structures with mud wattle walls and thatched roofs. Our mess hall and a headquarters building were of the same type. We had a shower soon after arriving, cold water, of course, but not bad.

Our nurses came to the [*rail road*] spur and were unloaded and sent to the hospital, where they put them up, gave them breakfast and lunch and at 3:00 sent them to the KARNARTIE ESTATES, an officer's club, where they are to stay for a while. We had a meeting that evening of Code Cs, where we were given some information. No provisions were made for messing the Officers separately. I don't think it is dignified, or good either, for an officer, a Lt. Col. to stand in food lines and in mess gear wash lines with all the men, but I have had to do that. Am arranging to have McCain, my orderly, wash my mess gear and Major Lamber's, too, and if necessary will get the Post mess Sgt. to get my food ahead of the line. We got revaccinated this day, too.

FRIDAY, MARCH 16, 1945

All morning was spent in the open air theater, all Officers and troops, listening to orientation talks. According to their statements the VD [*sexually-transmitted diseases*] rate among the natives is terrific, and among the G.I.s too.

> *Various diseases among the native populations and troops and inoculation polices are discussed in some detail in "Chapter XVII: China-Burma-India Theater" in* Army Medical Service. Preventive Medicine in World War II.[2]

Spent the rest of the day getting things organized. Dropped up to the Officer's club in the evening.

The nights have been nice and cool, necessitating a blanket. Lt. Budz [*Budziszewski*]—arrived today, his ship coming up the HOOGHLY RIVER to CALCUTTA. He surprised us, as we didn't expect him for 10 or 12 days yet.

SATURDAY, MARCH 17, 1945

Lt. Budz—and I went to CALCUTTA today. We went by courier truck at 0830 and drove about 40 miles, mainly through industrial suburbs. The road for about 1/2 the way was narrow, about 8' of macadam [*type of asphalt*] pavement and about 5 or 6' of dirt on either side. No pavements. In many places the native huts and storage are right on the dirt part of the road. They have a front part, about 10 or 12 or feet square for their business establishments and the back half about the same, for living quarters. The lower half of the road is wider, 2 laned [*sic*] and in better condition. Everywhere there are natives, walking along the road and squatting near the buildings. Dogs and cows walk around. There are numerous native 3-wheel bicycle taxis, one and 2 horse gharries and in the city, rickshaws and auto taxis, the latter usually driven by Sikhs, often in pairs. They are larger men, often nice-looking, beaked noses, beards and turbans. They seem to wear clean clothes, at least.

We attended a meeting at the <u>Hindustan Building</u> and afterwards we went to QM store, where they had very little to offer, and then to Rankin' s for a pith helmet. What few they had didn't fit. We went to Firpo's Restaurant at noon, where I had spiced hump [*from camel*]. It tasted somewhat like tongue. We drank bottled lime and soda, not bad. Later on we walked over to the <u>New Market </u>(or Thieves Market, or 40 Thieves, call it what you want). It covers a whole block and consists of numerous stores of all types, mostly little 20 ft. places. Bought Babbie some native jewelry there and a pith helmet for myself.

Everywhere are beggars and fortune tellers. These come up, as one individual did, and say, "Sahib, have good fortune to tell you. Soon get telegram." After saying no, they press something in your hand and say that it's a lucky piece. I accepted it and he immediately said "Baksheesh, Sahib." It was a little carved nut, so I said, "O.K., give you one anna." He said, "No, one rupee." I said, "No, only one anna," and gave it back to him and was rid of him. The streets are full of them, all kinds of vendors of all kinds of junk and have the usual number of beggars, and blind and lame. We had tea and cakes at the original Firpo's at about 4:00 p.m. Good cakes too.

Back at camp, there was a party at the Officers club, celebrating St. Patrick's birthday. O'Neil and Robinson really celebrated, too.

The following is a list of items bought and cost in terms of rupees and annas (ānā). R = Rupee, 16 annas= 1 Rupee.

(BAG R. -86/8 BRACELET - 27/ IVORY BR.-15/)
(PILLOW-15/ " -12 / NECKLACE-25/)
(" -15/)

SUNDAY, MARCH 18, 1945

We had our vaccinations [*for small pox*] read at 1000 this morning. Only 6 men had to have re-vaccinations. Otherwise the day was a lazy one. Lt. Col. Fry of the 18th F. H., which is acting as Station H. here, had Maj. Reed and me over for lunch. It was very nice, and he had a nice installation, all buildings of Indian type of construction, under British reverse lend-lease.

It is interesting to hear the jackals call at night. Not unmusical at all, something weird and unfamiliar.

MONDAY, MARCH 19, 1945

We are gradually getting things organized. Saw Lt. Col. Rugheimer, the Post CO of troops and got a few things straightened up. An order for all our extra items such as blankets, sun helmets, etc. were put in today. We are also getting candles and kerosene.

THURSDAY, MARCH 22, 1945

Received the winter clothing items for our EM. Capt. Peterson to hospital for a few weeks, and to rejoin us later on. The evenings are nice here. A cooling wind, moon shining and very pleasing after hot day.

FRIDAY, MARCH 23, 1945

Drivers sent to town today to pick up our vehicles from CALCUTTA Ord. depot. Took train to town, paid 2/8 [*2 rupee/8 anna*] for a one-way ticket and sat in II class carriage. No one came to collect tickets. Most of our Officers had no tickets and just paid R 1 [*one rupee*] to ticket taker at gate of SEALDAH station. Four of us rode to HINDUSTAN building in a gharrie, a rickety one at that.

Saw Capt. Eyler, Top Movement Assistant who checked over our next move. Met Lt. Bornemann and helped her to get requisition started for the nurses. Hope this gets results. They are to go by air and are limited to 172# baggage. We will pick up their footlockers and excess luggage on Monday at KARNARINE ESTATES. This is the Officer's club, and there must be quite a pack of wolves there. One even broke down a door to one of the Nurses rooms one night.

We had hamburgers and coffee at noon and Capt. Hagan, McAuliffe and I took a Red Cross conducted tour in the evening. Was at the temple of KHALI (CALCUTTA Actually is a "KHALI" ghat.) [*series of steps leading down to a body of water*]. A toe of the goddess, KHALI is here, making it one of India's 51 holy places for Hindus. Saw the burning ghat, where a woman was awaiting cremation. Next saw SIKH Temple and was greatly impressed by their faith which is like Calvinism without Christ. We saw the HOOGHLY RIVER, botanical gardens and government houses.

After this we went shopping. Bought a brooch for mother at Whitehall and Laidlaw's and then we toured the New Market. What a slick bunch of traders they are. We really were dehydrated and drank tea and lemonade at Firpo's and had a very good filling supper there.

Road back to SEALDAH station in taxi driven by 2 SIKHS. They wanted R/4 but got only R/2 as meter read R/1/14. Somehow or the other, I have a soft spot in my heart for those, fierce-looking Indians, despite their usual Indian wish to cheat. We had to stand up all the way back to CHANDIMARI stop, our camp stop.

SATURDAY, MARCH 24, 1945

Finished our clothing distribution today. No final word on move, except that it's scheduled for Wed. 28th. Tried to get special service equipment, but didn't get any. Went to club in the evening and drank some gin and grapefruit juice. Everyone got to bed fairly early.

SUNDAY, MARCH 25, 1945

Palm Sunday, but hot enough for July 4. O'Neil got me some British India stamps for R/3/8 to send home to mother.

More troubles. Major Reed, of 95th F. H. told me shortly after noon that our departure had been delayed 10 to 14 days. Got in touch with Major Clubb, post adjutant, who corroborated this, but qualify his statement by, that this wasn't final, and we should go ahead with our preparation for Wednesday departure.

Another beautiful evening. The moon was nearly full and I got my field glasses out and I looked at it. Good glasses, magnify about 6x.

MONDAY, MARCH 26, 1945

Received word this morning that we are to move as previously scheduled on Wed. 28th at about 0800. Good. It seems that all are to accompany the truck convoy, which is put on flat cars at BARROCKPORE. Have been busy getting things ready and called a meeting of convoy staff to get started.

TUESDAY, MARCH 27, 1945

A busy day, getting supplies, etc. in. Our trucks were brought in today from MAIDAN race track in CALCUTTA where the motor pool is. Had morning for personal packing and evening for organization packing and preparation. Didn't quite get through in time and some work has been left for Wednesday morning. Had Officers and EM shave this evening so as not to lose time on morning of departure. Paid final calls on Lt. Col. Rugheimer, Post CO and Lt. Col. Fry, CO of the 18th F.H.

Lt. Budz was involved in accident in which his jeep was smashed when it was hit by a prime-mover [*forklift*] which of course wasn't even scratched. Sgt. Perry, a d— good man, had has nose broken and will remain in 142nd G. H. for several days. Nothing more serious, I hope.

Capt. Petersen [*Peterson*] will have to remain behind to recuperate from an operation for anal fissure. Col. Rugheimer will try to arrange his journey by air with the nurses when they come.

The moon is nearly full. Whenever I see it like this, it makes me think of Tarnwood. [*MacMillan's home in Oakmont, Pa.*]

WEDNESDAY, MARCH 28, 1945

We were scheduled to leave at 0800 and did leave camp area before this time, but, for various reasons, our motor convoy got off 25 minutes late. At last minute it was discovered that truck #1 the lead, had no driver. Cook, the reg. driver, was in town with Lt. Budz to get a new jeep, so I hopped in and drove it. The only incident along the way was that I hit the end of a parked, empty and unyoke ox-cart, which was projecting into the road, with the side of my truckand jarred it well.

We drove to BARROCKPORE and to the RR siding of the Royal Calcutta race track, now used for airport and troops. Here I had to lead the convoy up a ramp and onto the flat cars, one for each truck. Quite a neat trick driving over every car, end to end. We hung around this place all the rest of the day and pulled out at 10:00 p.m. The last car on our train was a III class coach and baggage car. The benches were too narrow to sleep on, but McCain rigged up my sleeping bag and mosquito bar on a rack or shelf. Not too bad, either. McCain and Wurtzebach slept in one compartment, Budz and I in another.

THURSDAY, MARCH 29, 1945

Early this morning we crossed the GANGES river on our way N. we stopped at ISHURDI [*now in Bangladesh but located in Bengel, an Indian province, in WWII era*] from 0700 to 1000 where we washed up, shaved, etc. The entire trip, by RR was over a flat plain, endless rice paddies, with innumerable villages, patches of woods and bamboos. All along the track, which was built higher than the plain, or swampy areas where the dirt for the RR was dug out. The entire area was dry and dusty, though it seemed to be greener during the latter 1/3 of the distance. The flat plain, entirely without rocks or stones, seems to be an alluvial deposit of the GANGES and BRAHMAPUTRA rivers.

From PARVITAPUR [*sic, Parbatipur now in Bangladesh*] North, there seems to be a definite Mongoloid infusion. Some families very much so, in others just a trace.

The sun was obscured by both clouds and fog or mist. This fog seemed to be a mixture of smoke from home and field fires. It was also said that there were forest fires in the hills.

We arrived at SILIGURI [*located in West Bengal at the foot of the Himalayas*] at 10:00 p.m. where we were met by Lt. Moyer, who gave us directions and was in charge of our debarkation. We ran the trucks off the cars at about 10:45 and drove several miles out of town to our camping areas, where we bedded down for the night. DARJEELING, up in the hills, is a beautiful summer resort. On a clear day the mountains can be seen from her, but in the dry and dusty season, visibility is limited.

FRIDAY, MARCH 30, 1945

Good Friday! We are camped out and preparing to start our convoy journey. This morning we went to the nearby stream and bathed, the water was cool, not cold and we felt good about a bath. Pebbly bottom about 1 ft. deep and 20 ft. wide and a fair current. A hill stream and it looked good. As I'm writing this in the cab of #13 truck, of which I'm co-driver, I'm quietly perspiring and collecting dust. The dirty marks on the paper, wets it and stains it with sweat and dust wind. It's not uncomfortable, however, especially when the wind blows though it's likely to blow dust then.

XXX2 is having his troubles with the water situation. All our water must be boiled and chlorinated. It's difficult to do without proper stoves and installations. He likes to argue and say something is impossible to do, so I have to tell [*him*] to try it first and then find out.

Later this evening we saw the mountains to the North, the HIMALAYAS very faintly through the mist and smoke and dust. Chaplain Woods held a Good Friday service after sundown. My attendance to it was interrupted by the necessity of writing a letter to have Private Christian transferred by train to CALCUTTA, as the poor fellow had a bad case of dysentery, with bloody stools, which didn't respond to sulfaguaindine [*sulfa drug used to treat dysentery*].

I'm sleeping on the ground now, near the truck, on my bedding roll, not too bad, as I have my comforter and three blankets, all doubled up, to lie on. One blanket is needed at night, later on, for warmth.

It's rather roughing it, to take off a damp, in part, wet fatigue shirt and pants, roll them up for safety and for a pillow, and then on arising in the morning to put them on all damp again. However, the temp. is so mild, that it means very little difference anyhow; so far it hasn't hurt me.

SATURDAY, MARCH 31, 1945

We rolled out today at 0600, a nice cool morning, that is, cool for India. We drove north on the DARJEELING ROAD, paralleling the RR which is a 2' narrow gauge. Soon the distant hills came into sight and soon the road and RR followed a stream that ran clear and clean looking from a tropical gorge. It was quite a sight, quite a deep gully, with steep sides and a road on each side. The sides were wooded and looking jungelly [*sic*] with wild banana trees in abundance.

Several miles up the river there was a beautiful arched concrete bridge over which we drove, to go back downstream along the hill side and soon back in the plains again. We were in alternate areas of flat rice paddies, and gently rolling tea gardens. These look like carefully trimmed hedges, but in solid blocks, not single lines.

The people are getting to be more and more Mongoloid in appearance with all shades and types of mixtures of both Mongol and the Bengalese including both parent types.

The road was the narrow, black-top, macadamized kind, with wide shoulders, on which the people could walk or drive their ox-carts. There is always someone in the road and the sacred humped cattle, despite the reverence given them, are just as stupid as their American kindred. We don't see any signs of the cattle being revered, in fact, they are treated in a very undignified manner, for they are guided, when yoked to either cart or plow, by having their tails grasped by hand and pulled sideways for guidance.

Here and there in the plains of the BRAHMAPUTRA river valley are hills the usual, rounded type much eroded and arising from the surrounding plain, like an island emerging from the sea. The entire deltas of the GANGES and BRAHMAPUTRA rivers and their respective valleys are evidently a submerged area, the valleys of which have been filled with alluvial deposits.

We drove about 170 miles today and arrived at a British convoy camp about 5:15 p.m. An Indian soldier had me pointed out to him, and he came over, saluted smartly and said the convoy harbor CO would like me to come over for a cup of tea. Much to my surprise, I found him to be an Indian havildar [*sargent*], rank of 2nd Lt. He was very dark dolichocephalic [*long head*] and had a finely featured Denaric nose [*long and thin nose*] and corresponded facies [*sic*]. [3] He spoke English very brokenly and asked me if I could speak URDU, which of course I can't. He salaamed and we shook hands. He had a little folding wood table and several camp stools and reclining chairs in front of a native-type hut, his HQ. With him were 2 corporals, with Baluchi on his shoulder straps and he said that the other was from the frontier. He was a big fellow, about my size (the CO was about 6', as was the Baluchi). These two reminded me a lot of some Serbians in appearance except that they were very much darker. He invited me to supper pointing out a chicken, saying "chicken" and making signs of throat cutting. I first refuse, but then accepted.

At 7:30 the orderly came for me and I sat down at the little table with the havildar (?). He asked me if I wish to wash my hands and I said "Yes," so a soldier brought a little pitcher and poured water over my hands. On the table were 2 dishes of dark looking pieces of chicken, 2 dishes of gruel and 2 plates of bread. There are twice as large and look and taste like tortillas (bread). They are folded in quarters, then again and a piece pulled off by the right hand. I did just what he did, despite knife and fork on my plate and dunked the bread into the chicken gravy—was it hot and peppery! Then later, picked up pieces of chicken and gnawed at them and threw the bones on the ground where a cat was begging for them. Bili is cat in Urdu. Later we ate the gruel, which was rice, milk and sugar. Not bad, especially the chickens, which were well stewed. Then tea, with too much condensed milk in it for my taste, 2 cupfuls [*sic*] and what cups. They had never been properly cleaned since they were first bought.

After I left them, I went to the mess truck and got them some condensed milk and sugar, and danged if I didn't have to have another cup of tea. They seem to be pretty nice fellows, all in army 18 to 23 years. The Corps got 30 rupees a month, that's all. He wanted to come to America and join the American army. Don't blame him.

EASTER SUNDAY, APRIL 1, 1945

Here we are in the Brahmaputra Valley, at the Assam border of India, on Easter Sunday, half-way around the world from home. Had another cup of tea at 6:30 with my Punjab friend, then off on another day's travel. We crossed 2 combination RR and traffic bridges on the way to the ferry crossing of the Brahmaputra at GOOLPARA [*sic, Goalpara*], S. of BONGAIGON [*sic, Bongaigaon is a gateway to western Assam*]. We arrived at "JACKAL HILL," a few miles from the river before noon and had our lunch there.

Here Chaplin Woods held Easter Service under the shade of a big tree and had communion service. The Catholics had a service conducted by Capt. McAuliffe.

We left at 3:30 and on arrival on the river bank were told that we would cross at 1700. The river was over a half mile wide and had a fairly swift current. It was carrying with it a constant stream of water hyacinths and debris. We had a small shower in early part of day and I imagine that the water plants floating down were evidences of rain and freshets [*river flood from heavy rain in the mountains*], which cleared the pools in riverbeds. Most surprising were the school of porpoises or dolphins, we couldn't decide which, which were playing around in the river. Soon the ferry boat appeared. It was a river steamer, side paddles, with 2 barges on one side and one on the other. These barges were tied to one anchored to the shore, which acted as a pier, and a crew of English drivers drove our vehicles on board.

It was twilight when we arrived on the other side, where our vehicles were sorted out again in their proper order. We drove 9 miles to camp, arriving well after dark. This night I slept between 2 trucks on the hard beaten dirt of the convoy parking lot.

MONDAY, APRIL 2, 1945

We got up at 0430 today, to leave camp at 0500. The cooks didn't get up in time, and our departure was delayed till 0530. It sure was annoying. We traveled through the same type of country, hills arising from the flat plains, like islands.

Arrived at PANDU, just outside of GAUHATI about mid-morning and spent the rest of the day there. PANDU is a convoy relay point for trucks that are unloaded at BONGAIGOON [*Bongaigaon*], driven to PANDU, and then driven by another crew to the next station, NOWGONG, I believe. They have Negro and white trucking crews for this. Our convoy station was on the plain at the foot of a small group of hills, one of which was crowned by a native village of some type—someone said that they were temples.

TUESDAY, APRIL 3, 1945

We got off at 0700 this morning. I drove during the first part, as it was hilly and I needed the experience in shifting downgrade. The population is mixed Bengali and Mongolian, more admixture in some areas than others. The plains [*people*] seem to be mainly Indian, often pure, often mixed, while the Hill people seem to be more Mongolian. They are just as dark, are even smaller, and wear different clothes and have a different kind of haircut. Clippers up sides all around, and a big thatch of hair on top.

One village we passed had a road cut in it, where they were digging out the bank. I was very much interested to see some type of brick structure in the soil, some of it 10 ft. underground. Must have been a very old building to be buried that deep. Would have liked to investigate it, but only got a glimpse as we drove through.

We camped this evening on tea estate near DEARGAON [*sic, Dergaon*], which was being used as an airfield for cargo and passenger traffic. We had our vehicles on a flat strip, covered with iron runway matting. McCain got me a cot and set it up in the truck, and I slept very well there.

WEDNESDAY, APRIL 4, 1945

Started out at 0800 this morning on our final lap to CHABUA. It had rained a bit the previous evening and the air was considerably cooler. We were traveling near the center of the BRAHMAPUTRA RIVER VALLEY [*See map 1*] and saw very few hills. The land was flat and considerable areas were swampy. At one spot, we saw 3 old temples, red brick, and at another 3 or 4 more. They all looked old and decrepit, one in particular.

There are numerous tea gardens here. All seem to be planted with regular rows of large trees of the mesquite or locust type, legumes, whether for shade or nitrification of the soil, I don't know. Each has a large, white-washed building, probably for the superintendent; large tea-chuns, drying buildings, with rocks, etc. and the usual coolie lines, quarters and villages.

We camped near CHABUA, HQ, Intermediate Sect. Base Sect. II in a brand-new area, with pyramidal-type tents, shower and bath building, hall and kitchen, etc. This is also in the immediate vicinity of a tea estate [*See Map 2*].

This chapter from diary pages 22-36

ENDNOTES

---

[1] Romanus and Sunderland, *Time Runs Out in CBI* (Office of the Chief of Military History, Department of the Army 1958), vii, 28, 368.; Mary Ellen Condon-Rall, and Albert E. Cowdrey, *The Medical Department: Medical Service in the War against Japan* (Center of Military History, United States Army, 1998), 410-414.

[2] Kirk T. Mosley and Darrell G. McPherson, "Chapter XVII: China-Burma-India Theater," in *Army Medical Service. Preventive Medicine in World War II* (Office of the Surgeon General, Department of the Army, 1976), 634-657.

[3] Partha P. Majumder, "People of India: Biological Diversity and Affinities," in *The Indian Human Heritage,* ed. D. Balasubramanian and N. Appaji Rao (University Press (India) Lt, 1998), 47-49; Isurani Ilayperuma, "Evaluation of Cephalic Indices: a Clue for Racial and Sex Diversity," *Int. J. Morphol,* 29(2011),113-114.

Chapter 3: Hanging Around Chabua

Chabua, in the Assam state of India, was a staging area for transportation in and out of the CBI Theater. This town, east of Dibrugarh, was the headquarters of the district of Dibrugarh in the state of Assam and is on the Brahmaputra River. West of Dibrugarh laid the town of Dergaon, a proposed French refugee staging area and hospital (See Map 2). The CBI Theater was established March 4, 1942 and was broken into two commands— the India-Burma and the China Theaters in October 1944. Chabua was the Northern Area Combat Command Center Headquarters and Service of Supply (SOS) for Intermediate Section Number 2. Additionally Chabua was also the site of the 234th General Hospital, one of four general hospitals in this area and along the Burma Road (See Maps 2 & 3). [1]

The 96th Field Hospital had orders to establish themselves in Kunming, China and expected to spend only a limited time near Chabua. However, this was not meant to be. This delay and other tasks were the beginning of increased frustrations for the 96th Field Hospital, and its commander, Lt. Col. MacMillan.

THURSDAY, APRIL 5, 1945

Spent the day getting set up and arranging details. Were told yesterday that we were to stay here a month and were to send a detachment of men to CALCUTTA to bring back 56 vehicles. This requires about 85 men, leaving the rest here. Well, it's a nice place, if the men don't get too griped [sic]. They have memories like elephants for things they don't like in the post, and seemingly absolutely no remembrance of favors done them. The Officers are like goldfish in a bowl and everything they do is criticized. Many men don't realize that they are in the Army and resent any privileges according to an Officer not accorded to them.

Saw Lt. Col. Wallace, the Intermediate Base #2 surgeon today [*See Map 2*]. He's originally from Coraopolis, grad Coll. Pitt '29 [*University of Pittsburgh*] and M. D. from Western Reserve '33 and worked for a pharmaceutical concern in Albany.

Was occupied partially in finding Officers to substitute for those going on the motor convoy trip. Well, it will keep those fellows busy, many of whom haven't had enough to do.

FRIDAY, APRIL 6, 1945

Getting things well under control. Started Atabrine yesterday. *XXX1*, refused as was not unexpected. Lt. Budz is organizing his convoy detail for the trip.

> *To prevent malaria, which was a major problem in the CBI Theater, the drug Atabrine was used. In this theater, hospital admission for malaria was 180/1000 in 1944. Atabrine prior to the autumn of 1944 was available only in the combat zone, forward of Ledo. In the fall, however, a rigorous full-scale anti-malaria campaign was instituted which included Atabrine, draining swamps, and spraying for mosquitos. The hospital admission rate for malaria decreased almost in half to 95/1000 in 1945 after these preventive measures were instituted (See Chart 3-1).[2]*

> *The major cause of hospital admissions in the CBI was disease and it was higher compared to the Southwest Pacific Theater; over 90% of all hospital admissions resulted from disease in the CBI.*

44

Chart 3-1. Hospital Admissions, U.S. Army by Year in the CBI and Southwest Pacific Theaters of World War II

[Rate expressed as number of admissions per year per 1,000 troops. More than one admission by an individual soldier results in numbers over 1,000]

World War II Theaters	Year	All causes	Non-battle injury	Battle injury and wounds	Malaria	Disease Rate	%
China	1942	1,130	81	3	120	1,046	92
Burma	1943	1,081	84	6	143	991	92
India	1944	1,191	96	18	180	1,077	90
	1945	745	80	4	95	661	90
Southwest	1942	1,035	178	25	60	832	80
Pacific	1943	1,229	71	12	70	1,046	84
	1944	1,013	39	34	58	840	83
	1945	990	99	48	75	843	85

Table adapted from: Spurgeon Neel, *Medical Support of the U.S. Army in Vietnam 1965-1970* (Dept. of the Army, 1991), 33-35.

The Officers were paid this evening and afterwards we all went to SOS Officers mess and club, where we bought things at the PX. The distances here are great, our camp-site, the American staging area in CHABUA (1 1/2 miles away) is 5 miles from HQ SOS and about 3 from the 234th Hospital.

Heard that *XXXI* took his Atabrine like a little man today at breakfast today. Glad we didn't have to use force.

I have my field desk on a box and sit on a smaller box. This time I took the NE corner of the tent, as I roasted on the SW corner at camp KANCHRAPARA. Also took the NW corner in our sleeping tent, which is next to the Orderly tent.

SATURDAY, APRIL 7, 1945

Inspected the area this morning and found it to be in good condition. Kitchen area, not fully policed yet, looked pretty good, too.

We had a smart little shower this morning, not enough to create wind, just enough to lay the dust. And it was quite cool after the shower.

Saw Col. Owens of 234th G. H. which is 5 1/2 miles from our area [*See map 3*]. This hospital originally was the 111th Station Hosp. and was reorganized as a Gen. Hosp. in October 1944, thereby getting a number right next to 232 and 233d, which was activated at Camp Barkely [*sic, usually spelled* Barkeley] at this time.

Col. Owens said that the Japs were in the mountains about 30 miles S. of us from Feb. to April last year. We heard today that 5 O. and 27 EM were to leave on Sunday morning for CALCUTTA by train, before being paid. Capt. Hogan is trying to get them paid, if not, I have made arrangements that Sgt. Brojoc will be able to lend them R 30 apiece.

SUNDAY, APRIL 8, 1947

Have made arrangements to pay the men this morning, before their trip to CALCUTTA, so that part has been taken care of, making all feel better, especially the men.

Lober [*Lamber?*] and I went over to see Col. Owens, 234th G. H. Had a nice visit there and lunch as well. Saw a fellow who had been badly clawed by a tiger. He had wounded him the day before and found him next day in a ditch. The tiger jumped him before he could shoot and clawed him badly before his buddy shot the tiger. The story is going around about three EM who got drunk on "jungle juice," and decided to raid a small village for women. The natives beat them up so badly, that one died before he could be attended to, another had his skull fractured and the occipital lobe laid bare, and multiple fractures of arms and legs.

Another is a story of a Negro soldier who was in an engineering detachment and strayed off to some native villages. A few days later his headless body was found in front of the HQ door.

Broke up a crap game this evening; to be expected that they gamble but they should have sense enough not to gamble where I can see them.

Took the men to a USO show and to the final elimination boxing matches at "Madison Square Garden," an area near the polo grounds and the ATC [*Air Transport Command*] flying field. There were really some fine matches and everyone enjoyed them.

MONDAY, APRIL 9, 1945

We sent the remaining men to CALCUTTA this morning, about 47 of them where they will pick up some more vehicles. Have started our schedule again, calisthenics, Chinese classes, etc. Our TO/E equipment is arriving now and we will have to send a crew down to pick it up.

Hardly any men here this evening, as they are all on pass, as my pass policies are very liberal. We got a per diem allowance of $7.00 a day, total of $52.50 for our trip, not bad at all [*About $683 in 2015 dollars*].

TUESDAY, APRIL 10, 1945

Last night Baurnhardt and Nowell were hypnotizing some of the men, among them *XXX14*, our bugler. While under hypnosis, they suggested to him that he blow taps in the morning instead of reveille. They bet McAuliffe 2rs that he would, or at least want to play taps. Sure enough at 0700, *XXX14* got out his bugle and started to warm his bugle up by playing notes of taps! Then he must have realized that this was the wrong call, for he actually did play reveille then, in a badly botched manner, as he isn't a good bugler at best! It rained heavily last night and this morning is cloudy and cool.

Went to the Officer's QM sales store, and I got myself a fatigue cap just a little small, but their only size. O'Neil got 5 1/2 yards of Chino cloth for a "Bush jacket." If it turns out well, I'll get some too, and get one of the native tailors here to make me one. A lazy day, nice and cool with occasional rain squalls in clearing up at 1600.

WEDNESDAY, April 11, 1945

Had O'Neil get me 5 1/2 yds. of 8 ounce china cloth for a bush jacket. Might as well get one, I guess. Was measured for it by Indian tailor, who looks like Bengali, but has hooked nose, and is from the PUNJAB, and speaks URDU and is a Mohammedan [*Muslim*].

This evening went to our warehouse, 15 miles away, where our stuff and the 95th's is being stored. As it was only about 6 miles further to DIBRUGHAR [*sic, Dibrugarh, Assam, India near Chabua*], Feldmesser and I went there.

There is quite a native shopping district here. The town itself is the official gov't seat for upper ASSAM. The stores are of the usual native-type, usually 10 x 10, open spaces in front of their dwelling places very frequently. The town is much less Europeanized than Calcutta, streets narrower and dirty, full of ox-carts and foul smells.

Watched a native group of jeweler's at work, one was beating out a silver tube over a piece of wood. Another [*was*] gold plating a chain by putting gold filings on the chain then melting them on by means of a small mouth tube heated by a flame made by cotton wick in some sort of vegetable oil. Another was engraving a ring and the oldest was cutting a flower design in a pair of brass bracelets, embedded in wax, with a little hammer and chisel.

Around the corner was a jewelry store, where I found a flexible silver weave bracelet for Babbie. It weighed 13 1/2 tolas (35 tolas to 1#) and sold for R/2 per tola–R/27.

At sunset, we had quite a severe thunderstorm. No nearby flashes but many in the clouds. Later a real storm came up. Thunder and lightning and a real gale. The tent shook as if it were going to fly away and lots of hail came down as well as a heavy rain. Inspection later on showed very little damage.

THURSDAY, APRIL 12, 1945

We went to DIBRUGHAR [*Dibrugarh*] this evening and bought a hollow pair of bracelets and some Hindu religious post cards. Some stuff, elephant-headed gods, monkey-faced gods, blue-colored gods, looking cyanotic, and something other religions don't have, such as gods with 4, 6 and even 8 arms.

FRIDAY, APRIL 13, 1945

Received the sad news of President Roosevelt's death this morning on the radio. Died at 1600 in U. S. at about 0230 our time, next day here.

We received 21 of our 39 authorized officers and nurses watches, today. On our way back, Sgt. Feldmesser and I attended a Seikh service, in commemoration of the anniversary of the founding of their religion (See letter to Babs).[3] Had a nice cool evening, amused by Zeit, who had bought a beautiful ivory box for R/65/0 and was being kidded into believing that it was bone not ivory. Tried all kinds of tests on another little ivory elephant, even breaking it with a hammer and charring it, to get the odor.

Touching a heated pin to ivory does not produce a smell, but touching a heated pin to bone smells like burning hair.

SATURDAY, APRIL 14, 1945

Forgot that this was inspection day and only got to inspect the kitchen which was in excellent condition. Gave the men a talk on the Sikh temple experience and a sort of general outline of Sikh history.

Gave the finance office $225.00 for three $100.00 war bonds. Will have to try to send as much home as I can. I guess, though we'll be able to save pretty well with Babs in Sydney and our home rented and becoming more of ours each year.

His wife, Barbara, was from Sydney, Nova Scotia, Canada. During his time overseas in 1945 she and their son, Donald, lived with her parents in Sydney.

SUNDAY, APRIL 15, 1945

A quiet day, nothing doing at all, except that, on order of Gen. Cranston all units, including ours hold memorial services for President Roosevelt at 1130 this morning. I read the order and the proclamation of Sec. of State, Stettinius [*and*] had the men stand in silent prayer, and prayed aloud for the new president.

MONDAY, APRIL 16, 1945

In the morning got a box from our TO/E stock and expected to find a 350 watt generator instead found an X-Ray transformer, so had to make another trip in the evening to get a generator this time. This little generator is a honey. It is powered by a 1 cylinder gasoline motor of 1/2 h. p. We cleaned it up as directed and got the motor running, but, couldn't get any electricity out of it. We took off generator shield, and found nothing wrong and then pared off its little switchboard, and found nothing wrong there. After supper Eckrote had it running. This was the trouble. We just didn't have the motor going fast enough. Don't know why, but they had the motor going, too fast and had a lot of trouble throttling it down and running smoothly. Finally we succeeded pretty well in regulating speed and voltage. The little machine actually delivered 250 volts, instead of 110, when going too fast.

This evening Capt. Sopka asked me if we could move to adjacent tents as the 10th Air Force were moving out, and 8000 men were to move through our little area. The 10th is moving out after over two years in China. Lots of joy to them on their return to the U.S. Well, we'll move first thing after breakfast. Had meeting with officers and appointed Lt. Wurtzebach as O in charge.

TUESDAY, APRIL 17, 1945

We moved this morning and were pretty well set up in 1 hour. Of course, it took the rest of the morning to get the tag ends [*last details*] in order. The O and EM left the old position in nearly perfect order. I complemented the O on the good appearance of the area they left. For some reason or the other, the O are the worst offenders in such matters.

At officer's call had to tell those for whose promotion we had put in, that SOS HQ #2 wouldn't accept them, as we are only transient here and not assigned to them.

This evening we had our wire stringers at work, putting our wires up on the tent poles, so that we can use our power for lights and a few radios. Saw Maj. Sloan and Lt. Zanotta at SOS HQ and found out that our convoy was on its way, and was expected back about 21st. Lt. Z. questioned me on how many days rest the men would need and I told him 4 or 5 would do.

WEDNESDAY, APRIL 18, 1945

Had our generators up today and lights in Ord. Room [*orderly room*] and 1st two Off. [*Officers*] tents and 3 tents used for Dispensary, Supply and Special Services. Worked very nicely. Had my own radio on enough to find out that it works and wasn't damaged by transit.

The days are getting hotter, though the nights are still good and cool. No rain now for several days.

This morning Hogan and I drove to the British Officers' shop, beyond TURSULKIA where I bought 2 pairs of long stockings to wear with shorts and a bush shirt, which is worn with tails out, in latest U. S. feminine style.

We hit the jackpot in mail today getting four bags full. This is the mail that preceded us to KUNMING where we figured that we would be now. Received about 6 letters from Babs, one each from mother and dad and Gordon [*his brother*] as well as a letter from Kay Ramsey. She had APO 494 and must have looked it up in official records as that isn't the proper APO#. It was nice to get all these letters. There still are some magazines to be distributed yet.

Took my bush shirt over to get the sleeves cut down and got a pair of cotton pants cut down, too.

THURSDAY, APRIL 19, 1945

Went with Sgt. Feldmesser to Ordinance. We will get 100 carbines and 2 pistols to take over the road with us and then turned over to Ordinance in KUNMING. These arms and some ammunition will be issued to us a few days before we leave.

Mail today brought me 2 more letters from Babs, as well as a few magazines. My old cotton blouse arrived, as well as some plumbers' candles, pipe and pouch and Yardley's shaving soap. The box they came in was completely demolished and the candles were all out of shape.

Last night while checking up as O.D., Capt. Hogan found one guard post empty and another guard sitting in an ambulance. That's bad business and court marshals will result from this. It's too bad that some things just can't be relaxed.

Am wearing shorts and bush shirt today (also wore bush jacket this morning when it was cold).

FRIDAY, APRIL 20, 1945

Heard today that our convoy is to arrive tomorrow as scheduled. Also heard that they may have to make another convoy trip later on to which I voiced my disapproval, stating that we hoped to be on our way by that time, and furthermore I wasn't sure about the men's condition, after being on crackers and peanut butter and C-rations for nearly 10 days. We nearly lost our 6 big generators, as they had been shipped, just this day, to Ledo. They located them, however, and promised to give them back to us tomorrow. We will try to get 10 rifles for instruction purposes. Heard that Chinese bandits had attacked a convoy on the road. Gosh, we would be white meat for them if we had no arms [*guns*].

SATURDAY, APRIL 21, 1945

A dull drizzly sort of day. Inspected the area this morning and found it generally excellent, except for a few tents especially in cooks' row. The mess department had trouble due to lack of water—none in pipes.

Our 6 KVA [*kilovolt amp*] generators came in today. They are large, boxed-in boxes 10' x 6' x 4' and weigh well over a ton. There were only 5 on the truck and trailer and the driver said that the other one had fallen off! I had visions of the box being all smashed up, but there was no visible damage done. Only some dirt and scratches on the box.

At about this time our combat drivers came. They had a rather rugged time of it, especially as they hadn't been given sufficient rations to last them the entire trip. They didn't seem to mind it very much, however.

An issue in the overall India-Burma Theater was a lack of supplies including food. For example, the men of Merrill's Marauders and other jungle fighters in Burma became extremely malnourished.[4] This in turn led to weakened troops who more easily succumbed to tropical diseases such as dysentery which caused severe diarrhea and prevented absorption of food. Malaria, as previously mentioned, was also a major cause of morbidity (sickness) along with other tropical diseases.

They had a slight scare when someone at JACKAL HILL, warned them that a man-eating tiger was in the neighborhood. The other [*story*] followed their hitting and killing a calf. They made two mistakes, one in stopping, and picking up the calf, and the other in gutting it and putting it over the hood of a truck and carrying it in public that way. At one stop, an excited group of native surrounded them as they thought that it was one of their calves. A shot, fired off into the air scattered them, but they kept a double guard around the camp all that night.

We had a late lunch for the men, and supper for all at 6 o'clock. The drivers all went to bed early for a good night sleep. Have been having considerable trouble with little Anza radio [*radio purchased at Camp Anza?*]. Brummett had the tubes checked and found two of them weak. We did a lot of switching of tubes in the evening and got Barnhardt's SS tubes and mine all mixed up.

SUNDAY, APRIL 22, 1945

Overcast this morning and clearing as the sun rose. That doggone radio is working well this morning and so is Barnhardt's too.

The trouble is with the weak oscillator tubes, which evidently need higher voltage before they begin to oscillate.

A lazy day, hot and sunshiny. At about 1530 the loudspeaker summoned me for a phone call. Urgent. The transportation O. wanted to know our strength in O and EM, as DELHI [*Theater Base Section 1 Surgeon's Office; See map 2*] wanted the information immediately. Don't know why, but, we hope it is in preparation for further travel.

MONDAY, APRIL 23, 1945

Had a written report by Lts. Budz [*Budziszewski*] and Ostroff on the troubles with our motor convoy from CALCUTTA, here. Signed it myself and turned it over to Lt. Zonatto. Told him that the report was rough, and I'd be d—d if I'd send my men out under such conditions again. He was in a hurry (he is a busy man) and said that he had a report to send into the G–6 [*Assistant Chief of Staff for Information Management*]. Left the report with him. However, he wants us to go out on another such trip as it appears that we will be here till after first of June. That's pretty tough, as I had hoped that we would be over the road by then. He claims that we should have been kept at Camp KANCHRAPORA and not sent here. Well, here the climate is a lot more pleasant and I prefer it very much to the CALCUTTA region. My radio is working fine now, and Barnhardt has his loudspeaker working again and so he is happy.

Am having the O and EM who made the trip rest up now and take it easy for the next day or two.

TUESDAY, APRIL 24, 1945

A rather quiet day, hot in the evening as usual. The usual cumulus clouds over the HIMALAYAS too. The O and EM played ball and the O won 3-2. Barnhardt hypnotized Bromberg, quite a neat stunt.

WEDNESDAY, APRIL 25, 1945

At SOS HQ saw Lt. Zanotta, who told me that there might be a convoy trip to China for some of our drivers. We really will be the 96th F. H. and I. M. Trucking Co., yet.

This evening Capt. Anderson called me and wondered if we could supply 50 men for ordinance work. I told him that he could have 100 if he needed them. Our baseball team was defeated 5-3 by the 95th F. H. Was a close game, will lick e'm next time. Our officers beat our EM again after the 95th game.

Recreation and games were encouraged to keep troops occupied when not busy with military duties. Sports also provided some physical exercise.

THURSDAY, APRIL 26, 1945

A quiet day. Got a collapsible chair from British Officer's shop. It's very nice and comfortable and a big help, much more comfortable than sitting on boxes and bedsides.

FRIDAY, APRIL 27, 1945

Saw Capt. Anderson, Gen. Cranston's adjutant, and later met Gen. Cranston, Col. Ireland, Lt. Col. Donovan, Lt. Col. Morris, Maj. Monk, etc., in the transportation section of SOS HQ + H 2. They all seem to be very nice and knew me, due to the rather rough report I put in on the convoy trip from CALCUTTA, but they didn't seem to be displeased and complemented us on our two convoys and our men volunteering to do extra driving for the T. C. at JACKAL HILL.

We are to furnish men for a convoy, every other day, starting Monday, to drive in the morning to DIRGOON [*sic, Dergaon, Assam in the Brahmaputra river valley*] where they will pick up trucks and drive to our nearby dispersal area.

Rain this morning, cooling the air and clearing up at noon. We sent 50 men at 1330 to the 199th Ordinance Depot near MAKUM to work there supervising the coolies and help around.

In the baseball game between us and the 494th AA [*anti-aircraft*] outfit, Clemo received a nasty contusion of his right arm when hit by a slung bat. Received our monthly ration of a case of beer per man today. The beer really got a workout this night. Other outfits receive their ration, too, and there was singing and shouting all over the camp from some of the d—fools who drank probably their whole case this evening. Many were staggering around and when the Red Cross girls came in their truck, after the movies with coffee and donuts, some of the remarks and shouts of those birds must have been embarrassing, to say the least. Otherwise the soldiers were not too badly behaved.

SATURDAY, APRIL 28, 1945

Major Monks and his Sgt. arrived this morning and talked to the drivers. We'll be able to have 2 sets of drivers, so each man will only need to drive every 4th day. Not bad, just enough to keep him busy on occasions and to break up the monotony of our sojourn here.

While I was inspecting the kitchen here, a Lt. Col. Verder and a Capt. Cole, the former from the 14th were inspecting the area and dropped into our kitchen. It looks as if they are planning to take over our area. We may be kicked out, hope not. Or maybe they can hasten our trip out of here.

The rifles were being cleaned today. We have 100 .03's, Winchester and Remingtons. Our troops will get lots of training with the rifles. The officers beat the drivers today 19 to 2. What a licking they took.

Here's a story to make one's hair stand on end. It seems that a C-47 [*Skytrain*] was taking 40 wounded Chinese and their baggage over the hump from KUNMING to ASSAM. They hit icing conditions and the Co-pilot went to tell the Chinese to lighten the load. This was done and the plane made a safe landing. When the pilot checked on his cargo he found only 32 Chinese left. They had thrown out the 8 heaviest man, rather than jettison the baggage! Sent Babbie's box by parcel post today. Wonder how long it will take before she receives it.

SUNDAY, APRIL 29, 1945

A busy day indeed. While I was still loafing around in bed, Capt. Sopka came in the tent and told me that he had some news and this was it. How would we like to examine and take over medical care for some French refugees coming in from China? 200 a day (until 2000 or more are taken care of). Okay, that suited me. He told me what building to use as our dispensary and examination room and said that he would put them in tents in our area and would feed them, though he needed 4 of our cooks and 2 O and 7 EM to work registering them. I looked over the building and found it suited for our purposes and told Capt. Remy to take charge as supervisor.

At 1000 we had a meeting–Capt. Sopka's office, attended by Maj. Keith, Lt. Col. Marshall (SOS surgeon), Lt. Col. Radcliffe, SOS S-4, W O. Downs S-2, etc. They also discussed the old British hospital at PANITOLA and we all drove out there and looked at it. Not too bad; the buildings were in good state of repair, mostly of Indian type, stucco sides, but 4 were thick brick structures, more or less bombproof. One operating room and 3 wards. The engineers were working on the kitchen, which will be too small for our purposes, I'm afraid. The lighting system and the water systems were in bad shape. The latrines were a disgrace, even the squat-type ones were all stopped up and all the good bowls had been taken away. Really, as far as sanitation was concerned, the place was a mess. The most incongruous sight was that every room had cow-pads in it, without exception. What entices the sacred cattle in rooms with concrete and stone floors is beyond me.

At 1330 Ostroff and I went to SOS HQ and met Maj. Langer, S-4 to talk over our Q.M. supply problem. What a job that will be, too. Met Mr. Shepherd, ARC, and discussed its function.

Forgot to mention the most important thing. The collected officers said that I was to be CO of the refugee camp. "It's your baby," they said. Well, from just being in charge of physical exams and dispensaries I was elevated, just like that, to take charge of housing and health of 2000 French refugees. What a job! Well, anyhow, that's not too far from running a hospital, at that, though much less interesting from a medical view-point, 2000 women and children. Wow! We are now the 96th Field Hospital, Quartermaster Trucking and Refugee Camp outfit.

MONDAY, APRIL 30, 1945

Had Sandlin check the old British hospital for accurate bed space; Brummett checked the water and electricity; Browne the sanitation, and O'Neil the mess facilities. We're running a real hotel–but yet, a hospital is a hotel anyhow, so we are well set to do that job.

Gen. Cranston came to our area this morning and I talked to him while he sat in his car. From the way he talked, it appears that I'll have charge of the refugees in our BOLIJON staging area. Well, I can handle that part too. Understand that 4 CIC [*Counter Intelligence Corps*], one O and 3 EM will start working with us in registering the people. That will be quite a help to us.

Capt. Hogan will have quite an administrative job and will have lots of forms to fill out and lots of paperwork to do. This evening saw Maj. Williams, C. E. [*Corps of Engineers*] and he will see that the latrines are cleaned and will furnish us electric light bulbs on requisition. Lt. Col. Radcliffe helped me get 25 coolies for one day, tomorrow. They will work under Capt. Browne.

Heard that our nurses will arrive today and the 95th's as well. Quick work! Notified yesterday and on the way within 24 hours. They will be stationed and housed at the 234th G. H. and most of them will work there. They have 2 wards set aside for possible need of the refugees.

We had the nurses' baggage sent to their quarters this morning. One of our trucks, on the way to DEERGOAN [*Dergaon*] got off the road, side-swiped a tree and two men were hurt. Balcercak lost a finger from his right hand, poor fellow. He's a barber and plays a saxophone. Beckman got a crack clavicle and scapula. Too bad.

TUESDAY, MAY 1, 1945

Had Browne off this morning to supervise the tea-garden coolies who were cleaning out the wards. Ostroff was drawing supplies and light bulbs for the place and Brummett was working on the utilities. Then, a phone call with the message that the Pantolo hospital deal was off, that we were to take care of them here in our BALIPAN staging area, and also, that some delay had developed, and the refugees weren't being sent over so soon.

Spent a while this evening on the consideration of the opposing views Budz and Stotzberg had on the accident of the previous day.

Nurses haven't arrived yet. Saw Beckman and Balcerak at hospital, who weren't doing so badly. This evening it developed that the entire refugee deal may be off, as De Gaulle [*French General*] has decided that they could remain in the interior, near Indo-Chine, Burma and China border.

Lt. Crawford, MP's, dropped in this evening with a Pfc. who claims that his truck was pushed off the road by one of ours. Had *XXX12* up and he admitted cutting close, but didn't feel any blow from hitting other car, else he would have stopped and ascertained damage.

Well, we'll just have to take them off driving and put them on KP for a while, which may make them come to their senses.

WEDNESDAY, MAY 2, 1945

A lazy day, didn't do much, though there were a number of inconsequential phone calls that kept me trotting over to HQ orderly room.

Early this morning, 24 O and EM left by plane to DIRGOAN [*Dergaon*] to drive trucks back, while the other 16 had to go by truck and then drive back 240 miles altogether, which is quite a tough grind.

We're going to put up an X-Ray generator for power and have some men rooting through our boxes for them. They asked for 24 additional men to drive trucks today and wanted their names and ASN [*Army Service Number*] and weight for an airplane ride down to DEERGOON [*Dergaon*].

Our other drivers for today were pretty well disgusted, as they had been given British Dodge 1 1/2 ton trucks to drive. These trucks were in bad condition and caused trouble because they have double gas tanks, which the drivers didn't know about and which have to be turned on, the second used when the first is empty.

The latest rumor has it that there will be 4000 refugees, but no one knows when they will appear.

TUESDAY, MAY 3, 1945

Our 24 men left this morning by plane and drove the trucks back, getting back at 1400, tired and dusty. A quiet day. They want 2 men to work at CHABUA radio station, *VU22V*.

Our X-Ray generator is in commission now 2 K.W. [*Kilowatts*]. Due to our small load and the generator rated to put out

126V. [*Volts*] we have to run it at a slightly slower rate of speed and in consequence only have about 50 cycles per sec.

I'm figuring on taking the DEERGOON [*Dergaon*] convoy trip tomorrow.

THURSDAY, MAY 4, 1945

Arose at 0400 in the dark for our convoy trip. We drove 2 trucks with our 18 men and 2 officers in them. Browne and I drove one truck alternately. We went down without any incidents. It was dusty, but soon it started to rain a bit, which laid the dust and made travel easier. Near the DEERGOON [*Dergaon*] airstrip, we found our trucks, new Studebakers, loaded each with 18, 50-gal. drums of gas. After checking our vehicles, we drove in one of our trucks to the area mess hall where we had lunch at 1100.

On our way back it rained some, which was bad, as it didn't rain enough to stop the dust from rising, but made the windshield wet and the dust stuck to it.

SATURDAY, MAY 5, 1945

On our way out, Capt. Sopka stopped us and said that there was a phone call for me. It was Lt. Downs and I told him that I would be down to see him. He stated that the refugee plan was hot again, this time we were to take over an old British troop area near DIBRUGHAR [*Dibrugarh*]. Met Mr. Reed and Mr. Rutledge, the latter police officer for this area. Then Lt. Downs, Capts. Hogan and McAuliffe and I ate lunch at the Polo Grounds and then we drove to DIBRUGHAR [*Dibrugarh*], 4 1/2 miles over a very rough road. We came to the "Reinforcement Area," a place laid out in 4 squares, around two crossing streets with an oval space in the middle where 2 office buildings were. The area to be used by our troops was at the far end of the main road. Its buildings are adequate for our use as HQ, mess, dispensary and Officer's quarters. The EM will occupy tents in the former officer's area.

Later in the evening I met Maj. Woolamb, the British officer with whom we will work on the project. On our way back, I met Lt. Col. Welty, executive officer, who said that he would be glad to help us out with any problem we had.

> *Technically the overall command in CBI was Vice Adm. Lord Louis Mountbatten who was appointed as the supreme Allied Commander of South-East Asia forces in October 1943. Mountbatten was an uncle of Prince Philip, Duke of Edinburgh. During the war years, India was part of the British Empire and thus had British troops stationed throughout the country.[5]*

This chapter from diary pages 36-52

ENDNOTES

---

[1] *"Dibrugarh,"* Wikipedia, *Accessed February 5, 2015.*
http://en.wikipedia.org/wiki/Dibrugarh; Charles F. Romanus and Riley Sutherland, *Time Runs Out in CBI* (Office of the Chief of Military History, 1959), 6; George L. MacGarrigle, *Central Burma: 29 January–15 July 1945* (Army Center of Military History 1996), 6-7.

[2] Spurgeon Neel, *Medical Support of the U.S. Army in Vietnam 1965-1970* (Department of the Army, 1991), 35; Mary Ellen Condon-Rall and Albert E. Cowdrey, *The Medical Department: Medical Service in the War against Japan* (Center of Military History United States Army), 292-294.

[3] This letter is unavailable.

[4] Charles F. Romanus and Riley Sunderland, *Stilwell's Command Problems*: *U.S. Army in World War II* (Office of the Chief of Military History, 1956),189; MacGarrigle, *Central Burma: 29 January–15 July 1945* (U.S. Army Center of Military History, 1996?), 6.

[5] Charles F. Romanus, and Riley Sunderland, *Stilwell's Mission to China* (Office of the Chief of Military History, 1953), 360; MacGarrigle (1996?), 4, 7-8; Philip Ziegler, *Mountbatten: The Official Biography* (Collins, 1985), 241-278.

Chapter 4: Still in Assam: Flying over the Hump

SUNDAY, MAY 6, 1945

A group of us; Capt. Browne, sanitarian; Capt. Brummett, utilities; Lt. Ostroff, supply; Lt. O'Neil, mess; Lt. Stalzberg, water and a few others went down to our new area, looked it over and measured the buildings and mapped out our campaign and laid our plans out.

MONDAY, MAY 7, 1945

McAuliffe and I went to see our 50 men who are on D. S. with 199th Ordinance Depot near MAKUM. Only saw Sgt. Olsen who reported that all were in good spirits and seemed to be satisfied with their jobs. On the way back, I bought some coasters and ashtrays, all brass.

Tomorrow we are sending a number of men out to help drive a convoy over the Ledo-Burma Road. This is the first of three groups we are sending out.

On Tuesday, May 8, 1945, the British, French, Scandinavian countries and others celebrated V-E, or (Victory in Europe) day for the ending of World War II in the European theater. It is curious that MacMillan is silent about this most important day. Not only did a number of members in his unit have radios, a newsletter to the troops, called Jungle Jargon: Assam's Leading Publication *was available. This four-sided mimeographed newsletter, published every two days, had a variety of information. It included local, state side and world news, a comic strip, cartoon, movie and USO schedules, sports news, and censored information of what was going on in the war on the Western, Italian, Eastern, Burma, and Philippine fronts. This newsletter also had programming for the local military radio VU2ZV which included news, music, entertainment and sports.*

A yellowed copy of Jungle Jargon was found with the diary dated April 18 and April 19, 1945. The leading headline on the front page was "American Armies battering 4 Nazi cities." Another article states that "a total of 1674 Jap aircraft shot down since Mar. 18. Adm. Nimitz announces that Amer. now control two-thirds of Okinawa."

TUESDAY, MAY 8, 1945

Our men left, about half of them armed with .03 rifles - didn't look much like a medical outfit when they left. Good luck to them, wish I were going along. About 0930 there was a call for Drs. over the TP [*telephone*] system. A truckload of coolies had upset and injured quite a number, some severely, most however were unscratched. We gave them first aid and sent 4 ambulance loads to St. Luke's Hospital down the road. Here an amusing incident occurred. The gate was locked, so some of our boys took the gate off the hinges and just drove in. The elderly missionary lady Dr. came out, as mad as a wet hen, and, among other things she said, was that we were "jungle-burglars."

The heat is off the refugee deal, so were just putting our plans away for a while. We will have to move to the southeast of our camp soon, and are laying plans for it now.

For May 9, 1945 there was no entry in the diary.

THURSDAY, MAY 10, 1945

Our second group of drivers, under Lt. Budz left this morning. The rumor mongers are coming out again with the story of a convoy of 40 vehicles, which disappeared without trace on the highway [*Ledo-*

Burma Road]. This rumor is heard from time to time, probably started to scare some men going for the first time. It's in the class of rumor which states that 1 of every four vehicles goes off the road and smashes two pieces at the bottom of 1000 ft. drop.

Heard today of an ordinance outfit, which had come across with us on the U.S.S. Mann, and had been sent to KWEILIN (*Guilin*), CHINA, was back here at camp again. They thought they would be sent to KUNMING, but were sent here instead.

SATURDAY, MAY 12, 1945

The end row of our new area is being prepared for Bombay type tents . The old squad tents are being removed and natives are putting up poles for the new ones. Will move in on Monday, so will work on the tents tomorrow.

SUNDAY, MAY 13, 1945

We put up 11 Bombay. tents today. They are definitely cooler, due to the extra fly and the resultant airspace between. They must be good cold weather tents too, as they are quilted and have 3 or 4 layers. They have sides, with windows and the sides can't be rolled up, but have to be looped over the tent and guy ropes.

Heard from our nurses today. Lt. Bornemann and 5 others arrived about 4:00 p.m. by airplane. They had a rough trip, as they ran into a thunderstorm. 4 of the girls are patients at 234th G. H. in CALCUTTA, where 3 of the poor things came down with amoebic dysentery and the other received an electric shock while ironing.

MONDAY, MAY 14, 1945

We moved two rows of our tents today, the officer's row, and the dispensary and supply row. O'Neil was all hot and bothered, because I had told him I was thinking of putting the cooks in the only two Bombay tents in the second row, and had promised the cooks that they would get them. My final decision was to use one of these tents for dispensary and special services with Lt. Lorenz and Barnhardt sleeping in them. To bring about peace to all, I had another Bombay tent put up for the cooks. Then, of course, others wanted Bombay too, but none are available. If we can get 3 more, will put one up for the Sgts. of each platoon.

Hogan and I went down this morning to see the nurses and found that some from the 95th had come in, too. We chatted for a while and they invited us for lunch and we ate at the officer's mess of the 234th. They had their troubles at the 234th. They were robbed 4 times while housed in one basha. That's a shame. Lt. Bornemann, my chief nurse, asked me for permission to get married (that's Army routine) and I very gladly gave it to her. It seems that her fiancé is in the CBI Theater, MYITKYINA in particular, just an hour or so away by air, and this will be her opportunity. It's been hot all day and cloudless, till about 4 p.m. when a high haze and some distant clouds darkened the sun. Looks like a good old monsoon rain on the way. We'll find out how good our tents are—have the best hopes, as they are brand-new.

TUESDAY, MAY 15, 1945

It didn't rain during the night, but it rained all day, clearing at sunset. The rest of the nurses have arrived and I met some and invited them for lunch tomorrow.

The remaining 3 rows moved to the new area this morning. The O and EM recreation tents were struck, but not erected, due to the rain. The Hofling [?] affair reached its climax, as I thought that OR [*oral reprimand*] punishment would be better than Summary Court, as [*summary court*] would lead to trouble and personalities due to the feeling engendered by it.

Wednesday May 16, 1945 was not entered in diary

THURSDAY, MAY 17, 1945

Capt. Remy and I had an appointment with some British officers at the old reinforcement area, near DIBRUGARH. We arrived there on time, but no Britishers [*sic*] showed up. We located the latrine areas and left at 1115. We stopped at DIBRUGARH and did some shopping. Got Babbie some earrings and a bracelet to match, silver, with little bangles on it that sound a little like bells. Also got 6 chrome-plated coasters. We had lunch at the "Golden Dragon," a Chinese place. Had tea and "Eggs and Chips." We called on Maj. Woolam, the British O. in charge, and told him that we hadn't seen anyone at the new refugee area. He checked on why his men weren't there and found that the telephone line was down and his men hadn't been notified.

On the way back, stopped at CHABUA, and got a big Oriental decanter, 6 brass goblets and a big tray—R 55/0/0.

Friday, May 18, 1945 no entry in the diary.

SATURDAY, MAY 19, 1945

Inspection very good this morning, only Dispensary and Special Service tent area looking bad.

Sunday May 20 through Tuesday May 22, 1945 no entry in the diary.

WEDNESDAY, MAY 23, 1945

Had a sort of party at bungalow #1, Officer's Club, with most of the O and nurses attending. We just sat around and talked and drank rum and Coca-Cola and John Collins. Met Miss Bornemann's fiancé, Capt. McAndrews, MC, who is with the 20th Evac. H. in MYITKYINA, where most of the patients are Chinks. They're hoping to get married soon. He is about 45, an ex-football player and divorced.

Bashas were used as officer's quarters, hospital wards, and other community buildings. From: A. Steven Graham, "Chapter XIV: India-Burma and China Theaters," in B. Noland Carter, ed, *Medical Department, United States Army, Surgery in World War II. Activities of Surgical Consultants, Vol II* (Department of the Army, 1964), p. 923

THURSDAY, MAY 24, 1945

Much rain last night and quite cool today. Found some of my tobacco to have become moldy and there is some mold on the edge of the soles of my dress shoes. Just the beginning of what we'll have soon.

Had a phone call from Capt. Anderson, SOS HQ adjutant and he told me that I had clearance from "Hump Reg." for a flight over the hump and that my due date was Monday 28th. Am to pick up orders tomorrow.

FRIDAY, MAY 25, 1945

Was told to give my weight (215) and baggage weight to control office. One guess said that baggage weight was 65# so rolled up bedding roll and Val PAC, which came to about 68#, so I took out the briefcase and the blanket. Later that evening a messenger brought over 2 baggage tags. I expected to receive a call anytime, but nothing happened and was planning on retiring, when a call came for me to bring the baggage to the orderly room. I went up with it, and was told that I would leave at about 0530, Sunday morning. Thus I had to sleep on a bare "charpoy" [*woven Indian bed*] without my bedding roll. Did all right, sleeping on raincoats, etc. —having 1 blanket for cover—and using a mosquito screen from a tent as my own mosquito bar.

Saturday, May 26, 1945 no entry in diary

SUNDAY, MAY 27, 1945

Awakened at about 0530 and got dressed. It was raining and very muddy, so I took the jeep over to the orderly room and left it there. We stood around a while and about an hour later got into jeeps and trucks and were driven down to the airport. Here we awaited our turn in line to be fitted up with parachutes and an oxygen mask. After this we were briefed. The back rest part of the parachute is packed with all sorts of things for an emergency landing, anything felt necessary, even presents for natives, as well as written notices in several dialects.

No breakfast and we were hungry and no breakfast in sight, either. We soon boarded the plane and I was fortunate enough to get a seat near a window. We sat in two rows, about 20 of us, with our backs to the sides of the plane, and, the middle part of the floor occupied by our lashed luggage.

Shortly thereafter we taxied off, load 103 of May '45, for a trip over the "hump." After taxing around for a while, we got on a good runway and we were soon picking up speed. The ground rushed by faster and faster and the bumps got harder and harder. Next thing, the bumping stopped, and the big plane was off in its own element at 0950. We gradually rose, and soon hit the level of the low flying clouds. Soon we were through these, into another layer and then above the clouds. They were like a layer of cotton wool, with the sun above and the rain below. We could glimpse now and then the land below. Flat areas of rice paddies, tea gardens, patches of jungle and roads and streams.

Visibility was poor as we flew east. We crossed the SHAN and BURMA mountains without seeing them and flew over the flat areas around MYITKYINA. As we cross the ridges of the Burmese and S. China Himalayas, visibility increased, as more and more rifts formed in the clouds. What I saw of the jumble of mountains was not too wild. Everywhere, especially in valleys, but anywhere there was more or less adaptable land, were numerous patches of rice paddies, most of them steppe-like, as they follow the contours of the hills.

There were numerous trails and tracks all over the landscape. We saw no forest or jungle, but many patches of wooded areas with sparse tree growths, the trees solitary, like checkers on a board, but not quite that regular.

After 2 hours of flight—most of the time wearing oxygen masks—we came down a little lower and saw the big lake KUNMING is situated on. This is a big, flat valley, every bit of which seems to be used for farming, village sites, cemeteries, and recent military areas and dumps. The slit trenches, zig-zag for protection, are seemingly scattered haphazardly. We circled the airfield once, and soon were bumping along the runway.

We disembarked and went to the passenger terminal where they directed us to a nearby mess hall. Had my first Chinese cooked

American meal here. Stew meat, potatoes, eggplant and coffee. Returned to the office, where they figured out where I should spend the night. They decided on the 95th Station Hospital, and I was soon on the way there in a weapons carrier. Here the OD said that they had no room and suggested that I go to the SOS surgeon's office at HQ. Here Lt. Simpson gave me a slip to see Lt. Davis at "tent city," near the Provost Marshal's office. It was located on a hill top that had recently been cleared of the small, round, Chinese grave tumunli [*mound of earth and stones raised over a grave*]. I was assigned to a tent, where I deposited my baggage and soon found the washroom where I washed and shaved.

It seems that most of China is a graveyard. The coolies had dug a ditch near the tents and had unearthed several skulls and numerous human bones. I was told that there was quite a stench in this area where they first leveled the ground with bulldozers.

MONDAY, MAY 28, 1945

Met Maj.Thomas, Surgeon SOS HQ, Kunming, with whom we will be working one of these days. He showed me the general area in which we are to be put to work and told me that we probably would not work with our nurses, but that the 95th [*Station Hospital?*] would keep their nurses Well, that's one headache I won't have any way, though it probably means few G. I., but lots of Chinese "bings" [*soldiers*]. The major is to be transferred to the 22d or 27th F. H., nothing on B.[?] yet, and I revised dates on the promotion list I turned in, though don't expect any action on this for a while yet.

Maj. Thomas kindly invited me to share his quarters and take the bed of Maj. Stewart, SOS, Dental Surgeon, who will be away for a few days yet. Had my baggage moved over and made myself at home.

This evening, after supper at the Field Officer's [*rank of Maj. through Col.*] mess, Maj. Thomas and some Navy friends of his and I went over to the 95th S. H. for their weekly medical clinic meeting and

73

heard an interesting paper on "psychoneuroses and psychoses." They served lunch later, but we had just eaten supper and weren't hungry.

THURSDAY, MAY 29, 1945

Had a few conferences with Maj. Thomas and spent most of the day just loafing around and reading "Forest and Fort" by Hervey Allen.[1] I like this book a lot, as I'm familiar with the territory around there.

Tried to check on our missing materials, but could find out nothing. All they had was a lot of shipping papers on the 95th F. H. equipment.

WEDNESDAY, MAY 30, 1945

Memorial Day. Met Lt. Col. Roy Miles today, as one of my cabin mates, who told me that most of that crew [*from USS Mann?*] was here at Kunming. Had lunch at hostel #1, at MW corner of KUNMING, it is located at the erstwhile Agricultural College, a nice looking group of granite buildings, with the typical up sloping roof ends. Met Col. Crawford, theater surgeon and also saw Maj. Kagle, who taught sanitation at Carlisle barracks—a clever speaker.

On our way back, we drove through Kunming, mostly enclosed in its medieval walls and on a small mound, surrounded by the inevitable graves, which are now interlaced by trenches and foxholes. The city itself is a rabbit warren of crowded, narrow, crooked streets, swarming with people. There are lots of little stores and sidewalk merchants. There are quite a lot of new, modern buildings, mainly banks, which look out of place among the mongrel Chinese buildings. These new buildings have arisen as the result of Japanese bombings, the last on Christmas day, last year.

THURSDAY, MAY 31, 1945

Have little else to do now, so went to the airport to engage passage back. Here, I noticed a couple of parachutes that had evidently been opened and then bundled up. I then was told that these fellows had to bail out several miles from the airport, when the plane caught afire and an engine fell off. Hope I never have to bail out, better than crashing, however.

FRIDAY, JUNE 1, 1945

Was called up on phone and told that a plane would leave at noon. Got a jeep and had my baggage put in it. Shortly after I arrived, I noticed that I had forgotten my Val-pac, so got a ride back in a weapons carrier and retrieved it. Got back in time and discovered that I had time to spare, as the departure was delayed, due to lack of oxygen, which they had to refill.

We were off, after the usual taxiing round and had a nice trip back. It was bumpy in spots, especially when we went through cumulus clouds. The visibility was fair through breaks in the clouds and I got glimpses of the terraced country side and saw the lake at YUNAN-FU [*Kunming suburb*]. Also saw some stretches of the Burma Road, too. When we came to ASSAM, I could see LEDO [*and*] TINSUKIA and we passed over our camp area and I could plainly see our tents.

It has been cold in the plane, even with the field jacket on, and a blanket over my knees. When we got off the plane at CHABUA, the heat was noticeable as if I had stepped into a spot just in front of an open hearth furnace. Called up for a jeep, and Dorsey came for me. He told me that the thatched roof of the mess hall had caught fire when some gas in our water heating stove had exploded. Well, it's an ill wind that blows no good. The engineers sent some Indians over to put on a roof—we had been trying for weeks to repair; as it leaked badly in spots.

Everything else looked o.k. the 1st convoy group, under Capt. Inman, had returned. They had had a good trip, no accidents or incidences, and seemed to be proud of themselves as being a good outfit, better than their convoy mates (better disciplined, if they had given it any thought). Major Lamber's orders, transferring him to the 27th F. H. at KWEIYEN [*Kweiyang*] had come in that morning. He seemed quite pleased. Hope it works out well for him—should work out better for our outfit as he is unhappy in his old assignment.

SATURDAY, JUNE 2, 1945

The refugee deal actually has occurred, but we are to play only a minor part. We are to supply 1 MC [*Medical Corps officer*] and a couple of clerks at CHABUA airport and to send 1 O and 30 EM to the British, probably in DIBRUGARH. We are also to erect 3 pyramidal tents, with 12 cots, at the airfield. This evening, Capt. Remy went over and saw 16 [*people*] being unloaded, 2 litter cases. Saw Capt. Anderson and Lt. Zonatto telling them of my experiences in KUNMING and our need for trucks when the orders come in.

SUNDAY, JUNE 3, 1945

Had a call from Lt. Col. Ratliffe to have the 3 tents erected this evening and to send an officer to see Maj. Woolam, British Officer, at 10:00 tomorrow. At about 3:30 p.m. had a phone message to send a MO [*medical officer*] and some ambulances to the airfield, to evacuate refugees, so I ordered Capt. Remy and 4 ambulances to be there at 5:00 p.m. as directed.

They had an early supper and left in time. About a 1/2 hour later I got in my jeep to go to the field and was just driving away, when Capt. Remy and the ambulances were seen returning. Things had been messed up again. The patients had arrived at 3:00 p.m. and had been transported to DIBRUGARH. What a life!

MONDAY, JUNE 4, 1945

Maj. Lamber's orders have been rescinded and he has been put on DS with the 27th instead. We are expecting the convoy men and O back sometime soon. Lt. Stalzberg and I went to see Maj. Woolam, Br. O [*British Officer*], about the refugee deal and found that we did not have to furnish any men for this.

JUNE 5, 1945

The first group returned today with some ugly rumors of a CID investigation of some of our O and EM on the convoy to KUNMING for selling rations and Cigarettes. Also that *XXX3* had severely cut *XXX4* with a knife in a fight at YUNAN-FU] [*now Yünnanfu a Kunming suburb*]. Bad business, especially the CID part. Hope it isn't so.

It was illegal for military personnel to sell, barter, or trade their rations of food, cigarettes soap or other items to the locals. This was also true for rations in the homeland during World War II. However, in war-torn areas where food and luxury items were rare, it was common in all the theaters, during and immediately after the war, to engage in this type of behavior. A lively black market existed in United States, also. Although every family was supplied a ration book with ration stamps, books or stamps were bartered, traded or sold which could result in stiff penalties for the individuals if caught. In many ways this activity, among the troops and on the home front, is similar to individuals in the United States under the age of 21 buying and consuming alcoholic beverages which has been illegal since 1987. Among their peers this behavior is not considered an issue, however, among their superiors and the police forces it is considered a crime. The men in Macmillan's unit, however, all denied taking part in black market trade.[2]

We are checking into our equipment that was sent to the port as shortage replacements for us.

WEDNESDAY, JUNE 6, 1945

Early this morning another body of convoy men arrived by plane from KUNMING. Just before supper all the rest but four, left behind as mechanics, arrived back. Capt. Browne, Lt. Budz and Robinson came back with them and denied complicity with illegal dealings [*of selling cigarettes to the Chinese*]. A bad business.

Nearly everyone had something stolen from them by the Chinese along the road. (Will have to take drastic steps against this when we travel later on this month).

THURSDAY, JUNE 7, 1945

Checked with Lt. Robinson on trip this morning. From what he says, nothing too serious occurred, though it seems that some irregularities occurred. Heard a good one. Chaplain Schultz of the 95th F. H. says that Tokyo Rose broadcasted that the 95th F. H. had suffered severe casualties while traveling over the Ledo road! Wonder if she did say that, or if it's another type of 95th rumor?

Tokyo Rose was the name for a group of English speaking Japanese women of a Japanese propaganda show to undermine the morale of American servicemen in the Pacific and CBI Theater. Although several women made the broadcast one Japanese-American woman, Iva Toguri, who had been trapped in Japan at the beginning of the war was imprisoned for treason when she came back to the United States after the war. She was later pardoned.[3]

FRIDAY, JUNE 8, 1945

Am getting some more reports on the troubles on the convoy trip. Sgt. *XXX15* denied all the charges [*of selling cigarettes*]. It's really hot today, and I gave permission for the men to eat without shirts on. All we do during meals is just to drip, drip, drip.

Had Chaplain Woods get me an EFAR gasoline stove, Swedish make, that can be used for making soup, coffee, and the like. Very handy in cool weather when one can't get a hot meal. From the type of weather were having now, it doesn't look like a good investment, but it is sure to come in handy at some time.

SATURDAY, JUNE 9, 1945

Another hot, sunny day. Inspection this morning generally excellent, but a few spotty places. This morning 3 O and 13 EM went on a boat ride on the BRAHMAPUTRA. The general has turned his yacht over to S.S. [*Service Supply*] on Saturdays, and to show his appreciation of our services here, let us be the first group to get a ride on it.

Capt. Margison, convoy commander of the last group, came over to see me, but had no additional Information.

SUNDAY, JUNE 10, 1945

Had a good thunderstorm last night. Just a shade cooler this morning. Had a meeting with drivers of previous convoys and we drew up general plans and appointed officers for our projected trip. This time I'll act as convoy commander myself, maybe a bit of rank will help things along the way. There is supposed to be a pretty snooty MTS [*Motor Transport Service*] Major on the road. We hope, by good organization, to greatly reduce the usual thieving by the Chinese along the road.

MONDAY, JUNE 11, 1945

Met Sammy Kay, Maj. MC at 234th G. H. today, didn't know he was here. Has been here for about 6 weeks now. Was glad to see him.

The Bn. [*Battalion*] at the replacement depot may be broken up and sent home, there rumors stating that they are not going to China as they had expected. Well, I didn't think they would use ground troops in China anyhow—India based.

TUESDAY, JUNE 12, 1945

We had the nurses over for supper, giving them steak and corn-on-the-cob. Afterwards we saw "A Tree Grows in Brooklyn" at our staging area movie.

We're going to send *XXX5* for psychiatric observation. He does a lot of babbling, saying that we are to get a unit citation for our help at ordinance, that they need more men up there and that he himself is requesting them, then he will get a direct commission, but stay with us, in the guise of an EM, with a CID commission; etc. He was seen going around with all his buttons unbuttoned, shirt and pants. Also, he had a collection of many boxes of ordinance equipment and tools, for which he had no use whatever.

THURSDAY, JUNE 14, 1945

Checked on the need of our men and tents at the CHABUA air base, but they still seem to need them there, although they had done no work at all. Capt. Anderson wants 4 clerks to work at SOS HQ and we're sending them over.

FRIDAY, JUNE 15, 1945

The 95th F. H. received its clearance for travel last night and they are busy preparing for their travel. We should hear in a week or 10 days about our travels too.

There was no entry for June 16, 1945

SUNDAY, JUNE 17, 1945

We're going to rearrange our TO/E equipment, so as to enable us to pack it better, and to have a system of loading. Still in the doldrums.

MONDAY, JUNE 18, 1945

Tried to find Col. Cook, Ord. to get an "A" frame [*lifting mechanism*], for lifting a [*?*], but didn't see him and left message with his assistant, a major.

Today received copy of radiogram from KUNMING, telling us to release 32 of our men for duty with another unit, probably Signal Corps—6 cook's helpers, 3 barbers, 14 hospital orderlies and 9 basics. Gosh, we don't have 32 men we want to part with, though this will give us an opportunity to get rid of most of our 8-balls, who belong to those unskilled categories.

TUESDAY, JUNE 19, 1945

Worked on SOP [*Standard Operating Procedures*] rules and regulations this morning and went with Lt. Ostroff to see Col. Cook, Ord, about an "A" bar and got permission to get it this morning.

Well, we got our clearance this morning and gave him a list of vehicles needed. Will be able to get them all without any trouble, good old USA trucks 6X6 2 1/2 ton trucks, probably 6 MC's [*Mack*], open cab jobs (easier to jump out of it, if it rolls over the side of a hill).

Have been working on rules and regulations for our trip, and have the work delegated to my assistants. The plan should work out smoothly I hope. Met Maj. Heisler QMC and Lt. Kilgore, QMC, of two small ordinance outfits, who are going in our convoy as serials 5 and 6. Read my rules and regulation and let them know that I mean business, as far as keeping to these same rules and that I am convoy CO, even if I am a MO.

A serial is a unit of several vehicles within a convoy. The units are in numerical or alphabetical order and travel in this order to their destination. An Ambulance and tow truck are usually at the end of the convoy.[4]

THURSDAY, JUNE 21, 1945

Some more planning and regulation writing. We have called our men in from MAKUM Ord. Depot, SUKERATIN [*both in Assam, India*] and the radio station.

Two sergeants came over this evening and stated that Maj. McCrary had sent them over to join our convoy. This morning we went to Ord. Motor dispersal and picked up our trucks, all new GMC's [*General Motors*], many driven only 33 miles, all open-cab jobs. They look good.

Today we got an extra beer ration and two cartons of cigarettes.

This chapter from diary pages 53-66

ENDNOTES

---

[1] This historical novel is based upon the Siege of Fort Pitt in 1763 at Pittsburgh, PA, MacMillan's home town.

[2] Kevin Conley Ruffner. "The Black Market in Postwar Berlin: Colonel Miller and an Army Scandal, Part 1." *Prologue Magazine*, 2002; "Rationing: A Necessary but Hated Sacrifice." *Life on the home front: Oregon's Response to World War II*, 2008.

[3] "BioTokyo Rose Biography." address as of February 10, 2015. http://www.biography.com/people/tokyo-rose-37481.

[4] U.S. Department of Transportation. "Appendix B. Military Convoy Movement Facts," *Coordinating Military Deployments on Roads and Highways: A Guide for State and Local Agencies* (Department of Transportation, 1985). Address as of March 15, 2015. http://ops.fhwa.dot.gov/publications/fhwahop05029/appendix_b.htm.

Chapter 5: From Assam, India to Wanting, China: The Ledo-Burma Road Myitkyina and Needless Death

In February 1942 Japanese incursion into northern Burma (also called Myanmar) cut off the southern part of the Burma Road, the primary supply route from India to Kunming, China for General Chang Kai-shek's Nationalist Army. In December 1942 construction of a new road began to bypass the Japanese occupied territory (See Map 1).

The first section of the road began at Ledo near the Indian Burma border. Col. Lewis Pick, Chief Road Engineer, was appointed to oversee the highway's construction. The road was built with Chinese laborers and American troops. About sixty percent of the American troops were African-Americans. The Ledo road included sharp hair-pin curves and steep drops. As the Japanese were forced to retreat south in the ensuing months, the Ledo Road was extended until it connected with the old Burma Road It met the Burma road at the Mong-Yu road junction, 465 miles (748 km) from Ledo. The total length of the highway from Ledo to Kunming was 1,079 miles (1736 km) in length (See table next page).

On January 12, 1945, the first convoy, led by Col. Pick, departed from Ledo and reached Kunming, China on February 4, 1945. The convoy contained 113 vehicles. Over the next six months following its opening, trucks carried 129,000 tons of supplies from India to China. Twenty-six thousand trucks that carried the cargo (one way) were handed over to the Chinese.[1]

Medical convoys also traveled the road. This included MacMillan with the 96th field hospital [See map 4].

Table 5-1: Mileage from Ledo, Assam, India to Kunming, Yunnan, China and major points in between along Ledo-Burma Road

Name of town WWII	Modern transliteration if different	Country	Miles	Km.
Ledo		Assam, India	0	0
Shingbwiyang	Shin Bway Yang	Burma [Myanmar]	103	166
Warazup		Burma [Myanmar]	189	305
Myitkyina		Burma [Myanmar]	268	431
Bhamo		Burma [Myanmar]	372	600
Namhkam		Burma [Myanmar]	439	708
Mong-Yu		Burma [Myanmar]	465	748
Wanting	Wandingzhen	China*	507	816
Lungling	Longling	China	560	903
Paoshan	Baoshan	China	625	1,008
Yungping	Yongping	China	755	1,218
Yunnanyii		China	876	1,412
Tsuyung	Chuxiong	China	959	1,547
Kunming		China	1,097	1,736

* All towns in Yunnan Province

FRIDAY JUNE 22, 1945

Loading today – about 15 trucks of TO/E equipment from SEALKOTTEE warehouse and about 5 miles from our present area. Special services, our lighting system, etc. are being loaded on too. It was discovered that we were 6 vehicles short, and that we had 6 duplicate tallies, so we got this all straightened out.

The dispensary, special service and the rest of the departments were packing and loading, all going on well; also supply, kitchen and utilities. We have made arrangements to have our little generator put in operation every night for our kitchen truck and Brummett's radio and loudspeaker.

SATURDAY, JUNE 23, 1945

Loading and packing at a great rate. We really have a good bunch of men, am very proud of them, and the officers, too. They all pitch in and work. The extra tents, such as the recreation tents, etc. have been struck and loaded. Lt. Ostroff picked up our personnel pyramidal tents this morning and loaded them, too, and we'll pick up the jungle hammocks too. Our 32 men who are leaving are rather sad, they are to leave by train at 0930, Sunday morning and we are to go back to camp Kanchapora near CALCUTTA. We drew and distributed 4 days' K-rations for them, too.

This morning I went up to HQ to bid my many acquaintances, goodbye. Did not see Gen. [*Joseph*] Cranston or Lt. Col. [*Frank*]. Ratliffe. Saw Miss Bornemann, chief nurse, and several of the girls, now at the 234th Gen. Hosp. Sweeney is still pretty sick, poor kid.

Saw Lt. Budziszewski too, he appears to be quite subdued. The noon meal was our last in our mess hall. The mess detail was busy loading and cleaning up all afternoon. Did a good job, too. Inspection this morning found the area to be in good shape, all but one tent, the grounds were well policed, too. Packed my footlocker and Val-pac this evening. I now have about a dozen cartons of cigarettes and 3 bottles of whiskey as well as about 1 1/2 cases of beer. Sgt. Bauer tied up the two dogs that we want to take with us, and constructed a crate for carrying them along. These dogs whimpered and whined all night, and made me feel like getting up and letting them go, as they interfered with my sleeping.

SUNDAY, JUNE 24, 1945

A wet, rainy morning, after two nice days for our loading. Most of our work is done, just the personal packing and loading of baggage later on.

Our 38 men left about 0900 for CHAUBA RR station. Sorry to see most of them leave. Including our nurses, we are going over the road with 25% of our group gone. The nurses will probably not rejoin us and will probably be used as replacements in the IB [*India-Burma*] Theater.

The vehicles were all loaded by noon, with the exception of the luggage trucks, which were loaded after lunch.

The area was ordered policed and was inspected and found to be pretty good. A few of the officer's tents, as usual, were among the worst. Many fires were going as we burned a lot of our trash.

We were issued a cot and a jungle hammock apiece for the trip. We drew enough tentage [*sic*], pyramidal, for all our TOE strength including nurses.

In the evening, McAuliffe, McCain, my orderly, and I loaded up McAuliffe's weapons carrier with all our and Capt. Hogan's impedimenta. Hogan had left earlier in the morning to be our advance agent at LEDO. As all our trucks were loaded and packed in the SOS [*Service of Supply*] convoy area, we had none available for our Off and EM, so I went to Capt. Sopka, and was promised one or two at 1730. This wasn't enough, so the OD at the Replacement Depot was kind enough to help us out—just as we had helped him out on other occasions. His motor Sgt., however, was surly and uncooperative and Sgt. Bauer, in order to get the trunks, had to find the OD to get the Sgt. to let us have those trucks.

We were soon loaded and off to the convoy area, where we had to rearrange the trucks in numerical order in their respective serials. That was quite a job and took nearly 3 hours and we didn't get through until 2100. In the meantime, McCain had fixed my bed and mosquito bar for me in a nice Bombay tent near the area the 95th had vacated a few days before.

The weather at this time was hot and rainy and we were wet from rain and sweat both. Doesn't seem to hurt us any, however. Early to bed, as we have to leave at 0600, escorted by MPs.

MONDAY, JUNE 25, 1945

Awakened at 0430 today by *XXX14*'s bugle. It was just getting light but we saw no sunrise, as the clouds were thick and low. Had breakfast at 0515, hot coffee and desiccated scrambled eggs and bread. We were given three emergency K-rations as well, to be used in route, if it should be needed for missed meals.

The MP escort showed up at 0615 and we soon were on the way, our four serials and the other two trailing us.

We took the back road, past the motor dispersal area and came to the main road at TINSUKIA. We passed through DIGBOI, where they have a steel mill and oil wells, and reached LEDO about 1000. We arrived in our convoy area about 1030 [*See Map 4 for route from Ledo to Kunming*].

Capt. Hogan met us there, and showed us the sorry area we were to camp in. That was bad enough, but we were also greeted by the news that some of the bridges were flooded, or washed out, and that we would have to stay here, in this stinking mid-swamp for a week or longer.

I directed the parking of the vehicles and got them all properly spotted in part, so that we could pull out in proper order when we left.

The EM were assigned to their tents, and we went over to our area, where we were housed in Indian bashas [*thatched buildings*]. We have one log bldg. to ourselves about 50' long and 20' across, just the right amount of space for all of us and a corner for my desk and impedimenta. We had lunch across the street, and sat at tables, with white cloths on them, and were waited on by colored soldiers. Not so bad, after having to stand in line, with mess kits in our hands ever since leaving the ship at Bombay. It's just as hot here as at CHUBUA.

The area is a mess, unpoliced, and full of cans and trash. There are no showers or latrines handy to the EM area—"Chinese Parade Grounds." To make things worse, the water is off most of the time, being blamed on a pump breakdown.

TUESDAY, JUNE 26, 1945

Breakfast was 1/2 hour late and there was a tremendous lineup. I arranged to get our guards fed first, which is a help. They are driven up by jeep just before chow call, and driven back.

We were briefed at 1000 by Maj. Phillips. He gave us quite a lengthy talk and a mimeographed SOP. He was right when he called this a paper war. Several bridges are out or underwater and there are a number of landslides. We are to be prepared to leave day after tomorrow, and we will be ready at that time, but I don't expect the road to be open then. We spent all evening checking and tightening bolts and nuts on the vehicles. They weren't too bad, but we did discover that nearly all were low in grease in differentials and transmission.

The usual shower troubles again, no water till quarter to five. I didn't shave till after lunch and then had to shave in coffee colored water out of the spigot, that looked as if it had come straight from some branch of the BRAHMAPUTRA River.

We have to take all our oil and gas with us, 4500 gal. gas, 1800 gal. oil, and 200 # grease, as the pipeline is out as well as the road. We had 5–2½ ton trucks loaded with cord and rope assigned to China, so we got rid of them today and will get our oil and gas tomorrow.

Gasoline pipelines were laid along the Ledo Road to supply vehicles along the way and to China.

The men are complaining about the 1/3 mile walk across the fields to the mess hall and want us to get our kitchen started. They certainly have gotten lazy and spoiled, and the walk is no longer than it was from parts of the Regional hospital at Camp Swift to our mess hall. I really believe many are afraid to go through the tall grass and past a few remnants of the old jungle.

WEDNESDAY, JUNE 27, 1945

The rest of the trucks have been serviced and filled with gas. Today finishes up their repair and maintenance. O'Neill went for the extra oil and gas—five trucks of gas plus the extra oil and grease, probably 3/4 truck full. He forgot to get his oil and grease first, so had to unload my truck for this, instead of making two trips with one emptied truck

We had a good thunderstorm this night, cooling things a lot.

THURSDAY JUNE, 28, 1945

Nice this morning, not cool, but not hot enough to cause perspiration either. Had the area policed today, but they did a half-hearted job and will have to finish tomorrow.

This evening had a call from the 65th QM Depot Co, Lt. Hagan S-3. The 65th is to be air-lifted to KUNMING. That will take #5 serial out of our convoy except for their five 2 1/2 ton trucks, which we will have two interspersed among our own serials. We will have to feed the

6th serial with our men, now, but that will not be a hardship, as we can handle them without any trouble.

FRIDAY, JUNE 29, 1945

A lazy morning, till about 1030, when I had a call to go to the orderly room. Here was given a phone call message and on calling up, was given orders to be ready and at the IP [*initial point*], TOLYO Y, at 0700 the next morning. Well our plans were all made and we were all set and ready to go. I briefed the men at 1400 and spent about 3/4 hour in the talk.

Heard that the June 16 issue of LIBERTY, had an article on a troop ship going through the equatorial waters. Believe it was our ship as we had a LIBERTY correspondent aboard.

We are planning to get up at 0330 the next morning for our trip. Hope we have a successful trip, no losses of men or vehicles.

SATURDAY, JUNE 30, 1945

Up at 0330 bright and early, or rather, still dark and early. Everyone was up on time, and we have breakfast of coffee and K-rations. The MPs lead us out on time and we were at TOLYO "Y" at 0635. There was a heavy engineer convoy, caring pontoons and heavy equipment, that got in our road the first day.

We headed into the direction of the mountains, and soon were getting into the mountains themselves. There were numerous cloud-capped hog backs and peaks and while we were as high as some of them, we didn't get into the clouds. We climbed and climbed to Hellgate, near which was a bad landslide necessitating low-low gear; soon we were over the peak into a valley then up again. It was interesting to see our road, away ahead, and away up, on what seem to be a hilltop, and yet, when we reached it, found that it was only a shoulder of a yet higher peak. We were soon over the top, and went down into the second valley, where, at the river bottom, we gassed up at NAMYUNG [*Nanyung, Burma*].

Then up a long, long hill to KIM KIDU, where a wrecker was to join the end of our convoy. This place is on the very top of a small peak. We went downhill a short distance, and then up to the very top of CHINGLO HILL. Here we could see "KUM KIDO"[*sic*] way down and yet way up. The Northwest side of this hill had a bad landslide in it, but we got up all right. The Southeast slope of the hill is best known as CHINGLO HILL and is very dangerous. The hill goes down on a steep grade for miles, and has to be negotiated in second gear and still needs brakes.

This slope has numerous accidents daily. I saw one where a truck, which didn't make a curve, crashed into one parked on the outside of the curve, knocking both over and injuring both drivers and 2 passengers. A later serial saw another truck go over the bank not far from there. Further down the hill, we saw where a truck loaded with a gasoline-shovel, had gotten its left side wheels in the ditch and had tipped over.

After we had reached the level, narrow valley at the foot of the hill we reach the convoy area at SHINGBWIYANG [*Shin Bway Yang, Buma*]. This was a large, rectangular area, with a log shed near one side.

We pulled into lane 2 and parked here. This camp was a disappointment and very poor. There was very little drinking water, none to refill our trailer tanks, and absolutely none for washing. We were told that we could bathe in the creek. This creek was muddy which we didn't mind, but the banks were knee-deep in mud and that decided me against trying it.

O'Neill and I went to the water distribution point, several miles away, up hilly and winding roads. Just before we got there, the right front tire went flat, and we had to fix it. In the hot and humid late afternoon we worked at it. It really wasn't a hard job, but following a day of grueling driving, I was utterly exhausted and sweating buckets.

We turned at the 20th Gen. Hosp. [*See Map 3*] and came back. By this time the other serials had come in, all but serial "C," Capt. Inman in charge. We found out later that they had by-passed the camp and had settled down near a river crossing about 20 miles away, where they spent the night.

The mess was poor, and the Indian KPs washed the plates, etc. in dirty water and wiped them in filthy rags. An amusing incident occurred at breakfast next morning. We were griping about the food and sanitary conditions and there was a flight surgeon, Capt. Mc at the table with us. He took about 2 bites, turned pale, and suddenly left the table. We didn't mean to do it, but were amused by his reaction to our conversation.

After supper we gassed up and that caused a lot of trouble. My share of gas was mixed with water, and caused me a lot of trouble that night and the following morning.

McCain fitted up my jungle hammock and cot near the car. I had sweat so much that I had to change to another fatigue suit, but I was still sweating and soon had the clean one all wet and it was this way that I went to bed. About midnight it started to rain and it was not bad in the jungle hammock, except that a slight drizzle fell on my face. Well, I was using a sweaty damp towel as my pillow and covered my face with it. Pretty soon the hollow on top of the jungle hammock filled with rainwater and I pushed up on the top to drain it. The water ran down the foot of the hammock, which is waterproof, but, instead of running off onto the ground, it ran off on the cot and soon I was lying in a puddle of water and my right side was really wet. Now I was soaked and very sleepy, so I crawled into the cab of one of our open cab trucks and lay down on the seat, all curled up. I found a raincoat in the cab and covered myself with it, including an end of it to keep the drizzle off my face and head. What a night, but I did manage to sleep that way, but was still damp in the morning.

SUNDAY, JULY 1, 1945

Our serials had gotten mixed up during gassing up the night before, so we realigned ourselves at 0700. I was in the lead and my motor refused to run. More water in the gas and after clearing out the fuel cup, we got off again. Within a 1/4 mile, the motor stopped again and I let the convoy to go ahead, and caught them at the hourly halt. We were delayed at a small bridge and later on while crossing the TANAI River over a pontoon bridge. Just before this, we picked up the missing "C" serial.

Our ride was uneventful and over flat, swampy ground for most of the way, crossing some little hills near SHADOZUP and NAMTI [*Nanmati*], the watershed between the TANAI and the MOGAUNG, the latter a tributary of the IRRIWADDY.

There is a railroad crossing the road near NAMTI and there were about 3 dozen small, Indian-type freight cars of all types parked there. Many of them were burned, and all had bullet holes in them, first signs of the fighting near MYITKYINA.

The battle of Myitkyina had been fought between March and August 1944. The American and Chinese troops were greatly outnumbered by the Japanese. American special operations army unit, "Merrill's Marauders," officially named the 5307th Composite Unit (Provisional), unit Galahad, were specifically trained for jungle incursions and played a major part in the battle for Myitkyina. Although the Marauders and the Allies pushed the Japanese troops out of the area, many American and Chinese troops died, were malnourished and sick with dysentery, scrub typhus and other diseases by the end of the campaign. Their action

*enabled the Ledo road to be built through Myitkyina
and connect with the Burma Road.*[2]

*This road was later named the Stilwell Road in honor
of Gen. Joseph Stilwell although he was considered
controversial and recalled back to United States in
October 1944 by Roosevelt. The CBI was now split into
two commands; Lt. Gen. Raymond Wheeler became
Deputy Supreme Allied Commander South East Asia.
Maj. Gen. Albert Wedemeyer replaced Gen. Joseph
Stilwell as commander of all American forces. In
addition, Wedemeyer was Chief of Staff for Gen. Chang
Kai-shek, leader of the Nationalist Republic of China
from 1944 to 1945.*[3]

We reached the convoy area near MYITKYINA about 4:00
p.m. they had a basha for the officers and tents for the EM, as well as
drinking water and showers. We had to boil our own water, 90 gal. of
it for our trailers. We could do this due to the fact that breakfast was
over an hour late [*See Map 4*].

The chow here, supper, especially, was lousy and many men
didn't eat supper here at all, preferring their own K-rations. The
breakfast coffee, however, was excellent.

MONDAY, JULY 2, 1945

We started off at 0900 and several miles from camp came to
the IRRAWADDY, a stream about 1/3 mile across and went over a
big, prominent position bridge. This day's travel was very pleasant. It
was hot, but the roads were wide and flat, and we only went through a
few hills but these were bad, due to narrow, winding roads, many of
them wide enough only for one car at a time. This was in the hills near
NALONG, the watershed between the IRRAWADDY and its southern
tributary, the TAYINHO or NAM MU AN.

As we approach BHAMO, we were on good, level road again. There were numerous signs of fighting here and many temples were ruined and houses burned. The Burmese live in houses that are raised on stilts, the meaner type, especially among the hill people, being a thatched shed, with no sides, while the townspeople lived in what appeared to be the second floor, which was walled by bamboo mats.

We crossed the TAYINGHO a few miles above BHAMO, went through the town and camped about 8 miles below. The regular camp was being graded, and the mud was so deep that we had to park in a lot several hundred yards away. Here we set up our kitchen in a nice grove of trees and set up a HQ area and a vehicle parking area. By this time our bivouac SOP [*Standard Operating Procedure*] was functioning pretty well. I had my flag up, desk and table set up, and when it got dark, got my kerosene lamp going.

Our mess put out a good meal and Brummett's generator gave the kitchen some light and ran his radio. It was a nice set up and camp. We got boiled water for our trailers and hauled water for boiling purposes.

It rained during the night, but I was quite comfortable in my bedding roll, under my mosquito net, with a couple of jungle hammocks above to keep out the rain.

TUESDAY, July 3, 1945

Off bright and early to a good start. We drove for about an hour and then headed into a mountain range, the one separating the IRRAWADDY from another, more southern tributary, the SHWELI, called the NAM MAO in China. We climbed and climbed for about 2 1/2 hours, up 27 miles, mostly pretty good road, but narrow and winding, with many blind curves. There were quite a number of soft spot and mud holes, as well as landslides, mainly on the downslope. It took a long time to get down, though only half as long as to get up as this valley was pretty high. We reached a level spot and had lunch on a grassy bank, the nicest spot yet. The air was cool and invigorating, but the sun was hot just like many a spot in the USA the same time of year.

Soon after we started off again, we came to a new suspension bridge over the SHWELI, with the ruins of the old bridge in the water below it and several brick blds. near the bank, burned out and riddled with bullet and shell holes. A mile upstream, the gorge opens up into a wide valley, several miles across, through which meanders the stream now called the NAM MAO. It looks like a wide, filled-in lake, the flat bottom lands being intensely cultivated rice paddies.

After traveling about 7 or 8 miles, we came to Dr. Seagrove's [*sic, Seagrave*] "Burma Hospital," where he made history. We barely glimpsed it, on a bench of land, above the level of the road and the flats of rice paddies.

> *Gordon Seagrave, born in Burma, was the son of American missionaries. After medical school, he established a hospital in Namhkam, Shan State, Burma. When the Japanese encroached into Burma, Seagrave allowed his hospital to be used by the US Army and was commissioned as a major in the U.S. Army Medical Corps and later was promoted to Lt. Col. He, along with British and American physicians and Burmese nurses, trained by Seagrave, established field hospitals behind the front lines as the Allies attempted to push back the Japanese invasion. During Gen. Joseph Stilwell's retreat into India from the advancing Japanese in early May of 1942, Seagrave and his staff accompanied them.[4]*

> *When the Japanese army was later pushed south, Seagrave reestablished a new hospital at Tagap Ga in the Hukawng Valley of Burma; later, he established other field hospitals in a string down the Ledo Road to*

provide medical aid, not only to the American soldiers and Chinese workers building the road, but also to the local Naga hill people. One of his hospitals was used by the United States Army by the 44th Field Hospital near Mong-Yu, Burma where the Ledo joined the Burma road. [5]

By the early part of 1944, Seagrave founded a forward hospital near Shingbewiyang and cared for Merrill's marauder and allies as they forced the Japanese out of Myitkyina. This hospital principally took care of soldiers who could be treated and returned to duty. [6]

Dr. Gordon Seagrave and a Burmese nurse, treating a wounded Chinese soldier. From: Charles F. Romanus and Riley Sutherland, *Time Runs out in CBI* (Department of the Army, 1959), p. 82.

After about another 20 miles, the road turned off sharply to the right and started to wind up the rounded treeless and intensely green hills. After 3 or 4 miles of this uphill travel, we came to our convoy parking area, at a place (no native and habitations near) called MANG YU [*sic, Mong-Yu, Burma*]. Here we discovered that we were at the junction of the LEDO-BURMA ROAD, a scene that "LIFE" Magazine has pictured on its pages. Nearly on a hill, overlooking this junction is a Chinese cemetery and memorial.

This camp under Capt. Bowen, was the best we had been at. They supplied us with drinking water and had Bombay tents and open air showers. They had no messing facilities, but we were able to set up our kitchen right next to the vehicle parking strip on the level area below the tent area itself.

One of the first things we heard, was that there had been shooting early this morning, when one of the Kashin guards shot at some Chinese who were stealing a carbine. These Chinese are deserters and live near the Chinese cemetery. Later in the day, they grabbed a Kashin guard when he went down in a nearby village and kidnapped him. The Kashins swore vengeance on the Chinese, and delivered an ultimatum that their companion and stolen carbine be returned the next day or they would take matters in their own hands.

The next thing Capt. Ferris and Mr. Driscoll, of the CID [*Criminal Investigation Division*] came along and started to check the convoy for contraband and extra cigarettes, soap, razor blades, alarm clocks and all Indian rupees above 150. What a mess this looked like, as I know that everyone has been stocking up on just these on everybody's advice, everywhere, that these items were scarce in China, and we should take them along. I had quite a long confabulation with them, telling them that we all have extra cigarettes, etc., that we were on a permanent change of station; that no one had told us anything except for 150 rupees, that Major Morris CID in CHABUA had given us clearance on PX items; that I just couldn't stay with the outfit if all the extra items were confiscated; that most of the

extra items were packed away in baggage trucks and would not be available until we reached our final destination; etc., etc., etc. The upshot of all that was that they decided to postpone the investigation until the following day. I noticed quite a pile of confiscated cigarette, boxes of chewing gum, Atabrine tablets, soap, etc. that they had found the previous day. Some of this was from the 95th [*Field Hospital*], too.
7

> *A lively black market was found in China. The Chinese soldiers were often not well fed and many were malnourished. Limiting the men to only a small number of personal items, by the CID, was likely a method to prevent bartering, trading and selling food, tobacco, alcohol and luxury items to the Chinese and prevent soldiers from engaging in this activity.*[8]

We set up our kitchen below the vehicle area. The O and EM slept in tents higher up. Hogan, McAuliffe and I had a corner tent overlooking the area.

WEDNESDAY, JULY 4, 1945

We spent the anniversary of the declaration of Independence working on our vehicles, greasing, oiling, changing oil, etc. It was a rainy day, cool and not too miserable, clearing up in the evening.

At about 1500 a most deplorable accident occurred. Pfc. Peter Mungas was under his truck, greasing a few joints on the shaft, when he told Goodman to back up the truck. Goodman did so and backed the truck about 15 ft. Running the left front wheel right over Mungas' chest, crushing it and breaking the middle ribs on both sides. He was seen immediately by Lt. Lorenz and was in shock. He was taken to the 1st H. U. of the 44th Field Hospital.

As soon as the accident was reported to the MTS [*Motor Transportation Service*] office, the proper papers were brought up to me and I held an investigation immediately, questioning all who had witnessed the accident. With an injury as severe as this, we feared the worst.

Shortly after this, Capt. Ferris CID appeared and was ready to address the men. He and I talked to them and they had to turn in all excess cigarettes, soap, film and rupees over 150, to Capt. Hogan and myself to be returned to the donors on reaching our destination.

As soon as the collection was started, Hogan, McAuliffe, Sgt. Sleasura and I drove to the 44th F. H., About 20 miles down the road we had come up on the previous day. On our way there we met Lt. Baumhorst with the sad news that Mungas had died 15 minutes after leaving our area. Poor fellow, so needless a death.

We continued to the hospital, which is located in Dr. Seagrove's [*sic*] own historical hospital. It is on a bench of ground, overlooking the road and the broad NAM MAO valley, set under a number of huge banyan trees. There are several large, rectangular blds., 2 stories high and made of concrete, the outside built up of large cobblestones, giving the building a rustic appearance. The buildings had just been repaired and renovated and the F. H. had just moved in two weeks previously. There were no doors or windows in the place and there were bullet holes and marks on all the walls. Some even had the regular spacings of machine gun bullets, as well as the irregular marks of hand grenades and shells. Some of the old woodwork and rafters were still up showing that the place had not been burned down. This wood was well bullet-marked, too. The major in charge was operating on a man who had been slashed in the neck in a fight with a Negro, so we didn't see him.

We all had supper at the O mess, for 1 rupee, and then started back. We learned that the body [*Mungus*] had been sent by ambulance to BHAMO from where it would be taken by plane to MYITKIANIA where he would be buried in the American Military cemetery with proper honors. This unfortunate accident threw a pall over everybody.

Chaplain Woods and the 65th Ord. Depot Co. chaplain held a combined Sunday service (they missed Sunday at SHINGBWIYANG) 4th of July and funeral oration. Very good. The sleeping here at MONG YU was good, as we were at about 5000 ft. altitude. Our Indian heat rashes were clearing up rapidly and it felt good to be able to sleep under blankets and not to perspire all day.

THURSDAY, JULY 5, 1945

Up at 0515 this morning, in the dark. Had a good breakfast and left at 0645, after a poor start, as they forgot to awaken the bugler, so all our preparations were rushed-but we still got off on time. Took some pictures of the BURMA-LEDO road junction just before starting.[9]

After about 1/2 hour drive, we came to the Chinese border, near "Wanting" [*Wanding*]. Here a few hundred yds., on the Burma side of the little boundary Creek, there was an MP station and a gate. We had to turn in our Border passes here and check the vehicle passes and tallies, too.

This area shows some signs of fighting. The few mud brick houses blasted, shell holes, wrecked vehicles, dugouts, foxholes and even one wrecked tank, Japanese?

WANTING is a tiny and miserable looking Chinese town, with the usual loafing Chinese soldiers in it. Our drive was miserable, mostly up and down, which I don't mind much, nor the sharp corners, but what annoyed me was the condition of the roads. The Chinese don't bother with maintenance and the road was so full of holes, that we couldn't go much over 10 miles an hour, even on the level stretches. The road originally was macadamized, in some places there was less macadam than original dirt surfaces.

Our way generally followed the course of the NAM HKAWA until we came to TOFA, 104 miles from the MONG YU. This was the roughest ride yet.

> *Parallel to and preceding the Ledo Road was the so-called combat road, in some places quickly bulldozed out of the brush, in others merging into an improved section of existing road or trail. The combat road stretched 139 miles from Shingbwiyang, in the upper Hukawng Valley, to Mogaung. An old oxcart road was rehabilitated from Mogaung to Myitkyina, which added 51 miles. By the time the 96th Field Hospital traveled the road, the stretch from Mong Yu to Hsipaw, temporary bridges were built and the road maintained.*
> 10

The convoy area at TOPPA, as usual was in preparation, and we parked on a big field, which, until recently was an emergency airstrip. Our particular spot was off to one side, in a little valley, right by a cemetery. There was quite a crowd of Chinese peasants around, trying to trade eggs, etc. or to beg, but I didn't notice them having any success.

The MPs at WANTING had told us that some bandits had shot at a Chinese general and his driver the day before, while they were riding in a jeep, killing the driver, and given the general a scalp wound.

Another tale was that an American major had been kidnapped on the Burma Rd. not too far from its junction with the Ledo Road about the same time, and subsequently murdered. It's a very bad stretch of road, no doubt of it. Believe we could see the Salween River Valley from our stopping place.

This chapter from diary pages 67-81

ENDNOTES

[1] C. M. Buchanan and John R. McDowell, *Stilwell Road: Story of the Ledo lifeline* (Office of Public Relations, India-Burma Theater of Operations, USF in IBT, 1945-1955); George L. MacGarrigle, *Central Burma* (Office of the Chief of Military History, 1996), 9; Charles F. Romanus and Riley Sunderland, *Time Runs Out in CBI* (Office of the Chief of Military History,1990), 136-137.

[2] Historical Division, *Merrill's Marauders: February-May, 1944* (Center of Military History US Army, 1945), 112-113; Barbara Tuchman, *Stilwell and the American Experience in China: 1911–45* (Macmillan, 1970).

[3] Romanus and Sunderland, *Stilwell's Command Problems* (Office of the Chief of Military History, 1956), 467-470; Stephens Graham, "Chapter XIV: India-Burma and China Theaters," in B. Noland Carter, ed, *Medical Department, United States Army, Surgery in World War II. Activities of Surgical Consultants, Vol. II* (Department of the Army, 1964), 895.

[4] Gordon Seagrave, *Burma Surgeon* (W. Norton Co, 1943), 115-118; Graham, *ibid.* (1964), 896-897, 901-903; William Boyd Sinclair, *Book 5: Medics and Nurses"* (Joe F. Whitley, 1989),14-32.

[5] Seagrave, *ibid.* (1943); Graham, *ibid.* (1964); Romanus and Sunderland, *Time Runs Out in CBI* (1990), 5, 123.

[6] Romanus and Sunderland, *Stilwell's Mission to China* (1953); Romanus and Sunderland, *Time Runs Out in CBI* (1990), 123; Romanus and Sunderland, *Stilwell's Mission to China* (1953); Sinclair, *Book 5: Medics and Nurses* (1989).

[7] The 95th field hospital preceded the 96th over the Ledo-Burma Road.

[8] Romanus and Sunderland, *Time Runs Out in CBI* (1958), 64-68, 164.

[9] These photos are not available.

[10] Romanus and Sunderland, *Time Runs Out in CBI* (1958), 98.

Chapter 6: From Wanting to Near Kunming

We started off at 0700 in a drizzle and had some difficulty getting out of the lot. After a short drive we started uphill, [*which*] has an especially nasty hairpin curve to get around. I was in the lead and got struck, but got out soon and the others had no trouble as they saw what not to do.

Truck Convoy heading to China on the Ledo-Burma Road
From: Mark D. Sherry, *China Defensive 4 July 1942–4 May 1945. US Army Campaigns of World War II.* (U.S. Army Center of Military History, Department of the Army, 1996), p. 25

All the hilltops were fortified with slit trenches, foxholes and dugouts and many spots showed shell craters. At about 0815 we noticed a road on a hillside or rather mountainside, miles away. This road was on the other side of the Salween River [*Lu Kiang in Chinese transliteration*] and we didn't reach that spot for 3 hours.

We stopped on the road near the little knoll for a rest, about 1 1/2 hours after starting out. McCain walked about 20 ft. from our halting spot and cried out, "there is a booby-trap up here!" We went up and looked and there was a chemical hand grenade in the grass. The pin was still in place, the grenade was caught in a couple of twigs between the body and the release handle. It really wasn't booby-trapped, but we left it severely alone. I looked around some more and soon saw a broken wooden scabbard. Near it was a human ulnar bone, with some yellowish khaki cloth around it. Next I saw a skull, the lower jaw, about 6 ft. away was the rest of a human skeleton! It had some of the same kind of cloth on it, with bone buttons. Around the middle was a piece of wire, rounded as if shaped by his body. Someone had probably put it around him just after he was killed, probably to drag him out of the way. About 10 ft. away was a shallow shell crater, from a 75 mm shell. This may have been the shell that killed him.

The skull was that of a young man. It was mesocephalic and in good condition. The incisors and the bicuspids had dropped out, but the molars were present and in wonderful condition, no evidence at all of caries. I took this skull with me and gave it to McAuliffe later on.

The shapes of heads are often used by physical anthropologists to classify various ethnic groups. They are classified according to a cephalic index, or head circumference measurement and are dolichocephalic (cephalic index up to: 74.9 cm.), mesocephalico (cephalic index: 75-79.9 cm.) and brachycephalic (cephalic index: 80-84.9 cm.). The most common head shape of the Indian population is mesocephalic (medium) and brachycephalic (large) heads. Asian skulls tend to be bradycephalic. [1]

The top of the west ridge of the SALWEEN valley, which is a narrow gorge at this spot, is about 5000 ft. high, and the road winds down around several smaller mountains to the stream level, which is about 2000 ft. above sea level. The west range, which runs due North and South is called the KAOLI KUNG SHAN [*Gaolingong*] range. It is remarkably uniform in height for hundreds of miles, averaging 11,000 ft. in height. The east slope is steep and the gorge of the river very narrow.

At 1/2 hour before we came to the SALWEEN river bridge, we glimpsed it in the distance. It looked even smaller than a toy, about as big as a splinter. Just before reaching this suspension bridge, the road was cut through the rock, with rock overhead, like a half tunnel.

The entire part of the Burma Road that we traveled from our junction at the MONG YU to the SALWEEN River showed evidence of battle, and was dotted by wrecked and stripped cars and trucks. They were especially thick on the down slope to the river. They were trucks and cars that have been driven up from Burma in early 1942 and had been abandoned along the road, mostly from mechanical trouble and lack of oil and gas very few from enemy action, except some that were caught on the road by the Japs, when the Chinese prematurely blew up the bridge and stranded hundreds of thousands of their own soldiers and refugees on the west bank.

The Burma Road, was built between 1937 and 1940, to provide material to China after the Japanese closed Chinese ports. This road crossed the Salween River. Due to a diplomatic agreement with Japan, the British closed the Burma Road for three months in 1940. However, as the Japanese army advanced from the west toward Paoshan (Baoshan), Yunnan, China, the Chinese army blew up two bridges in their retreat to prevent the Japanese from crossing the river in 1942. Although the Japanese were unable to cross the river, a standoff between the Japanese on the western and the Chinese on the eastern part of the river began. In order to recapture Chinese territory the Salween Campaign began on May 11, 1944. Chinese troops, assisted by American forces, crossed the upper Salween. After several months of fierce fighting and much loss of life on both sides, the Japanese occupied areas of northern Burma and Southwest China were liberated in the late fall of 1944.[2]

The mountains eastward are not quite so high or steep. PAOSHAN [*Baoshan, Yunnan*] is in a nice, wide long valley. The elevation is 5500 ft. and it was cool and nice for sleeping, although it rained a bit toward morning. McCain and I were very comfortable sleeping in the back of the truck [*See Map 4*].

The regular convoy area, as usual, was not properly prepared. Instead of staying in the proper area, in which CC-261 [*Convoy*] was parked, we were parked on a flat field near the airstrip, about 3/4 miles from the convoy area where the office, mess hall and showers are located. It was too long a distance to walk, so I borrowed a truck from the MTS officer. We shuttled the men back and forth from our area to the convoy area. It didn't work too badly, and was a big help.

I drove up with Capt. Hogan in his ambulance and had the first warm shower since landing in Asia. We slept well that night, though there was a small shower toward morning.

SATURDAY, JULY 7, 1945

Due to our having to shuttle men back and forth, we were delayed in starting out. This morning there was a nuisance of a Chinaman pestering around our vehicles; after shooing him away a few times, he persisted in coming back, so I literally ran him out and while chasing him, hit him on his back sending him sprawling. He stayed away a while, but believe it or not, was right back again just before we left.

We left in a drizzle and drove off through several herds of mules, being taken up to KUNMING by G.I.'s. These were the first of numerous herds we saw along the way, being both enroute, blocking up the road, and camping out on some level spot, where they pitched tents had their kitchens and even an ambulance and medical care. Was told that it took them about 8 or 10 weeks to make this trip.

Pack mules were used to carry equipment over the Ledo-Burma road by both Chinese and American troops.

PAOSHAN is a fairly large walled city, typically Chinese, with large entrance gates and projecting towers at each corner. There were the usual collections of suburban houses and huts along the main road leading into the town.

We didn't go through the town itself, but bypassed it, and were soon traveling up to the narrow end of the valley. When we hit the hills we came past a Chinese convoy going the opposite direction. As the road was very winding and had numerous sharp corners and bends, we had some ticklish moments, but there were no accidents.

We took the road to WAYAO and after traveling for about 2 hours, came to the LANTSANG KIANG or as it is better known, the MEKONG River. We followed it for about 10 or 15 miles. It is a swift, cocoa colored river, flowing in a narrow gorge. We had lunch in the drizzle on the road overlooking the river. There are two bridges crossing the MEKONG River and we crossed over the newer one, about 1/4 mile upstream from the old one. It was a suspension bridge and they permitted only one truck at a time to cross.

We started up the mountain by driving up a tributary valley. It was a 15 mile climb, and we soon were among the clouds, often with visibility of only 50 or 60 ft. It is interesting to note at these elevations, nearly 9,000 or 10,000 ft. that the vegetation is of a temperate type, none of the creepers, vines and tropical types seen at all. Numerous pretty flowers are in evidence, mainly blue and yellow.

After reaching the peak we descended into a high valley and before we had expected it, were met by MP's who told us that the convoy parking area was 1 1/4 miles beyond.

We gassed up at the POL [*Petroleum, Oil, & Lubricants*] station and were directed to our parking area on a little knoll. It was quite satisfactory. The mess equipment was set up just below the parking area on a flat spot near a little ravine. The HQ area was on a flat spot, level with the parking area and overlooking the mess area and ravine. The water supply was good. There was drinking water in lister bags and washing water from a large tank. When this tank overflowed, it made a good shower for some of the men.

A lister bag is a 32 gallon canvas water bag used to supply troops with drinking water which during World War II was generally purified with calcium hypochlorite or boiling.

The rain had ceased by midafternoon and we had a good view of this little valley in which YUNGPING is placed. The village itself was about 1/2 miles from us.

After supper time, convoy #261, started an epidemic of shooting at the tombs of the surrounding hillocks [*Chinese build their gravesites in the side of hills.* This epidemic, as I feared, became contagious and soon some of our men became infected with the shooting bug. I had to stop Lt. *XXX6* from taking some men away to shoot, which was against my direct orders laid down in the SOP for the trip.

It drizzled during the night and was raining again when we set out at 0700. Schlaybach, one of our men, had an attack of acute appendicitis today, so we decide to send him in an ambulance with Lt. Barnhardt attending, to our next stop YUNNANYI about 130 miles beyond. The 21st F. H. has a unit there and should be able to operate on him.

SUNDAY, JULY 8, 1945

We started out in a drizzle again, on our long 130 mile run. As we had expected, the first 1/3 of the way was the most mountainous, and we spent all morning on this part of the trip. For long distances I had to keep my truck in low gear. About 1100 we started to descend into the YANGPI river valley.

Just before we reached the village of YANGPI and the river crossing, we saw where the pipeline had sprung a leak and the gasoline had exploded and caught on fire. Several rice paddies had been ruined, several houses had caught fire, and along the ditches on both sides of the road, the grass and weeds were burned up. It must have been quite a blaze and numbers of Chinese were badly burned. We stopped for lunch on the east side of the river, which flows from N to S, and eventually empties into the Mekong River. After following this cocoa colored stream for about 5 or 6 miles, we turned left, up a tributary. This part of the road was very steep and in parts cut out of nearly sheer slopes. About 5 miles up, we came to a rapids and saw the building of a little hydroelectric plant there.

Soon we were on the floor of a little valley and came to a town SIAKWAN. It is at the S-end of a large lake the EOG HAI [*now called Erhai*] which is surrounded by mountains and skirted by a fine, flat plain.

We hit a beautiful stretch of macadam road and long stretches of fair, bumpy, dirt roads Soon we crossed the pass and saw ahead of us another nice valley, smaller in size than the first. We could see the road on the E side of the valley, but instead of our road cutting across the valley to this road, it was cut out all the mountainsides flanking the valley (HUNGAI valley?).

After leaving this valley, we crossed another ridge and soon were in the YUNNANYI valley. It has a little lake in it and is roughly oval in shape, several miles across. Here is the Army air base that the "Flying Tigers" used and the convoy area is close to the base.

The pipes of the POL station were dry and we were told to return in the morning to gas up. The convoy parking area is about 3 or 4 miles from the SOS HQ down a narrow one way road, which has a mud hole in it that can nearly be dignified as a "tank trap." Actually, it was a jeep trap and caused lots of trouble, many jeeps having to be hauled out.

The convoy area had some tents in it and quite a number of convoys. There was washing water in barrels nearby and lister bags in a tent. There was a mess hall for the EM and an officer's mess. The food was pretty good, although there were the usual number of gripes, who said the food was not fit to eat. This was the same gang that always complains about food. The chances are that they come from families that probably serve poorer food than the food served them in the Army.

One of our trucks broke down, loaded with a generator had broken down about 60 miles down the road and we had to send a wrecker after it. It came back during the night.

MONDAY, JULY 9, 1945

We had a good night's sleep and had reveille and chow call at 0630. Even then, many preferred to sleep in, rather than get up for breakfast. We had assembly at 0900 and started about 25 trucks and the HQ and O's vehicles out to the POL. They got stuck in the mud hole, sure enough, and were delayed several hours, until the engineers fixed it.

We greased the trucks and took it pretty easy the rest of the day. I wrote a couple of letters.

TUESDAY, JULY 10, 1945

We had reveille at 0445 in the morning, as usual, and chow call at 0500. Our breakfast was messed up, due to the fact that the camps cooks had gotten up late. I gave the mess Sgt. the devil for delaying us.

The ditch in the road had been fixed in a rough way. One of the stones got in between the rear dual wheels and had to be removed at our hourly halt. It was quite a job, too.

After leaving the YUNNANYI valley, we came to the mountains again. The villages here are so high, that our climbs are short compared to some of the previous ones. There are numerous small, flat valleys between the mountains and we drove through many. Our PM's travel was mainly downstream, following the course of the LUNG CHAIN [*Now Longquan*] River, which eventually flows into a main tributary of the YANGTZE KIAN [*Yangtze*].

The road was terribly rough and dusty and thus quite tiring. At YUNNANYI we picked up, to take to KUNMING, a Dr. Wei, president of Shantung [*Shandong*] University. He is a very intelligent Chinese gentleman and scholar, is an Episcopalian minister, a possessor of many degrees, has traveled around the world 4 times and has lectured at many famous universities. We also took along 3 American soldiers and a Chinese-American employee.

We reached our night's destination early and were told to gas up at the next POL, 7 miles down the road. It was a rough trip and put everyone out of sorts. But we had to do it as they were working on the driveway and if it rained during the night, we would be unable to drive in the next morning and would have to lose much time in gassing by hand.

The convoy camp at TSUYUNG is in a small valley, next to an emergency airstrip. It was fairly muddy, but not too bad. We parked our vehicles in our usual square, with the mess department on one side and the O and EM on the other. We fed our men there; after supper Dr. Wei gave us a very nice talk, until darkness forced us to halt the meeting. In the meantime many O and men had started firing at the tombs on the hillside and orders came down from base HQ to cease, so I had to stop them [*See Map 4*].

On several occasions we were complemented in the way we set up at nights, the comfort with which we traveled and with the way I set up the vehicles when parking, and with the excellence and proficiency of the mess.

WEDNESDAY, JULY 11, 1945

Off to a good early start for this, the last lap on our trip to KUNMING. Before we left, we found room for a Chinese Col. Lee and his adjutant, a captain. They wanted to go to KUNMING with us. The Col. was a nice chap, looked like a soldier and could talk good English. He was a regular saluting demon.

Our trip, during the morning especially, was from one valley to valley, over relatively low mountains. Before noon, we came to a small place called LU PENG and here we first came across the old, abandoned Yunnan-Burma RR. It was a beautiful mountain engineering job, following a branch of some river for quite a distance, through tunnels and bridges. Only the bridge piers remained and there was no sign of tracks, although later on we saw stacks of cross ties.

We followed the RR right of way all the way into KUNMING. We reached the traffic control point, outside of KUNMING about 1445. This spot is nearer the level of the valley of the lake TIEH CHIN [*now Dianchi Pool*]. The road comes down a notch in the mountains west of Lake. This range seems like an impossible barrier, but isn't. After waiting at the traffic control point for an hour for the MP's and for the last serials to catch up with us, we started out in a semi-circular drive around the N end of the lake, to our campsite east of the head of the lake. We didn't go through Kunming but drove around it. This was a busy road, full of military traffic, native buses, gharries and innumerable primitive carts, drawn by emaciated horses, steers and water buffalo. They just crawled along.

The hillsides are vast cemeteries, and the flat ground is used for rice paddies and truck gardens. They grow beautiful vegetables here and they wash them in the nearby pools and creeks. That really ensures them being contaminated with any and every type of germ in China.

We passed Camp Coombs, and were stationed at Camp McMillan! The trucks were parked on top of the hill. A nice, cool windy spot. In fact, as I'm writing this at my desk, the wind is blowing so hard from the west, that I'm having difficulty keeping this page from blowing away. As I sit here, I can see some foothills and the level plain. Beyond is the lake, and the mountains hemming it to the west. I can see the airport, with its many white, glistening planes and the airport with its dust clouds ahead of me.

KUNMING and the SOS area are hidden by sight by an intervening foothill, a bare desolate looking spot, with scattered tombs and many badly eroded gullies. The personnel area of Camp McMillan is about 1 1/2 miles east of our knob, in little valley. This area is right beside an old sugar refinery a mass of gray stone buildings. They have tents, a mess hall and showers here. I made arrangements to borrow two trucks to shuttle our men back and forth between the two areas. It worked out pretty well, and we soon had men down getting shaved, showered and later on eating.

Along the road, death seems to be quite in evidence. We saw quite a number of dead ponies, looking thin and emaciated. Dogs were tearing away at them. At one place, a truck had gone over a cliff, and was lying on its back, surrounded by the mules it had been loaded with, all bloated and puffed out.

Early in the afternoon, I saw a dead Chinaman, lying at the edge of the road, stretched out on his back. The others saw him, and told me of another, who was in a sitting position near the road, clothed only in a shirt. A third man was being carried on a litter, his legs dangling.

WEDNESDAY, JULY 12, 1945

They were late sending up the trucks and so we were half hour late in our schedule. I shaved and put on cotton khakis for the first time in weeks. Had a hair cut, too. Then had Baumgardner, my driver, drive me to SOS HQ. Here I discovered that Maj. Thomas, SOS surgeon, had been rotated to the USA. Maj. Garland had his job now, and Maj. Watson, MC is here now, and he had been our inspecting officer at Camp Swift, a very nice fellow.

Met Lt. Budziszewski here, too. He and Nagler were flown up from the 234th Gen. Hosp., CHABUA, a few days ago. He looks, sounds and feels ill. He runs a fever at nights and can't sleep. I believe that he has some infection in his herniotomy [*hernia operation*] wound. Nagler is completely recovered from his appendectomy.

Met Maj. Reed at HQ. Tomorrow morning all of us are going to see Col. Armstrong, theater surgeon, about our future plans and assignments. It seems that we are to unload our equipment into boxcars and turn in all our trucks, except TO/E vehicles. Looks as if the personnel is to be air-lifted.

We dropped in at the JADS [*Judge Advocates Division*] office, it looks as if Lt. Stoltzberg, MAC, is to get his wish and be transferred to JADS. They have been working on a case already, and I gave permission for the transfer. Met him shortly after this, and he had the written transfer already. Quick work. He had been left behind at LEDO, 20th Gen. Hosp. and had been flown over before we had made the trip. Hate to lose [*him*], but he'll be happier in his new assignment.

Lt. O'Neil returned from the 95th Station H. this morning. He had a bad eye, evidently a burn. I had removed the foreign body yesterday, but the burned area had to be removed by instruments, I didn't have with me. His eyes feel better today.

I saw the ordinance people and they want the trucks turned in, day after tomorrow. Will stay at Camp Coombs then and probably fly out.

Schlaybach, who we sent to the hospital with tentative diagnosis of appendicitis, returned today, too. He cleared up in a few days, undiagnosed, but all well again.

FRIDAY, JULY 13, 1945

Had taps blown last night at 10:30, but it didn't seem to mean much to some of the men, as an hour later, I had to break up a large, noisy crap game, a poker game and a singing and guitar party. Boy, was I mad, but it quieted the gang down. This morning, as usual, they didn't feel like getting up. We really do have nice weather for sleeping, two blankets aren't too much at all.

Saw Maj. Borland and Maj. Watson this morning, but they hadn't seen the surgeon yet, so had to return in the afternoon. Got down a little late to the meeting and they were in the S-3's office, and returned with definite information. #III unit to go to CHUNG KING [*now Chongqing*] and HQ I and II to go to NAN TAN [*Nandan, in Hechi, Guangxi*] on the road toward LIUCHOW [*now LiuZhou*]. As we had been told that we would lose our trucks and have to go by rail and regular, convoy route, I decided to get busy and see what I could do.

First I went to transportation, where I saw Capt. Phillips and found that the road was passable, up to and past NAN TAN, from there to LIU CHOW, it's passable only for weapons carrier's, due to bridges being blown up. The Chinese have just recently pushed out the Japs, after nearly 2 months of fighting.

Second, I went to HQ and saw Maj. Oliver and Lt. Edquist, who agreed with me that motor transport of our own was the best. They are from the Transportation division and are in charge of convoys from KUNMING-CHANYI to KWEIYANG and points east.

Third, back to transportation at SOS HQ and then to see Maj. Hewitt, S-4, who said "absolutely no!" The general was promised those trucks by the 15th and he's going to have them. I told him S-3 wanted us to leave in 48 hours and he talked with them, verifying this, and also learning that S-3 just wanted us out of Kunming, and didn't give a damn when we got to our destination, just as long as we left here. Well, I knew that, though I didn't tell it to him on purpose. Major Hewitt said that he knew a party who had 25 Dodge trucks that we might use. I kicked about them, telling him how unsuited they were, but didn't kick too hard and told him that they'd be better than nothing at all. He then called up this party and told me to meet him at transportation again.

So, fourth step, back to base station "A" Transportation section again and discovered that the 25 trucks belong to Capt. Sherman, with whom I had talked previously. Well, he had the 95th and the 96th confused a bit, but with the help of Lt. Col. Becker, we finally got it straightened out.

The plan, we are to pick up 25 British type Dodge trucks next morning and load our equipment into them. Then turn in all the ordinance trucks. Also the 3rd unit, is to unload their equipment at a depot and await orders at Camp Coombs.

What a day—a hectic day, but we go by our own trucks, and the 95th [?] have to go to NANNING by rail and Chinese convoy. Guess we got the best of them this time again.

SATURDAY, JULY 14, 1945

Up early this morning to see the transportation office. Took Lt. Ostroff and 26 drivers with me to pick up the 25 Dodge trucks. After some figuring, etc., and writing a note, Capt. Sherman told us where to pick up the vehicles. We went there, but found that we had been misdirected. Finally we wound up at the proper spot, the MTS motor pool, and drew the trucks.

The IIId unit, eventually bound for CHUNGKING, was starting to unload their trucks in a compound not far from the MTS area.

The checking of trucks, etc., progressed very slowly and but few were accepted. We would need all of the next day, Sunday, for loading and unloading, turning in our trucks, etc. Those not accepted by MTS are to be turned in by the IId unit.

Lt. Budziszewski is to go with the IIId unit to CHUNGKING. A radiogram from the 27th F. H. at KWEIYANG, stated that Maj. Lamber was not to be kept there, and that we were to pick him up on our way through there.

After supper, I went to see Maj. Watson and go into town with him, but he wasn't there, so I drove in myself, parked at the MP lot, and drove by rickshaw to the United Nations club. It was full of officers and some Chinese girls of, let's say, questionable character. The place is run like a stateside nightclub, tables and dancing, food and wine.

SUNDAY, JULY 15, 1945

We were busy unloading our TO/E equipment from our good 6 MCs, that had carried us into China over the LEDO-BURMA ROAD, into right hand drive Dodges, made in Canada, I believe.

It was a cold, rainy day, such as we've had most of the time in China. Our hilltop parking area is a lot drier than the lower, flatter plains. Our loading was accomplished by late evening and we arranged to turn many vehicles over to MTS, although they rejected many, of course.

Chaplain Woods, and his assistant, T/5 Calkins have been placed on DS at CHANYI [*Zhanyi, near Qujing*], our next stop. It seems that there are about 1700 troops there, without a chaplain, and that they need one quite badly. Well, will get them back soon, I hope. There are only 12 Protestant chaplains in all of China.

That afternoon, Capt. Brummett and I went to KUNMING to do some shopping. We were disappointed, because it started to rain, and rain steadily, as soon as we arrived there. We stayed at the American Red Cross till about 5:30 and then went out in the rain, no raincoats or field jackets on either, and got pretty well soaked, especially as we missed the "Cantonese Restaurant" and had to retrace our steps for nearly 1/3 of a mile.

The meal was good. I ordered sliced chicken soup, rice, tea and sweet and sour pork. Got a huge bowl of soup, enough for 3 or 4 and ate with a small, porcelain spoon. These spoons, small bowls, etc. were in a big bowl of steaming hot water as were the chopsticks. You should have seen us with chopsticks. Really, they aren't a bad eating utensil, as all Chinese food is cut small enough to handle with them. It was a delicious meal.

I spilled a cup of tea on my lap, but the tea was so weak and my clothes were so wet anyhow, that it was not noticeable when we left.

It had stopped raining and we wandered through many streets. We each bought a pewter carbide lamp and some carbide. I promptly dropped my lamp and dented its bottom flange. It will be easily straightened out again. Slept well in my jungle hammock that night.

This chapter from diary pages 82-94

ENDNOTES

---

[1] D. Balasubramanian and N. Appaji Rao [eds]. *The Indian Human Heritage*, 1998, 47-49; Ilayperuma Isurani. "Evaluation of cephalic indices: a clue for racial and sex diversity," 2011, 113.

[2] Charles F. Romanus and Riley Sunderland. *Stilwell's Command Problems* (Office of the Chief of Military History, Department of the Army, 1956), 329-360.

Chapter 7: Kunming to Tushan: The Beginning of Confusion

MONDAY, JULY 16, 1945

Our last day at camp McMillan. It had rained during the night and the ground was wet and the days slippery. My truck #1 was the first out and I skidded a bit in leaving. It took the rest of the vehicles over 1/2 hour to get off the hill. We started out at 0930, quite a late hour, for the 109 mile stretch from KUNMING to CHANYI [*Now Zhanyi in Qujing, Yunnan Province* [*See Map 4*].

Table 7-1: Towns traveled through from Kunming, Yunnan Province to Liuchow (Liuzhou), Guangxi, Province

Name of town WWII	Modern transliteration if different	Province
Kunming		Yunnan
Luliang	in Qujing	Yunnan
Chanyi	Zhanyi in Qujing City	Yunnan
Annan	Qinglong	Guizhou
Panshien	Panxian	Guizhou
Anshun		Guizhou
Kweiyang	Guiyang	Guizhou
Tushan	Dushan in Qiannan	Guizhou
Liuchow	Liuzhou	Guangxi

By old roads, it's approximately 675miles (1,030 KM) from Kunming, Yunnan Province to Liuchow, Guangxi Province.

About a mile out, our motor started to miss and we found out that a wire had come loose from a spark plug. It was soon fixed and we were on our way again.

CHANYI [*Zhanyi, near Qujing*], is a small village, with inevitable suburbs of cheap stores between it and camp. CHANYI is a rail head and a large QM depot and is a beehive of activity. Here we found that the MTS to be in worse condition than usual—which is pretty bad. Everybody was confused and the confusion was heightened by the presence of a party of generals, Gen. Weidemeir [*Wedemeyer*] and Simpson.

> *Wedemeyer and Simpson may have been planning the campaign using Chinese troops, with the training and support of the Americans, to open one of the Chinese ports. This proposed campaign is discussed in Romanus and Sutherland, "Chapter XII: The End of Wedemeyer's Experiment "in* Time Runs out in the CBI. *During this campaign, numerous Chinese troops died of starvation, cholera, and other diseases. However, the campaign was halted upon news that the Japanese would likely surrender in mid-August 1945.* [1]

There was no available area for parking nearby and no tents that were unoccupied, so we finally drove about 3 1/2 miles away to a flat, area beside the road, in a little limestone valley. And on our way there, we saw something that was a laugh. There was a sign saying "Convoy Parking Area Entrance" with "under construction" in small letters. A bulldozer had just recently made a small opening from the road to some terraced rice paddies and cornfields. 100 yards up the road was a similar "Exit" sign, also with a 20 ft. road leading to neighboring fields. Only fields in between. As everything was so brand-new, it was obviously eyewash for visiting generals, who might be fooled by them. I, who had a convoy to park, just laughed sardonically.

We borrowed 4 empty, shaky trucks from the MTS and shuttled the O and men back and forth to showers and mess. These latter were really good, the showers hot, and a good meal with excellent Chinese bread.

After supper we put up our jungle hammock and Capt. Brummett got his carbide lamp going. It really works well and even in a strong breeze throws a steady, brilliant light.

TUESDAY JULY 17, 1945

We tried to get an extra truck or two, or even some half-loaded ones from MTS, but no luck. We did however, have this luck; we are to gas up along the way, and in this way, can keep all the trucks and all our equipment together and be ready to set up as soon as we arrive. Also heard that the road, closed by a landslide is now open, and that we will be able to proceed in the next days, instead of having to lay over 2 or 3 days as they had told us yesterday.

Lt. Ostroff is trying to get parts for our hydraulic brakes. No less than 9 out of 25 of the Dodge trucks had their brakes go bad on them, that's about 1/3, too many.

We are to leave at 0900 on Wed. the 18th and a gas truck is to be out at our area shortly after 0800.

The generals and our officers had breakfast at the same time this morning and traveled on afterwards.

Capt. Pearl stopped in and surprised me by telling me that HQ had 2 units of the 22nd Field Hospital [*that*] were located 1/2 miles E of us, on the main road. I dropped over at 7:15 p.m. and met Maj. Yee, a Chinese American from California, who is now in command, and Lt. Col. Johnston had just left for the USA. (I met Col. Johnson a few days ago in Kunming). They have a nice set up on a small hill, and are putting up mud brick buildings and laying out crushed stone walls.

Their surgery is still being done in a tent. They have been overseas for over two years now and were in the SALWEEN river campaign.

After I was in bed about 1/2 hr., a messenger in a Jeep came in to tell me that the road was closed beyond ANNAN [*Qinglong*] and that we would have to lay over a day or two.

WEDNESDAY, JULY 18, 1945

Early this morning, gave orders that we were to lay over this day and were to travel the next day. This morning while at breakfast Capt. Hogan said that he had seen Lt. Shoemaker, Transportation O, in the latrine, and had been told that the road was open. So it was. At 5:00 p.m. the message came in that the road was closed, at 11: 00 p.m. that the road was open again. So, I quickly changed plans and we were ready to set out soon.

A POL convoy was supposed to leave at 0800, so we planned to leave at 0900. Shortly after we were shuttled down to our area, it started to rain, and it poured steadily all morning. Our parking area was a flat spot, below the road level, and I was afraid that some of our Dodges might get stuck, but they all got out without trouble, but very slowly, as the POL convoy trucks kept rolling by us. Pretty soon my pant legs were soaking wet, where the water ran into them from my raincoat. My helmet liner kept my head, but not my face dry. As I was directing traffic, I had to stay out in the rain and soon the water ran down my pant legs into my shoes and I was actually swishing in water every time I took a step. Wet and cold, I got into my truck when we took off that 0930.

We drove over the usual up and down, right and left turn road. For several hours we could see a mountain range to the N. that we were paralleling. At lunchtime it had stopped raining and we halted by the side of the road in the little valley, just outside of a small town. (Didn't see its name). While we were parked there, a Chinese driver's truck went through the stone wall of the nearby bridge, turned over, and tossed out its load and driver. The latter was miraculously unhurt, except for an injured finger, but was, of course, quite shaken.

We had quite a time getting through the little town. The Chinese driver's, according to custom, eat their meals at Chinese restaurants and they practically blocked the street with their trucks, and one spot in particular, by double parking. That spot was just passable, and most of our trucks hit one wheel of the offending truck and whenever that happened, the Chink driver made an awful fuss. That, of course, made us feel better.

About the middle of the afternoon, we came to a small, narrow, valley. At the bottom of the valley, we found our night's destination PANSHIEN [*Panxian, Guizhou Province*], a small-town, with the main suburban street of slopes and houses, of the usual squalid type.

The MTS people were bulldozing a parking area and it was entirely too muddy for us to use. Seems that we always are too early in nearly every step, to benefit from their ultimate arrangements. Coolies gassed and oiled our trucks there and then we were led to our parking area, which was a large, flat piece of ground, right next to the city wall and one of its main gates. It was a large expanse of black, evil-smelling earth, mainly a big mud puddle. We chose the higher dryer, area near the city wall. The place stunk and we soon discovered the same coolies had left buckets of fecal material standing nearby. To make matters worse, a mule came trotting along and upset one, a filthy, grueling mass, just swarming with maggots. We covered the spot with dirt and put oil in the remaining buckets. Bet the coolies were mad.

We really had a mob of spectators out to watch us. Just like the crowd watching a carnival setting up. Capt. McAuliffe had a rope put up, and the guards kept the mob back of this rope. They sure were a nuisance, especially one professional beggar, who had a baby strapped to his back. What made things worse, was the fact that the kids had firecrackers and were selling them to our men, who were throwing them into the crowd. I put a stop to this nonsense soon.

The Chinese city walls are interesting. Any town or village of pretension has a wall. The lesser ones have mud brick walls, the better ones, cut stone walls. These walls are not very high, often not more than 10 ft. in height and have battlements on them. PANHSIEN's wall was about 12 to 14 ft. high, cut stone face and the wall filled with rubble. It had a nice gate and gatehouse, with a pagoda on it. These gate houses are well built. The Chinese are good stonemasons. The entrance was like a tunnel, with a vaulted roof, about 12 ft. high and about 30-40 ft. long. The floor was paved and sounded hollow to the tread. There were a pair of swing-hinge, iron-plated doors just within, which, when swung open, fitted into a recess, so that they wouldn't narrow the passage. In the vaulted ceiling, just before the doors, were square holes, which looked like places through which could be shoved large timbers, to act as a grate, for added protection.

THURSDAY, JULY 19, 1945

Up at 0500 and on the way at 0715—a little late, due to our need for shuttling back and forth and also due to the fact that a POL convoy was to leave before us.

We went up the hill on the east side of the valley and soon reached a high, narrow, alpine valley with a flat bottom. Later we went down hill and then up another. We had lunch overlooking a branch of PEPANG KIANG [*Beipan*] River.

At about 2 p.m., we came to the foot of the famous 24 steps near ANNAN [*now Qinglong, Guizhou*]. The road winds up and up, 24 switchbacks and is the one that is so frequently photographed.

Sometimes the 24, or 21-steps, have been attributed to being on the Ledo-Burma Road. However, these hairpin turns were on the road that connected Kunming, Yunnan, China — at the end of the Burma

Road—to Chungking (now Chongqing) the Nationalist Chinese provisional capital and headquarters of Gen. Chang Kai-shek. Through much of its travel, after leaving Kunming, the 96th Field Hospital traveled approximately along what is now the G320 Chinese highway that goes through Yunnan and the Guizhou Provinces. Many parts of this highway, that begins at the Burma-Chinese border, was part of the old Burma Road[See Map 4] [2]

The town of ANNAN [*now Quiglong*] is on top, in a saddle between two peaks. I led the convoy right through and 7 miles past, by mistake and we all had to turn around in an old convoy area and return. Was I burned up! And so were the rest. When we finally returned, we found that we should have turned left on a Chinese alley. They did have a sign, but had taken it down to repaint it, and hadn't stationed an MP yet, because they weren't expecting us as early as the time we arrived.

This camp is a very nice one. We slept in tents and had good showers and mess. They even had a movie there. I must've been pretty tired, as I fell asleep before the lights were put out and one officer moved in, and I never even heard him.

FRIDAY, JULY 20, 1945

Up at 0600 and off at 0800. They claim that this is the worst day's travel, 106 miles, all up and down, except for the last 30 miles into ANSHUN [*in Guizhou province*]. The place we had spent the night in ANNAN, near the famous 24 switchbacks, is near the top of the range. We were traveling downhill and in 1/2 hours were at the bottom, a deep gorge out by the PEPAN KIANG [*Beipan River*].

We had seen this range east of the PEPAN KIANG River, ever since leaving ANNAN. This ridge was long and saw-toothed, with all the little peaks about the same height. We climbed over several foot-hill ranges and on looking back to the west, saw that the ANNAN mountains also looked saw-toothed. About 2 miles back of ANNAN we came on a truck on its back. The geology of this range is interesting. The west side slopes up toward the eastern sky, then there is a valley, high up and on the other side of the valley, the layers slope at 90° from the first, a clear indication of a definite break in earth's crust. We had lunch in this valley and then continued downhill to a more easterly branch of the PEPAN KIANG River.

Our climb up the east slope of this gorge was noted by our passing a convoy, westbound. We nearly had a head on collision, when one fool Chink tried to pass another on a blind curve. We just missed colliding and in the back sway he side-swiped the truck back of me, causing no real damage, however. Boy, was I mad and ready to force the next Chink off the road over the cliff. Our passing of this convoy was on a narrow spot, on a sheer cliff-like hillside and on most of it, we were on the outside and often the outside wheels were just a few inches from the edge.

On top of the hill, we came to a plateau. Here we had about 30 miles of good, wide, though dusty, road, all the way into ANSHUN. On this plateau were numerous rounded, conical hills, many perfect in shape. Well this is typical of all Chinese hills which are well eroded and treeless, these in particular look artificial, as they were cut from horizontal rock layers, and looked like a gigantic pile of pancakes, each one a little smaller than the one below. Something like an old-fashioned beehive.

ANSHUN is a walled town and looks cleaner than the usual Chinese town, as it has paved streets and sidewalks; it has a circle in the center and it's a good thing that I had received directions at ANNAN, as there were no signs in this town at all. We took the street to the left at the circle. The only sign was "Pro-Station." After 4 miles of China's bumpiest road, we came to the convoy area, located near an old airstrip [*See Map 4*].

We had a nice location, hot showers and a good mess. We slept by the cars in our jungle hammocks. McCain was late putting mine up, as the weapons carrier McAuliffe and Brummett were driving, and in which my bedding roll was, broke its fan belt and was delayed on the road. The moon was half-full and it was a beautiful night.

After I had gone to bed, I heard a loud argument, mainly one man inciting the other. I yelled for them to stop, but they didn't hear me, so I got out of bed, good and mad, put my boots on and went over to where I heard the altercation, but it had ceased before I arrive. I then discovered that it was *XXX7* and *XXX8*, the former who was loudmouth, while *XXX8* was a lot more quiet.

SATURDAY, JULY 21, 1945

Started off at 0800 sharp, as it was reported to me that the expected incoming convoy was not scheduled to run today.

The road back to ANSHUN was just as bumpy as before, and the rest of the way out of town was just as bad. The streets were nicely paved in well cut, rectangular blocks, but many of these blocks were depressed, probably from the weight of the trucks, as well as from age.

The road was still in this plateau valley and was wide and not hilly, but was very dusty. We drove along this valley most of the morning. The topography of our route and the map don't seem to agree, as was true of most of our journey. As well as I can figure out, we were following the valley of the LUKWANG HO, a north flowing tributary of the WU KAING. We crossed no sizable stream until we came to the one on which KWEIYANG [*now Guiyang, Guizhou*] is located. About 10 miles from KWEIYANG, the country became rough as we went down grade and finally we entered a deep gully and came to some buildings and to a sign "City Limits of KWEIYANG." We soon were out of this area and then around the corner, came to the real city itself. We followed the signs and came to our parking area at the "race track." That's what it was, too; we parked our trucks on the southeast curve. We found good tents and a good mess hall, as well as hot and cold showers.

It was hot all day, reminiscent of INDIA, but not as humid. Capt. Abelson, the base's surgeon came down to see us and asked Capt. Hogan and me to meet him at his office in about an hour.

We showered and cleaned up and McCain fixed up my quarters in a small tent that I'm sharing with McAuliffe. I even have my table and desktop now.

At 1500, Capt. Hogan and I drove to see Capt. Abelson. We had to take a guide with us, as the road wound around the hill and then came to the river and followed its course for about 1/2 mile. The surgeon's office is up the side of the hill and is very nice and cool and comfortably equipped.

Here Capt. Abelson told us that HQ and one unit would probably set up at TUNSHAN [*Dushan in Qiannan City*], about 1/2-way between KWEIYANG and LIUCHOW [*now Liuzhou, Guizhou*], while all the med. O. and some of the EM of the other unit would be put on D. S. for a while [*See Map 4*]. I didn't like that, but what could I do? It's common gossip at this camp that they have been awaiting us, just so that we could have these men on DS to relieve others, mainly from the 172d General Hospital, who are being recalled to the parent Unit at KUNMING. The 172d G. H. is to take over the hospital at KUNMING and to relieve the 95th station hospital there now.

The 27th F. H., stationed here at KWEIYANG, is to move to LIUCHOW and start a hospital there, and after starting it, is to be relieved by the 95th Station Hospital. What a mixup, and were in the middle as usual.

Maj. Lamber is on D.S. with the 27th F. H. at WANPING, and will probably stay there as long as the 1st Unit is being used on D. S. Well, we'll probably be here several weeks, so may as well settle ourselves down comfortably, as well as we can. Our trip from KUNMING to KWEIYANG was not too bad. I feel a little tired from the 1500 mile trip, not exhausted at all, but my eyes feel tired and heavy.

> Distance Table—Approximately
> Kunming—Chanyi 86 miles, Annan 80 miles
> to Pan Haien, 80 miles Anshun, 100 miles
> Kweiyang 85 miles

This confusing table appears to trace the mileage from one convoy camping area to the other along his route of travel from Kunming to Kweiyang. Google.com shows that from Kunming, in the Yunnan province, to Kweiyang, in the Guizhou Province, is about 326 miles (525 km) on old highways. The route of travel of the convoy was approximately along the G320, a primitive road at that time, along with other roads that may not exist anymore. It is unclear why he says 1500 miles in the preceding paragraph when in the next paragraph from his speedometer he says the distance was about 380 miles.

My speedometer, on the Dodge truck I drove all the way from KUNMING, registered 653.0 KM, or 380.0 miles. Well, don't know which to believe now, probably the speedometer, or well just split the difference, and call it 400 miles.

SUNDAY, JULY 22, 1945

This morning went over to SOS HQ [*Kunming*], where I had an appointment with Capt. Abelson. Here I met Maj. Brown, dental surgeon for Base Section #III: Lt. Col. Ricamore, executive O; Lt. Frank, Ord. O, and Capt.— ? MTs. O.

We went to the Chinese contagious hospital where they are taking care of the victims of the local cholera epidemic. A lot of the poor devils were dying here. These are the first cholera patients I have seen. They are very dehydrated and were given intravenous saline. Out in the yard, carpenters were busy making coffins, not a cheery sight for the patients, but they were too sick to care. Instead of beds, the patients were lying on wooden platforms, no mattresses or covers at all, and the floor was filling with vomitus, and partly filled, rusty bedpans were lying around the floor too.

MONDAY, JULY 23, 1945

What a day this turned out to be! First, a telegram from Kunming, ordering T/4 Down, our only stenographer, who can both take shorthand and type, to report to the JAD6 office in Kunming. I wrote a letter to the Commanding General, in which I stated that this man was not a court reporter and asking them to rescind the order. It will do no good, I know.

Secondly, the local-based surgeon's office is not satisfied with the number of officers and EM, especially MAC officers, that we can supply and threatens to force our supplying them by an order from the local HQ.

Thirdly, I lent Lt. *XXX9*, MAC, account inspector, a Jeep yesterday. The Jeep was found parked today with a broken windshield and a broken rearview mirror. He just left it there, without a word of thanks, apology or explanation.

Fourthly, I have had orders cut, putting the 3 remaining officers of the 1st unit, and about a dozen EM, on Detached Service [DS]. That ruins our 1st unit, just as we are ready for action. Capt. Abelson needs these O and men, and then some, from our unit, to fill in for those who are being taken away from him by the need of these men in their parent units, the 172d G. H. and the 27th F. H. What a day!

The PX supplies we brought with us, were unloaded into the orderly room tent, and are to be sold tomorrow. We had to guard them well tonight, as PX supplies are particularly unattainable here and they might be stolen by soldiers stationed here. An example of their value is given here. A soldier was ready to sell 616 film for $1.00 a roll (normally about .35 a roll) but was willing to swap two rolls of film for 1 can of beer!

McCain cleaned up all my leather goods today, as several things were mouldy[*sic*], especially my visored winter cap. It's raining now and cooler than it was yesterday.

Was pleased to find my little coin purse, given to me by Babbie, in my briefcase. I thought it lost on a trip from CALCUTTA, to CHABUA, the end of March.

TUESDAY, JULY 24, 1945

At 1000 we started to distribute our remaining PX supplies and most everybody received a carton of cigarettes, chewing gum, tropical candy bars, fruit juices and matches, about $3.00 worth of stuff. I bought a leather shoulder holster for my .45 automatic, why, I don't know. Had some laundry done, which was needed much more than the shoulder holster.

Arrangements were made for inoculating us with booster shots for typhus, cholera and plague at 1400 today.

> *Diseases including cholera, malaria, typhoid fever, amebic dysentery, scrub typhus, sexually transmitted diseases such and chancroid, syphilis and gonorrhea and even the plague were common in the CBI Theater and were endemic among the civilian population.*[3]

Capt. Hogan made a trip to see Capt. Abelson, SOS Base Sec. # III Surgeon Kweiyang this morning with a list of Ist unit O and EM to be put on D. S. When he came back from there, he had news. First there was a telegram from CHANYI, requesting the return of the 25 Dodge trucks they had lent us. That meant unloading them, but Lt.

Ostroff suggested that we drive them, fully loaded, to TUSHAN [*Dushan in Qiannan, Guizhou Province*] and unload them there, put the TO/E equipment in tents, and keep some men there to guard them, until the unit appeared.

Plans were laid for this, Capt. Peterson [*was*] assigned as O in charge and 25 drivers and 25 riders detailed for the job, 14 men and Capt. Peterson to remain with the equipment of HQ and units I and II. Arrangements were made to give these men their shots early, so our caravan could leave shortly after 1300.

Lt. O'Neil was to get rations for 15 men for 35 days and the ration truck was to leave later, after it was loaded.

Secondly, mail had arrived for the first time in a week, but, alas, no mail for me. Am still looking for Babs letter #49, which hasn't arrived yet, though #50 did come in.

Got my 3 shots for this evening, one of them really stung.

Capt. McAuliffe, Lts. Wurzetebeck and Nowell are to go on DS with 259th. Stat. Hosp. here in KWEIYANG, tomorrow. Had some films developed of our LEDO-BURMA road trip. They turned out pretty well, especially those of DIBRUGARH, Assam that the chaplain took, but doggon it, McCain left my head out of some of the best, those of me with the truck at the LEDO- BURMA road junction.[4]

WEDNESDAY, JULY 25, 1945

Receive some mail this morning, 2 letters from Babs, dated July 1st and 4th. Our mail is really taking a long time to arrive here. Our evening mail had a lot of broken packages in it, and was a wet mouldy [*sic*] mess every package broken and most of its contents broken up. It's really too bad.

Went over to the 295th Stat. Hosp. with Capt. McAuliffe and Lts. Nowell and Wurzetebeck, where they will be on DS for a while, hope not too long. This hospital, opened up about 2 months ago, is located in a group of 3 fairly large, 2-story stone buildings, which until recently was a school. It's located upstream from KWEIYANG and is one of the prettiest, little villages I have seen in China. The stream runs numerous water-life wheels for irrigation, and quite a number of Chinese mills, the kind with a horizontal water wheel.

Lt. Holzberg dropped in tonight, working on a JADS case and will be here a few days. He is tickled with his new assignment.

Heard tales of a high-ranking general being called back, due to his leaving here with a large quantity of money, which he can't explain away too well.

It appears, from what Capt. Hogan gathered from Capt. Duffy at SOS HQ [*Kweiyang*], that we will be given a fund of $15,000,000 CN [*Chinese*] for hire of labor and buying of materials for our new location. We will even be given a truckload or two of Chinese workers to take along with us. That sounds pretty good.

THURSDAY, JULY 26, 1945

Full moon last night and really bright. Saw Col. Oliphant, CO of Base Sect. # III. An affable gentleman, quite a conversationalist. It might be that we are to go to KWEILEN [*Guilin*] after its liberation. That wouldn't be bad at all.

Had lunch with Maj. Brown, DC, at SOS surgeon's office. They really are fixed up nicely. Capt. Avery, the new CO of the race track convoy area was over today, crying on Capt. Hogan's shoulder that he needed the space we are occupying for other transients. Well, isn't that just too bad? What do they want us to do, sleep on the ground? So that others can sleep where we are.

Cookie had done a nice job stenciling the proper numbers on our vehicles. Had McCain repaint our helmets and stencil our names on the inside of them.

The QM depot group that was serial "D" of our LEDO-KUNMING convoy #270, came in today. Poor devils had lost one man and one vehicle, when it was forced over a bridge. Driver was killed. Accident occurred about 1/2 day out of CHANYI.

Got myself some DDT dusting powder for the bites I got every night.

FRIDAY, JULY 27, 1945

Lt. Ostroff and the drivers returned safely this evening from their trip to TUSHAN, where they left our supplies. One truck burned out its bearings on the way, and Howell was left at TU YUEN [*Duyun*] due to minor injuries occurred when he was knocked down by a truck. They put up 7 or 8 pyramidal tents and several squad tents for the equipment. Don't know when we will need the stuff.

SATURDAY, JULY 28, 1945

Saw Capt. Abelson, base section surgeon, and Lt. Col. Cavanaugh, from surgeon's office, Kunming, this morning and had lunch with them. It seems that the 96th is destined, for a while at least, to act in reserve only and it looks as if we'll have to loaf around TUSHAN for a while. Well, if we do, we'll set up, even if we only have a few patients.

McCain and I will start out in my Jeep early tomorrow morning, and drive there. Found my alarm clock in Hogan's and O'Neil's tent. Neither know anything about its being there. Hmm-mm.

SUNDAY, JULY 29, 1945

McCain and I left KWEIYANG this morning at 0800. We took our jeep and a change of underclothes and bedding roll for a 3-day stay at TUSHAN. The weather was cool and cloudy, with occasional rain clouds. We stopped for lunch at MA-SHAN-PING and then traveled on again. The road was good, bumpy in a few places, but usually pretty wide and not too hilly.

At about 1500 we came to TU YUEN [*Duyun; See map 4*]. This was the farthest advance point of the Japs invasion last December. The first evidence of this was wrecked cars and trucks and bridges and culverts blown up by our OSS. The town of TU YUEN was badly bombed, ruined and burned up. The bridge over the river was partially blown out. The RR ends at this town and we saw wrecked trucks and cars, many of them burned up.

Just before we entered the town, I saw an ambulance in the ditch. It wasn't due to an accident, just got stuck going down to the river to be washed. We stopped and took one of the men with us, as he wanted a wrecker brought over from the 27th F. H. which has a unit near TU YUEN.

The hospital is about 5 or 6 miles from town, over a terribly rough and narrow road. The hospital itself is located in a nice, little valley, in some good buildings. Here we saw Pfc. Howell, who had his foot run over by a truck when Capt. Peterson was convoying our equipment to TUSHAN. Howell was doing quite well.

Saw a poor Chinese boy here who had found a Jap hand grenade and to set it off while playing with it. The poor kid was blinded in both eyes, his face was peppered with fragments and he lost his fingers from his right hand and toes from his right foot.

We arrived at TUSHAN at about 5:00 p.m. It was raining then. We first had supper at the airfield and then went to the convoy camp.

141

The airfield is a nice, high, one, large enough for landing C-46's [*Commando; cargo*] and P-51's [*Mustang; fighter*], being a fighter base for the latter.

The convoy camp was near a RR station and a former rice paddy. Capt. Peterson and his 14 men were there, quite comfortable in wooden-floored and matting-sided pyramidal tents. Our T/M equipment was in squad tents. Kitchen equipment was under a fly, and the cooks had made coffee and baked a fine chocolate layer cake. The camp had a latrine, but no showers yet.

I slept in Capt. Peterson's tent. It was quite comfortable and had electricity from one of our little surgical lamp generating sets.

MONDAY, JULY 30, 1945

Met Capt. Davidson, Airfield CO, and looked his place over. He was planning on moving his group and thought we could take over all the buildings here. It's a fine set up, but we would have no need of a hospital here. They do have a 10 bed dispensary here, with a couple of Chinese nurses in it.

Loafed around all day. Left an EM at the control tower to watch for Capt. Abelson's arrival. Doubted his coming, as it was raining all day.

This chapter from diary pages 95-111

ENDNOTES

---

[1] Charles F. Romanus and Riley Sunderland. *Time Runs Out in CBI. U.S. Army in World War II* (Office of the Chief of Military History, Department of the Army, 1958), 369-394.

[2] Mark D. Sherry, *China Defensive 4 July 1942–4 May 1945* (U.S. Army Center of Military History, Department of the Army, 1945), 6; The modern G320 Road is found on: Google maps: https://www.google.com/maps. Click on China road maps, go to Yunnan province, and then enlarge.
[3] Kirk T. Mosley and Darrell G. McPherson in *Army Medical Service. Preventive medicine in World War II. Volume VIII*, ed. John Boyd Coates, (Dept. of the Army, 1976), 635-636.
[4] The location of these photographs is unknown.

Chapter 8: Tushan to Liuchow and back to Chanyi, V-J Day and the 24 Steps—again

TUESDAY, JULY 31, 1945

Babbie's birthday, wish I had gotten her box of presents off to her in time. Loafed all day, Wednesday.

WEDNESDAY, AUGUST 1, 1945

Received telegram from Capt. Abelson advising me that he would come out next day and telling me to look over area occupied for 49th Portable Surgical Hospital and also telling me that the IIIc unit was coming to KWEIYANG, plans of going to CHUNGKING changed and to stage at TUSHAN.

Peterson and I had looked over the 49th area and found it not suitable. To get there we had to drive over narrow streets and under ancient gates in the city wall, which was too small to drive trucks through. The hospital was in a medium-sized, 2-story building in a compound. They were preparing to pack and move on. Their place was entirely too small.

Rain again, all day, occasionally clearing. The hills are beautiful, shrouded in patches of low-lying mist.

THURSDAY, AUGUST 2, 1945

Saw an L-5 [*Stinson Sentinel, a small two-person aircraft*] flying over and drove to the airport, thinking that Capt. Abelson might be in it. He wasn't, but soon 2 more arrived, and he was in one, and Col. Burbank was in the other. Another change in plans. We were to move to LIUCHOW [*Liuzhou, Guizhou Province*] and stage there as the 27th F. H. and the 95th Stat. Hosp. were to be set up there. We were just to remain in reserve and possibly take care of the operative work for a proposed Chinese Gen. Hosp. I was to drive on to

LIUCHOW, and he was to fly there and either meet me there, or leave word and plans with Col. Scott, CO of SOS in LIUCHOW. Capt. Abelson and Col. Burbank were to fly to LIUCHOW that evening.

They started out, but in about half hour, we saw them coming back and landing again. At lunch they told us that the weather had closed down, and they couldn't make it.

Mac [*McCain*] and I packed before lunch and were off at 1300. In TUSHAN, we saw a dead Chinese laying right on the side of the main street, with a bashed head, nobody paying any attention to him at all.

The TUSHAN RR station was pretty well rebuilt, but there were some burned-out freight cars right in front of it. We inspected one and it had a layer of ashes, about 6" deep on its floor. There were numerous potsherds and debris among the ashes, buttons, buckles, and even an iron scabbard. Must have been packed with belongings of refugees.

The road out of town was good, except for a few mountain passes. The RR was in bad shape, all bridges and rolling stock blown up. Our OSS must have been a TNT-happy bunch of eager beavers.

The hills were rounded and eroded, and near the 300 kilo-mark, we saw a hill with a hole right through it like an eye in a needle. The hills are all honey-combed with caves.

Places they stopped at on the trip from Tushan, to Liuchow, and back again were marked off in kilometers. Most of these areas did not have place names.

We drove on and stopped at a convoy camp at marker 350. Here we parked the jeep and put up our cots and mosquito bars under a big shed. It rained during the night, and we were glad of the roof overhead.

FRIDAY, AUGUST 3, 1945

The convoy camp could not give us breakfast, so we ate some C-rations, pork and beans and were off at 0710, hoping we could make LIUCHOW that night. (We didn't make it for a week later). We passed through NANTAN [*Nandan, Guangxi*] and CHICHEN, the former at one time considered a possible location. There were a lot of wrecked cars, trucks and motorcycles along the roadside.

One stretch of the road was down a long, steep grade. This is known to the GIs as "Dead man's hill," due to the fact that thousands of bodies of Chinese refugees were found here. They just didn't have strength enough in their weakened conditions to climb the hill, and died along the way.

We got to the ferry, Kilo 448, at 1030 and discovered that both this one and the one at Kilo 491 were out, due to high water. There was a bridge here, but are OSS demons had demolished it so thoroughly that even piers and abutments had been destroyed. The river here runs through a narrow, rocky gulch and flowed about 12-15 miles per hour. Capt. Leo A. Riordan, Burma Road engineer, was in charge of the camp, which was situated on a high, dry, bluff, overlooking the river. This spot was marked by 4 or 5 huge holes in the ground. He called them "bomb craters," but they were actually sinkholes, as they were not water-filled, and some had bamboo in them, 4-inches in diameter, which takes years to grow, since the bombing (?) could only have taken place last fall.

Capt. Riordan made us welcome. McCain stayed in a big squad tent, while I stayed in Riordan's Bombay tent. These quarters were also shared by Maj. McCandless, who was in charge of a Chinese convoy, which was stopped, just as we were. These Chinese drivers, as usual, had their women with them, some as passengers only, others as their personal girlfriends.

Ah, yes, earlier that morning we passed by a large column of Chinese troops, headed our way. While approaching the rear of one group, I honked my horn and this frightened a horse, causing him to rear and back up against the side of the jeep. Next thing, I knew, the rider had been thrown and was lying on the ground. Instantly, memories flashed through my mind of incidences which had been somewhat like this, that had ended up in shootings with Americans killed. I didn't know whether to drive on as if nothing had happened and to get away as quickly as possible, or to stop and see what would happen. I chose the latter course and got out of the jeep. I was glad to see that the Chinese soldiers were grinning and that the thrown rider had gotten up and was smiling, too. I waited until he walked up, leading his horse and asked him if he were hurt. He wasn't and it didn't even seem that his feelings were hurt. He wanted to ride in the jeep, so I invited him in and told him to climb upon our baggage. He did so after giving his horse to another soldier. He spoke fair English and said that he was a Sgt. Major. I thought he was an officer, as he was the only rider. He rode with us about 20 miles and then got out, probably at the point his men were going to march to that night. All's well that ends well.

SATURDAY, AUGUST 4, 1945

Was glad we were in tents last night as it rained. The river came up during the night, and unless it goes down soon, we will be stuck here awhile. It cleared this evening and the sun came out, so I did some washing in my helmet. The things really look clean.

A Lt. Col. Kelso, QM, came in today and had with him Claiborne and Carlson who had been assigned to the 3d QM Medical Depot on DS. Also received a telegram from Col. Oliphant, in which he wanted 4 EM to be assigned to the Burma Road Engineers camp at

410 under Lt. Fulton. Also one MO to take sick call every other day at Kilo 121.

SUNDAY AUGUST 5, 1945

Still raining and river still coming up.

MONDAY, AUGUST 6, 1945

Looked as if it might clear, but raining again in the afternoon and river still up. We have a pleasant group of officers in our area. Col. Delano, who moved in when Lt. Col. Kelso, moved out, Lt. Fleiger, very interested in hunting and fishing. Lt. Henderson, a construction lineman officer and a few others.

Food is running short, but we are expecting some in from KWEIYANG.

TUESDAY, AUGUST 7, 1945

Still raining and river still high. A scared bunch of EM here, as one of the 2 prostitutes hanging around the camp developed cholera and died last night. Some of them really are worried, as well they might be. Orders given not to bathe in river, or to shave in unboiled water.

WEDNESDAY, AUGUST 8, 1945

Still cloudy and raining at intervals. 2 of my men on DS arrived here this evening from kilo 410, and proceeded to give everyone a cholera shot. I was busy initialing the #81 forms. We inoculated everyone, soldiers, coolies and their women, and even some Chinese soldiers. The cholera scare really has them going.

THURSDAY, AUGUST 9, 1945

Elinor's [*his sister*] birthday. Clear this morning, river still high, but assault boats have had motors put in and the jeeps and weapons are to be taken across. Ours was the second across, at 0930. We soon were driving along nicely, under a kindly sunshine. Several miles along, however, the motor started to misbehave and we found water in the gasoline filters. We had to drain and clean these out twice and then were able to travel on smoothly.

We had lunch along the road, opening a big can of fruit cocktail. We crossed the ferry at 491 on a big native barge, poled and rowed over very smoothly. The river here is wider than it was above, but not quite so swift. The town here was badly battered up and burned.

About 15 or 20 miles north of LIUCHOW, we noticed that many of the valleys were uncultivated, and the rice paddies overgrown with weeds. Whole villages were deserted, many of them showing few signs of damage and burning. When we entered the broad, hill-studded valley near LIUCHOW, we saw several big cargo planes in the air and a big dust cloud. I thought that this dust came from the highway, but as we approach, saw that we were looking at the airfield dust cloud, as we could see planes on the ground. The airfield is next to a chain of little hills that rise sharply out of the little plain.

LIUCHOW ITSELF WAS BADLY BATTERED, not a single building intact, very few with roofs. The few intact places were hidden near the hills and under trees.

Went to SOS HQ and met Col. Scott there. He had received a telegram about the 96th, but knew nothing about it. Capt. Abelson never did get here, so I had to explain the situation to the Col. He and I drove out to a couple of spots he thought might be suitable for a hospital site. The best one was a group of buildings near a couple of hills with big caves in them.

Mac and I put up our beds in some tents in the SOS campground. I share a tent with Maj. Alcam and Dr. Chung Kwa, both engineers and both likable. They are looking over the RR situation.

FRIDAY, AUGUST 10, 1945

This day started quietly. Capt. Koble and I went out to another area, near the river. This area was poor and I didn't like it, told him that I preferred the "caves" area. LIUCHOW is on both sides of the river. The part on our side seems to be smaller, but nicer. Paralleling the river is a wide road, with a parkway in the middle. Every building smashed. The dises (?) of this road, and the center tree strip, and hovels erected in and about the wrecked buildings are a mass of small stores and booths and tea shops.

About the middle of the afternoon there were rumors of the Japanese acceptance of the terms, after experiencing another atom bomb or two. Later on this report was confirmed and we all listened to the radios all evening. We were really excited.

On August 6, 1945, the American B-29 bomber, Enola Gay, dropped the world's first atomic bomb ("Little Boy"), over the city of Hiroshima, On August 9 ("Fat Man") was dropped on Nagasaki.

About suppertime, there was a rumor of a riot among the Chinese coolies. The paymasters ran out of money and the coolies tried to storm the compound. McCain was there and he really worked hard keeping them out, even using a club on them. They finally were paid and quieted down. Col. Seedlock had his bottle out, and we drank a few "Ben Gays." Very few of us got much sleep that night. Our nerves were too tense. There was considerable shouting and shooting and the Air Force group set up many flares.

SATURDAY, AUGUST 11, 1945

Today is my birthday—41. It started to pour during the night, and poured most of the day. The sun never did come out.

The radio news was discouraging. The report said that minister of war, Tojo [*Tôjô Hideki*], had pulled a palace coup, and was refusing to obey the Emperor's orders for surrender. Everyone was in the dumps and the wet weather didn't help. Later on radio reports didn't mention the revolt and said that the United Nations were still considering Japan's exceptions to the surrender.

The Allies demanded Japan's unconditional surrender. After a few weeks, the Allies agreed to allow the Japanese to retain the Emperor.

SUNDAY, AUGUST 12, 1945

Radio this morning states that Allies have accepted Japs surrender, including the exception of the emperor's remaining on his throne. Well, it still looks good and we can presume that the war is over.

Rain, rain, rain! Parts of our mud walls—sundried brick, are falling in and there is a huge gap in our main stonewall, which was held together by mud instead of mortar. The Sampan people, river men for generations, state that the river is the highest they had ever seen. No additional war news.

MONDAY, AUGUST 13, 1945

Still no order that hostilities had ceased, only bombing of Japan. Col. Scott returned this morning and had a meeting of all O and EM at 1300. At this he told us to sit tight, and start inventorying all our supplies, so that they can be properly accounted for and turned over to the authorities, who will turn most over to the Chinese.

He said that the Chinese had held up American soldiers crossing the river at NANNING and had taken their trucks from them. Fine business. We have to guard our lives and properties here from our "friends and allies."

Rain, rain and about 5-min. of sunshine. Looked over the airport and saw the big C-54's [*Sky Masters*] come and go. They really are huge.

TUESDAY, AUGUST 14, 1945

Rain again, nearly all day long. At last THE NEWS, at 3:00 p.m. we heard that the war was actually over. Everyone felt good, but there was no excitement. Guess the news is pretty much of an anti-climax. Everyone is wondering when and how we'll get home. Some think that we'll go back by plane to India, the majority think that we will be flown to Canton and embarked there.

We have orders today to go about armed (when leaving our compound) and to go in pairs. The higher authorities feared there may be trouble, mainly due to different Chinese factions fighting over our equipment and we may be in the middle of this.

Despite facing a common foe in Japan, Chinese society had been polarized before the beginning of the war. Tribal groups, marginally supporting Chinese Nationalist headed by Chang Kai-shek and communists headed by Mao Tse-tung battled for control of Chinese territory. The U.S. Army's main role in China was to keep the Chinese in the war against Japan through providing advice and materiel assistance. As long as China stayed in the war, large numbers of Imperial Japanese Army soldiers could be tied down on the Asian mainland. As soon as the war ended, however, various warring Chinese groups wanted materiel in order to resume fighting for control of territory at the wars end.[1]

WEDNESDAY, AUGUST 15, 1945

This is the day; at 0830 Col. Scott, CO of LIUCHOW SOS called a meeting of all O and EM and told us the war was officially over. Chaplain Lampson held a prayer service. Very fitting I thought.

After lunch we drove around a bit, as it had stopped raining for a while. We saw the airport, which is closed, as the runways are too muddy to be used. The river is up 60 ft. and nearly overflowing into the flats on which the town is located. During suppertime we had a severe, but short downpour. Maj. Allen RRE, [?] tried to get to the ferry at 491, but was stopped 40 kilos from here, due to torrents running from the hills onto the road, flooding it over 4 ft.

We took a walk through the town, and saw a Chinese lying on our pillbox [*concrete round bunkers with defensive armaments*] right at the busiest intersection. He was thin and covered with flies. We thought that he was dead, but he moved occasionally. He probably will be dead before morning. None of the Chinese paid a bit of attention to him at all.

THURSDAY, AUGUST 16, 1947

Clear nearly all day. Life is going on here as usual. Asked Col. Scott if it would be a good idea if I suggested that the 96th F. H. be put on duty at the port of embarkation. He thought so and said that I send Col. Armstrong, theater surgeon, a telegram. I did this, requesting that he give the 96th F. H. consideration for this duty. It's the least we can do as a unit for the war effort.

This evening took a walk to town and got Babs "Chops."[*Seal marker*]. It's quite a neat job, but did cost $6000 Chinese—about $2.50.

The dying Chinese was gone, but on another street we saw several that if they weren't dead, certainly look so. The river is down about 20 ft. today, but the road to KWEIYANG is still flooded, ferries washed away and they are going to air-drop food to the crossings at 448 and 491.

FRIDAY, AUGUST 17, 1945

A week here already and the road still closed. This morning a dead Chinese was found by the motor pool. They seem to have quite a death rate here, much of it probably disease, rather than starvation, as is usually thought to be the case.

Tried to get a call through to Capt. Abelson at KWEIYANG, without success. It's really stupid, but I'm getting a real rest. Do wish I had my mail, though.

A heavy shower this evening, otherwise a very pleasant day.

SATURDAY, AUGUST 18, 1945

Tried again to get Capt. Abelson, got KWEIYANG operator, and gave him message to have Capt. Abelson and Capt. Hogan call me. Loafed around all day. Censorship is off, as long as troop movements and Chinese politics are not mentioned. Just loafing around. Still can't get my calls through to KWEIYANG.

SUNDAY, AUGUST 19, 1945

Just reading and loafing all day. Whether good, just one little shower. River going down.

MONDAY, AUGUST 20, 1945

Went to L-5 strip, and got a ride, hoping to get to TUSHAN. No luck, had to turn back in the vicinity of CHO-CHI, due to thick cloud formations.

The ferry crossing at 491 was in operation, but the crossing at 448 looked rather forlorn, as all their boats had been washed away, and new ones hadn't arrived yet. The river was still high.

Several bridges along the road had been washed away and were being worked on, as were two landslides on the road. The worst spot was where the railroad, highway and the creek all ran through a little gully. Back again, after mess in the liaison air group mess hall.

TUESDAY, AUGUST 21, 1945

Tried again to go by L-5, started out at 0800. No luck, we nearly got there, getting as far as NANTAN [*Nandan, Guangxi*], and had to return. Clouds low on the higher hills.

Col. Scott would like to have my jeep, giving me a Tally-In [*receipt*] for it, and an order for a replacement at KWEIYANG. I could leave it here, and go back by plane. A L-5 would be all right, but they can't take McCain, so I don't like the idea.

WEDNESDAY, AUGUST 22, 1945

After supper last night, Lt. Col. Henderson and I went to A-3 [*Operations and Planning Directorate*], 10th Airborne and saw Lt. Col. Taylor there, who had a load of engineer equipment at the CHIN-CHENG airport, 20 miles from KWEIYANG, which he had to airlift to LIUCHOW in a few days, so he decided that he could transport us there and get his stuff back.

Capt. Bye, MAC, supply officer for SOS, LIUCHOW, wanted some Atabrine from KWEIYANG, so I told him that I could telegraph that order into Capt. Hogan and have him deliver it to the airfield, when he called there for McCain and me. Mac was glad when I told him that we would fly back together, as he was feeling low at the thought of being left behind. We packed in the morning and I called Col. Taylor back and he told me that a plane would be ready for us at 1215.

We arrived at the airport at 1130 and were told that the plane was not ready yet. Later we were told its number and where it was. We went over and discovered that it hadn't been unloaded yet, and had to wait over an hour for this to be done.

We finally got off at 1340. There were 4 passengers, McCain, Lt. Henderson, Lt. McCarthy and myself. This Lt. "Charlie" McCarthy is quite a character, well known in China. He's a small, seedy-looking little Irishman. Red-haired, blue-eyed and a snub nosed on an Irish face. He has built, and blown up most of the airfields in China. Quite a guy. We had a nice trip and the coolness in the plane was a relief after the heat in LIUCHOW.

China is certainly mountainous, old, worn down mountains, all looking velvety from the sky, as they are usually bare of trees. When trees are present, they usually are in gullies on the mountain side. We flew over the race track and saw it clearly, our four ambulances standing out in particular.

We arrived at the airport at 1500, where Capt. Hogan in a jeep and Capt. Brunsen in the weapons carrier met us. On the way back, Hogan told me the news. The officers of the 3d unit had been ordered to CHUNGKING [*Chongqing*], but not the EM. These officers were there now and [*the EM*] had been left behind at Kunming when we left, all but Capt. Inman, who had a bad case of infectious jaundice. Too bad, as he probably will be ill for quite a while, and may have to be evacuated to the states through India.

Lt. Holzberg, one of our unit, was down with an attack of malaria. I met him later on in the day, and he was better, but still a little weak. He said that he had stopped taking his atabrine. We are still on ours.

Capt. Abelson, Base Section III surgeon, was ill with an enlarged spleen, no diagnosis. Lt. Col. Driscoll, CO of 95th Stat. Hosp. is taking his place for the time being. Lt. O'Neil is now working up at the surgeon's office and enjoying it. Good thing, as he has not had enough to do.

It certainly felt good to get back to the unit again. It really feels like getting back home, and it was nice to take a shower and get in clean clothes. Also to get mail and be able to use my desk again, as well as all of my other things.

THURSDAY, AUGUST 23, 1945

Went to surgeon's office, where I saw Driscoll and Abelson both. Nothing but rumors. It seems that the 95th F. H. is to send one unit at least to some POW camp, while it's tied whether the 96th F. H. or of the 95th Station Hospital are to set up in SHANGHAI. No one knows anything yet.

After that Hogan and I went to SOS HQ, where I saw Col. Oliphant the base CO. He had nothing definite to say either.

Received my pay too so I now can have something in my pocket book [*wallet*]. Lots of mail and magazines, too. The area and the men look sloppy, so I had orders issued for sprucing up and will have an inspection on Saturday morning. The men seem to pay no attention to malaria control. Well, I'll stop that.

It was a struggle to implement public health prevention methods as young men often did not think they would catch these tropical diseases. MacMillan likely had to

*order all his personnel to continue taking Atabrine and
use mosquito bars/nets as prevention against malaria.*

FRIDAY, AUGUST 24, 1945

Took it easy and enjoyed the weather. Went to 259th Station
Hospital this evening where I saw a couple of eye patients for Lt.
Wurtzebach. When I arrived back, found that Capt. Browne and Lt.
Butziszewski had returned from CHUNGKING [*Chongqing*]. Sandlin
and Baumhardt were left up there, doing professional work. It seems
that the theater surgeon's office was recently moved from KUNMING
for a week or so, and then going to SHANGHAI, which will be the
American Center in China. Rumor in CHUNGKING has it that the
18th F. H. is to land its equipment in SHANGHAI, and that we are to
set up the hospital. (Our only orders so far, are to turn in our
equipment, and prepare for airlift to place where new equipment will
meet us). It seems that the 10th F. H. which was at camp
KANCHAPARA, INDIA, was on board a ship which was part of a
task force that was off the China coast, ready to seize HONG KONG
and CANTON. They'll probably be sent home, we'll take over, and
later the 172d G. H. (Now at KUNMING) will take over from us.

SATURDAY, AUGUST 25, 1945

Last night I heard some of the sad sacks of the outfit bitching
about the forthcoming inspection. Guess there always are some dumb
bunnies in every group who resent everything and anything that
interferes with their own selfish ideas of what or what not to do.

The inspection was very satisfactory. The men looked good,
the tents were clean and orderly and their clothes and equipment in
good condition. The shortages were surprisingly few, too.

Loafed around and had a box made for my electric iron and
gasoline stove.

SUNDAY, AUGUST 26, 1945

A quiet day, nothing unusual. Loafed and read all day long.

MONDAY, AUGUST 27, 1945

Went up to base surgeon's office and found no one in. No new rumors.

TUESDAY, AUGUST 28, 1945

Had to get Babs' box remade as it weighed 361/2 # and the limit is 15#. Will have 3 boxes made. Lt. Budziszewski had a severe vomiting spell last night and feels poorly today. He blames it on some Polish sausage he got from home. Wouldn't be a bit surprised as that stuff has to come through India.

WEDNESDAY, AUGUST 29, 1945

Good news today. Lt. O'Neil, who is on temporary duty at the surgeon's office said that the 96th was alerted and should be ready to go on short notice. Destination: SHANGHAI. Fine, but I just can't get excited over it at all. I've seen too many plans and orders changed here recently. However, it's nice to think about, anyhow.

Lt. Budz is better today. Had to take Pvt. Hordison to hospital for malarial smears, as he had a chill last night.

Capt. Hogan and I gave the men a little talk this evening. QM food has been stolen from the warehouse, right on the beat of our guards. Hope they haven't been stealing. It's either that or they aren't guarding the place properly.

THURSDAY, AUGUST 30, 1945

Guess that alert we received yesterday meant something after all. This morning I received a message to go up to the base surgeon's office. Here Capt. Abelson told us that we had orders to take our men, their weapons and personal equipment, and our TAT equipment, which is our bivouac stuff, records, etc., to CHANYI–that's backtracking, as we came from there 5 weeks ago. We are to go back by the block convoy system and to fly from CHANYI to, it is rumored, SHANGHAI. We figured on the 20 trucks, 16 for men and 4 for baggage and TAT equipment. We were to be driven there by G. I. drivers not Chinese, of which we were glad.

Later on in the afternoon, we received a message from Col. Farmer, that we would drive these trucks ourselves. Just that much better. Will have 3 drivers per truck 4 hours driving and 8 hours off.

We are to leave at 1:00 p.m. on Sunday, Sept. 2, 1945 and drive for 39 hours, arriving at CHANYI at 0500, Tuesday, 4th.

Lts. Ostroff and Lorenz returned from TUSHAN this evening. Ostroff is really going to be busy the next few days, turning in our good hospital equipment and our trusted trucks.

Went to 259th Stat. Hosp. to treat an infected corneal foreign body and a severe, ulcerated conjunctivitis.

FRIDAY, AUGUST 31, 1945

A busy day today, getting ready for our trip, and getting rid of a lot of stuff that we have accumulated. We cleaned out the trucks and ambulances, separating the things we needed as TAT equipment, which included some food, athletic equipment, and of course, our official records. The remaining stuff we gave away to the different organizations, or will turn back to the depots.

Pay day, too, so I guess the GIs will have a lot of gambling going on tonight. Some of them squandered their pay this way month after month.

McCain was in his glory. As boxes were opened, or as ambulances or trucks were cleaned out, he was right on hand to look things over. He didn't do badly either, as he found a new field jacket, with the tags still on it and a pair of rubber boots, among minor discoveries.

Lt.'s Ostroff and Budz packed the IIId unit equipment in trucks and brought it down to our area, for distribution tomorrow to the proper depot.

My eye patients at the 259th Stat. Hosp. are getting better, but still have bad eyes. As I'm writing now, after supper, the EM are lining up in anticipation, as a big stock of boxes, filled with PX supplies, are being opened and gotten ready for sale. Bet they run out of change again.

SATURDAY, SEPTEMBER 1, 1945

Last night had an enjoyable evening, after dark, burning up a lot of trash and old boxes and watching the flames. It was not hot and the occasional heat surges from the flames felt good.

The supplies have been loaded on trucks and unloaded in their respective warehouses, so they are off our hands now.

The men that were stationed at TUSHAN have returned, as well as the three officers from the 259th S. H.

I've been packing and arranging my stuff, quite a job. McCain stenciled my desk and my collapsible chair case. The men are to be relieved from guard duty and kitchen supervision for the night, so that they can get a good night's sleep.

SUNDAY, SEPTEMBER 2, 1945

This is V-J day, the day of the official surrender signing and we are preparing to return to CHANYI by truck and airlift from there probably to SHANGHAI.

Everyone is busy this morning, packing bags and discarding unnecessary things. The trucks were sent for, at the airstrip at 0900 and soon rolled into our area. What a sorry sight they were, too. They all look badly battered, and few had no bows or tarpaulins. None had spares, and few had seats, so our drivers had to scout around and take enough from other trucks to make up for the deficit. The trucks were loaded by 1100 and the men went away for 1130 lunch. On inspection, the area was well policed, with the exception of a few tents of course.

We left the race track at 1245 and soon arrived at the airstrip, where we got the missing tops, and waited for our turn in the block convoy system [*A system were trucks could run 24 hours a day*].[2]

We left at 1400 and were soon rolling on the road to ANSHUN. The weather was clear and sunny and the road good, though dusty. At one point on the road, we saw a dead Chinese, just lying there covered with flies.

We reached ANSHUN at about 1700, where we had supper, washed up and got a few flat tires fixed. They have a new convoy camp here now, right on the road, saving us the rough 3-mile ride out to the old airstrip.

We left ANSHUN at 7:00 and soon were driving in the dark. We were held up about 1/2 hour after leaving by a 6X6 truck that had skidded into a cut bank, and had its left fender dented. The Chinese driver had disappeared after this accident and had just run off, even though the damage done was slight.

Hogan's truck wasn't behaving well and he had no power at all. Part of the trouble was his using an alcohol-gasoline mixture by mistake. It was quite a sight to see the vehicles of the convoy on the switchbacks, going back and forth. We could watch ours coming back of this, and also other convoys approaching us.

We reached ANNAN (*Qinglong*) about midnight and ate fried eggs and drank coffee there. We were really making good time, and were looking forward to arriving at CHANYI late the following day, Mon. Sept. 3, '45.

We left ANNAN at 0200 and soon were descending the famous 24 steps. It was quite a sight to see the vehicle lights zig-zagging down. A few miles further on, we came to a road fork. That's where we made our mistake.

The 24 steps near Annan (Qinglong) along the road from Kunming to Kweiyang. From: Charles F. Romanus and Riley Sunderland. *Time Runs Out in CBI. U.S. Army in World War II* (Office of the Chief of Military History, Department of the Army, 1958), p.68

The right fork was narrow and had a lot of Chinese trucks parked in it. The left fork was wider and more inviting, so we took it instead. We didn't know it then, but we were on the wrong road. I tried to sleep on the floor of the truck and managed to get some rest; it wasn't bad at all.

MONDAY, SEPTEMBER, 3, 1945

On awakening, the road and countryside didn't look right at all. We soon arrived at a town called CHINGLIN [?] and there discovered our mistake. Were we upset! We were 75 kilos away from the main road. 4 hours wasted and it would take more than 4 more hours to return.

We turned around and met some of our stragglers. Everyone had made the same mistake, even those who started late, due to motor trouble. This side road, which goes toward NANNING and the river was one of the hilliest and winding roads we had ever been on and was quite narrow, too.

We arrived back at ANNAN [*Qinglong*] at noon, and ate there again. We left there again at 2:00, this time 2:00 p.m., a disgusted lot.

Back down the 24 steps again, not in as happy a frame of mind as the previous trip. The only consolation we had was that hardly a day passes, that someone doesn't make the same mistake and take the wrong turn. D— those Burma Road engineer's, using their power equipment to turn a side road into a better road than the main highway.

The section of road from ANNAN to CHANYI is one of the hilliest on the Burma Road, but we made good time and arrived in CHANYI at about 1830. It was raining now and we found out that they had tents only for the officers and a few men. Our men had to sleep in their trucks, which they didn't mind. The only trouble was that there wasn't room in the trucks so they had to sleep in other trucks parked nearby.

My cold, which I thought was better, had blocked my ethmoid sinuses and I felt mighty miserable. Every time I coughed, or was jolted, a severe pain shot through my head. I was glad to get into bed, as I felt feverish, and had a little chill soon afterwards.

TUESDAY, SEPTEMBER 4, 1945

Felt better this morning, but still had sinus pains and a stopped up nose. We started out on our final lap about 0900, in a slight drizzle. Just as we were ready to leave, a Chinese convoy rolled by, the 7th tank battalion, a truck convoy outfits. We followed them in about 1/2 hour, and soon caught up with them. They were just poking along. Soon, however, we passed them when they halted for a rest, and then were able to make good time.

About 35 miles out of PANSHIEN [*Panxian*], our truck, with T/5 Nepelli driving started knocking; then the motor stop. We discovered that we had run out of oil, and had burned up the motor. Too bad. Sgt. Deming towed us for a few miles, but couldn't get traction on a steep hill, despite putting on chains. I ordered the truck pushed over to the side of the road and abandoned here, at the 400 kilomark. It could be pulled in later on by a wrecker.

We all piled ourselves and our luggage into Deming's truck and took off. We had to abandon a couple of McCain's chairs that he had dragged along from CHABUA, INDIA.

Near the 415 kilomark near the village of PING-YI, we saw a truck in a cornfield, on the level about 15 ft. below the road bed. It had gone over the bank and had rolled over once. The bows were all broken and the sides muddy. We didn't stop, just slow down when we saw no GIs there, and traveled on.

About 10 miles further on, we came up to one of our trucks and stopped. We learned with horror that this truck was one of ours, carrying 9 men. Sweazy and Sendori were lying on cots in the truck, we halted. They had back injuries, and were being taken along slowly, awaiting the arrival of an ambulance that had been sent for. The other 7 men, including Capt. Westerfelt, were only bruised and shaken and had gone ahead in other trucks. With them were 3 Chinese boys who had been hit by the truck, and were seriously injured.

167

Sgt. Deming said that Sgt. Bauer had said that 2 men had been left behind with the wrecked truck. I didn't want to leave these men there, and despite our not seeing them at the trucks, had Deming turn around to pick them up. There were no men there, and later on I learned that none had been left behind.

When we came to the 22nd F. H., about 5 miles east of CHANYI, we stopped there and saw the injured. They were being x-rayed, but the MO didn't think that they had any broken bones. The Chinese kids were there, one in particular in a bad state of shock, with a compound fracture of his left leg and a fractured pelvis.

We were soon at CHANYI, and found ourselves beds and tents then. We reported the two abandoned cars and were told that wreckers would be sent out in the morning. It appears that it's nothing unusual to have to get trucks out of ditches and from over hillsides.

This chapter from diary pages 112-131

ENDNOTES

---

[1] Mark D Sherry, *China Defensive 4 July 1942–4 May 1945* (U.S. Army Center of Military History, Department of the Army, 1945), p. 8, 25.
[2] See: "Truck Transport," Address as of February 28, 2015 http://www.history.army.mil/books/wwii/persian/chapter16.htm.

Chapter 9: From Chanyi to Shanghai: The Kicked around Field Hospital

<u>WEDNESDAY, SEPTEMBER 5, 1945</u>

Felt a good deal better today. Hogan, Ostroff and I went to SOS HQ and the transportation division. Hogan talked to Col. Armstrong at KUNMING, who told us that we were to be flown to a "great Chinese port," where HQ and 2 units would be set up, while the remaining unit would go up the river a few hundred miles. Hell, that can only be SHANGHAI and NAMKING, the erstwhile capital of China. Took things easy the rest of the day.

In October 1944 when the CBI Theater was divided in two, Col. George E. Armstrong, MC, became both chief surgeon and USA SOS surgeon for China. He later became Surgeon General of the Army.[1]

<u>THURSDAY, SEPTEMBER 6, 1945</u>

Nothing to do, except to be lazy and rest up and listen to rumors, which are thick here. Received word that all EM who had been in the Army a long time, and in grade a long time, should have their names turned in for possible promotion. We held a meeting on this and have 16 names to report.

<u>FRIDAY, SEPTEMBER 7, 1945</u>

Held another meeting this morning to consider promotions that would fill our T/O vacancies up to 100%. While this meeting was in progress, a Maj. Bates, MC and a 1st Lt. Donley, MAC, reported to me, with the information that they were to be assigned to our unit. Both seem to be good men, though I was hoping to be able to promote Capt. Petersen.

The radio states that field grade officers need 100 points for discharge, CO.[*Company*] Grade Off. 85. Brummett is all hopped up, as he has 85 points, and is very anxious to get out of the Army. Well, I'm just anxious to get back to the states, as long as Babs and Sandy [*nickname for his son*] and I can stay together, I'm willing to serve in the U.S.

Rumor has it that the 172nd Gen. Hosp. is going to SHANGHAI, I hope we won't get squeezed out again. I'm tired of being pushed around and just let lie around.

O'Neil and 8 EM arrived today from KWEIYANG. Only 4 men are still on DS. They are at LIUCHOW and are to be flown in by plane. Maj. *XXX13* is also on D.S. and as far as I'm concerned he can stay there. This is also the opinion of most of the officers of my command, too. A beautiful, hot summer day, cooling off nicely now as the sun is setting. C-46 [*Commando*] and 47's [*Skytrains*] are arriving and departing from the CHANYI airport in great numbers, seemingly every five or 10 minutes. Received package from Babbie.

SATURDAY, SEPTEMBER 8 1945

Hogan talked with Col. Crawford, theater surgeon, in KUNMING this morning. Nothing new, except that Maj. Bates, MC, a MO, will probably be exchanged for a captain who is a surgeon.

A nice, quiet, peaceful day, until I went to SOS HQ to receive a message. Then I did burn up. G-3, Col. Weyrich, of KUNMING wants us to go to LULIANG, a former B-29 [*Super Fortress*] bomber base, about 60 miles south of here, and bivouac about 10 days there, before being airlifted to SHANGHAI. That's ridiculous, we are in no shape or condition to bivouac, as we don't have proper equipment. Furthermore, I don't like the idea of being kicked around again. I'm sick and tired of it. If you have no use for us here, for God's sakes why not send us home?

I'm to call up G-3 in the morning. Hope he has other plans then, or changes them, because I'm fed up and won't take it anymore. He can relieve me of command or court-martial me, the 96th isn't going anywhere from here, except to SHANGHAI by direct airlift. Enough is enough.

SUNDAY, SEPTEMBER 9, 1945

Well, I feel better now, as I've learned the reason for our being moved around again. The airfield here is too small for the heavily laden ships that have to take off for our SHANGHAI run. We are to leave here on Tues., day after tomorrow, for the 60 mile run from LULIANG. We hope to be airlifted on or about the 15th.

Yesterday, Chaplin Woods, and his assistant, Calkins were formally transferred back to us again. We were glad this was done, though we were expecting it.

Woods had quite a tale of a happening yesterday afternoon. A convoy was being driven to LULIANG, and the next to the last truck, driven by a Chinese driver, plowed into a group of marching Chinese soldiers, killing six of them and injuring about 10 more. The Chinese promptly shot the driver and hauled him off into a patch of scrub, where they probably made sure he was dead. The maintenance truck, driven by a C-I [?] was right back of this truck and of course stopped. The Chinese soldiers hauled him out of this truck and wanted to shoot him, as they erroneously considered him to be in charge of the convoy and they wanted to hold him responsible and shoot him too. The only thing that saved him was the fact that their injured comrades needed hospitalization and he was the only one who could drive them to the hospital. He drove them to the 2nd F. H., and while they were busy tending to their injured companions, hopped in the truck and drove away in his escape, shaking off a few Chinese who attempted to stop him.

This case was soon being investigated, and the Chinese general in command, demanded that the driver, an innocent man be turned over to him. He would have been shot in quick order if they had gotten him. At SOS HQ, Lt. Col. Duff and his staff tried to placate the Chinese general. He still insisted in his demand, so Col. Duff said that he would make out a warrant for the arrest of the driver and gave the general a receipt. The Provost Marshal was given the warrant and he tore it up in the presence of the driver it was written out for. What a life!

Maj. Lamber returned today. He has a chronic case of amoebic dysentery and was as mad as a boiled owl. About the first thing he asked me was, "Did you volunteer to set up a hospital?" To which I replied, "Yes, but I doubt if they paid a bit of attention to it."

He seems to think that this will delay our trip to the States, as we are a superfluous unit. I doubt it, as there are hospitals here who have been overseas for over two yrs. and they are bound to be the first to be sent home. Lamber said he got the horselaugh from the MO of the 22nd F. H. because I had volunteered. Lamber has it all wrong. 13 of the 17 officers there are going home in a few days because they have been overseas so long and for no other reason. Maj. Brinsmead [?], recently adjutant of the SOS HQ at KWEIYANG came by today, to see if we would let him have 15 drivers to drive the trucks he had borrowed, back from KUNMING to CHANYI. I let him have Lt. O'Neil and 15 men. The Major's convoy had gotten up a collection of about $150 and I wouldn't be surprised if that were given to these 16 drivers.

MONDAY, SEPTEMBER 10, 1945

Heard echoes of rumors today that I had volunteered the services of the 96th F. H. for duty in China. That's not true. The basis of this rumor is a telegram sent to Col. Armstrong, requesting the 96th F. H. be considered as a field hospital to be placed at the port of embarkation. I had information that the F. H., at this port, would be replaced by either the 95th S. H. or the 172nd G. H.

I called a meeting of the EM at 1400, and explained this to them. Hear that Budziezowski and Browne saw this letter to Col. Armstrong's office and not having the background, spread a false version of it among the O and EM.

TUESDAY, SEPTEMBER 11, 1945

The 20 trucks to take us to LULIANG arrived on time. Loading was a bit messed up, due to the poor liaison between Budz and McAuliffe, the former in charge of the men and latter in charge of baggage. We got off at 0920, but had to stop just outside of town, due to the fact that 2 trucks hadn't been gassed up. We left Capt. Hogan behind to check out with the adjutant of SOS HQ.

We bypassed the town of KUTSING, a typical walled Chinese city, with innumerable, crooked, narrow streets, teaming like the proverbial rabbit warren.

The road to LULIANG was extremely rough, and it became progressively worse. It took us over 4 hours to make about 50 miles. Our two injured men, Sendori and Sweazy, were brought along in an ambulance borrowed from the CHANYI dispensary.

Fortunately, I didn't get lost finding my way into the airport, and brought the convoy to a halt at just the right place. Budz and I went to the billeting office and found a guide, who showed us where the men were to be quartered. They had 3 big barracks, which formerly housed the MARS task force. The EM unloaded all their baggage and then the trucks that had officer's baggage in it drove to the officer's area.

The MARS task force, or the American 5332d Brigade (Provisional), a long-range penetration unit, was activated July 26, 1944. It contained three regiments including survivors of Merrill's Marauders, the 124th Cavalry, other infantry units and a US trained and equipped Chinese Regiment. They along with British, Indian, and Chinese units pushed the Japanese south of Myitkyina. By late January 1945, the Japanese 33d Army was forced back to Wanting, near the China-Burma border, and was captured by the Allies. The Ledo, or Stilwell Road, was now connected to the old Burma Road and restored to Allied control. [2]

They gave us 2 ward tents, one a double-roof Bombay tent, which was fairly cool, the other an American type, which was not. Lt. Budz, billeting O, put the low-ranking officers in the better tent and himself and the higher ranking officers in the poor ones. I didn't like my quarters, so the billeting Sgt. got me space in a room in the barracks. It had three double-decker bunks in it. I took a lower and Maj. Bates, Capts. Petersen and Westerfelt took uppers.

The Priorities and Travel Officer of the base, Capt. Dilts, didn't know about our projected travel, so I showed him the orders on which we came here.

Col. Stellings, AC [*Aircraft Commander*], is the base Co. He is a fine fellow, an Eastern Airlines pilot of many years experience and an old reserve officer. He invited me up to his quarters on the "Hill," into which he had just moved. He has a little living room, with an open fireplace in it, and an adjoining bedroom. This barracks room was once the quarters of the A.V.G., (American Volunteer Group) the famous American Flying Tigers, who at one time flew from this group.

Clair Chennault, a retired American Army Air Corps Captain and a friend of the Nationalist China leader, Chang Kai-shek, was asked to form a Chinese Air Force to protect the Burma Road. This road between Lashio, Burma and Kunming, China was the only supply route from India to China after the Japanese had occupied the Chinese ports. India and Burma were part of the British Empire. China was a protectorate of the Empire. Under the authority of President Franklin D Roosevelt, in July 1941, one hundred American Navy, Marine, Army Air Force and a few civilian pilots were recruited to join the American Volunteer Group (AVG). Enlisted ground crew to maintain the aircraft were also hired. One hundred Curtis P-40's (called Warhawks in the United States, Tomahawks or Kittyhawks in Britain and other countries) pursuit aircraft were diverted from the British lend lease program to Burma along with the men for training.

The AVG painted the nose of their aircraft with shark's teeth and after the news media began to call them the "Flying Tigers," they adopted the name. The Disney studio drew a cartoon of a flying Tiger for their aircraft. Beginning December, 20th 1941, three squadrons of Tigers protected the Burma Road as the Japanese push north into Burma. When the Japanese gained possession of the southern portion of the Burma Road during spring 1942, the AVG flew transport aircraft and also acted as protection for cargo planes flying material over "the Hump"—the southern Himalayan's—from Ledo, Burma to Kunming, China and other airports. The group was disbanded July 4, 1942 and most of the men went back to the United States and rejoined their military groups. A few stayed in the CBI Theater or went on to other assignments they were initially replaced by the 10th and then the 14th Air Force.[3]

23 officers live in this building and have their own mess here. The best mess in China, I guess. We had steak smothered in onions, green beans, potato chips, apple pie with cheese and coffee. The best

Army meal I've eaten since leaving the states. We really didn't need the two drinks of "Haig and Haig" scotch just before supper. A pilot had bought this bottle in Shanghai a few days previously, at $9:00 a quart. Not too bad for good pre-war liquor.

Met a Maj. Howes here, who had been stationed at GOOSE BAY, LABRADOR, several years ago. He vaguely remembered David McCurdy [*MacMillan's brother in law*].

Col. Stellings had me move into better quarters, quarters incidentally occupied by Hogan, but usually reserved for field grade officers. It's handy to store rooms with the adjutant anyhow, so I was quite pleased.

P-40 Tomahawk

The P-40 was used by the "Flying Tigers" or AVG to transport supplies and equipment over the "Hump." Image courtesy of the National Naval Aviation Museum archives, Pensacola, Fl.

WEDNESDAY, SEPTEMBER 12, 1945

This is a nice space and the men are enjoying their stay here. Capt. Dilts still has no definite information on us from WING [*Air transport?*], but a call Hogan put through to KUNMING, set our departure at 0500, Monday 17th. Hope it works out O.K.

They had a nice custom here of serving coffee at the Red Cross at 1000 and selling coffee and donuts from 3 to 4 o'clock. That helps pass the day.

THURSDAY, SEPTEMBER 13, 1945

It seems that the 4th COM-CAR outfit (Combat Carrier) is to take us to SHANGHAI by a stop at LIUCHOW for fuel. Played ball today, for first time in many years. The officers vs. EM. Maybe it was my participation but this is the first time the officers were beaten in the 6 or 7 games that they played. I was up at bat three times and struck 3 singles, right in the hands of the infield. Incidentally, I stone [*sic, stung*] the ring finger of my left hand, when a fly ball bit its tip. Yes, I made enough errors, but at least, I didn't strike out.

Brummett has 84 5/6 points, so will put one in for his going home on 85 points.

FRIDAY, SEPTEMBER 14, 1945

Another day of unsettled orders. At, about 3:30 p.m., I talked to Col. Weyrick, G-3 [*Operation and Plans*], and he had nothing special to say, except that there was a temporary stoppage of troop movement to SHANGHAI, which wouldn't affect our first consignment of 58 O and EM, yet, an hour later, Lt. Lee [*Yee ?*] came in and said that the whole hospital would move on Sunday and that 9 C-46's [*Commandos*] of the XI Combat Carrier group was coming in and would fly the whole bunch to LIUCHOW, where we would transfer into planes for SHANGHAI. He had spoken to G -3 this morning.

Everyone seemed to be utterly confused. There seems to be a lack of liaison and cooperation in staff work of the brass hats. What a life!

SATURDAY, SEPTEMBER 15, 1945

Things have cleared up a bit. It seems to be certain that the advance party is to leave early Monday morning. An M. P. outfit is to precede us and all other troop movements to SHANGHAI are temporarily suspended, due to troubles of some kind or the other with the Japs in SHANGHAI.

It seems that we are to fly to LIUCHOW in C-46's and there to transfer to C-54's [*Skymasters*]. The latter are big, four-motor jobs, much better suited for the job.

The radio first, and a news bulletin next, stated that Medical and Dental officers are eligible for discharge under any of the 3 following categories: (a) 80 points, I have 69, (b) 48 years of age, and (c) Pre-Pearl Harbor Service. This last one included me and really does sound good. Hooray!

Had O'Neil and Donley working on our weighing and loading project for tomorrow. We hope the planes to take us will be in by noon tomorrow. Bet my luggage comes to at least 250#. Five pieces (1) Bedding roll, (2) Val-pac, (3) Foot locker, (4) Duffel bag, (5) barrack bag.

SUNDAY, SEPTEMBER 16, 1945

A busy day, preparing for our flight tomorrow morning. Had O'Neil and Donley pick up the baggage of O and EM starting at 1500. They weighed each man and his baggage and after supper sorted out and weighed the TAT equipment [*equipment needed by troops during transport*], too.

Only 3 planes came in and between them, they only had 58 parachutes. If no more planes come in, we can't go at all, or only just a few of us.

Lt. Yee wasn't too hopeful of either more planes, or more parachutes. He had to leave 30 men behind from yesterday's shipment, due to lack of parachutes. The local ATC [*Air Transport Command*] has very few extra parachute and doesn't want to lend any to the COM-CAR outfit.

Went to bed, pretty much convinced that we wouldn't be awakened early for our planned trip.

Sure enough, was not awakened for any trip, so know that the expected planes have not arrived. Lt. Yee confirmed this later on, so there's nothing to do, except to sit around, and hope that we get off tomorrow morning.

Three planes arrived this evening, and before supper, and 2 later on. These latter had been misdirected to KUNMING and therefore were late. These 3 planes only had 39 parachutes among them, so we could only take 34 of our O and the EM on the projected trip, as the 84th Veterinarian Inspection group had 5 of their men to travel with us. We figured on leaving 24 men behind to follow us.

Went to bed for a few hours sleep, after our equipment had been loaded in planes.

TUESDAY, SEPTEMBER 18, 1945

Was awakened at 0200. No more planes or parachutes had arrived, so only 34 O and EM of the IIId unit could be taken this morning.

At 0245 we had breakfast at the "line mess"—scramble eggs, rice cakes and coffee. I was surprised to be hungry at this –time.

The 3 planes took off in the dark at 0435. It was interesting to see dawn approach and see the sky gradually grow lighter, bit by bit. As we were heading due east all the time, it was more noticeable all the time.

We landed at LIUCHOW at 0730, having covered about 360 miles, as well as we could determine by the map. It was broad daylight by then, and the sun was rising in a practically cloudless sky.

We were driven to the ATC transient area where we had breakfast. Hardly anyone had their mess kits with them. Breakfast consisted of pancakes and fried eggs and cocoa. We put the fried eggs between the two pancakes and ate a fried egg and pancake sandwich! Not too bad either. Our C-46 planes were unloaded into trucks and our equipment loaded into the C-54's that were to take us to SHANGHAI.

I took a seat up front, where I could look out the window. We departed at 1015. China certainly is a mountainous country, just like a wrinkled old apple. It made me sorry to see how overpopulated the entire land is. There is hardly a square foot of arable land that isn't cultivated, and it's no unusual sight to see a whole hillside terraced, often rising several thousand feet from the flat plains and their narrow valleys.

At noon we opened some "10 in 1" rations and I had some cold ham and sweet potatoes, as well as crackers, butter and strawberry jam.

About 1430 I noticed a broad, winding river in a large valley, and had a hunch that we were approaching the vicinity of SHANGHAI. Soon we flew over a large city, situated on this river, which by this time had entered an area of large mud flats. I went up to the pilot's cabin and was told that this was HANCHOW [*Hangzhou*] and that the river flowed into HANCHOW BAY.

The land from here on was low and flat, flat as a tabletop. It was cut up by canals, creeks and narrow sized ponds. The fields looked fresh and green, except for the spots where the rice had been cut and stacked in yellow rows. Near SHANGHAI the flatness was relieved by about a dozen little hills which stood out like dark green islands in the patchwork sea of lighter greens.

Soon SHANGHAI showed itself in the distance skyline as a scattered group of white spots. As we flew closer, these resolve themselves into individual and scattered groups of moderate size skyscrapers. I was very much reminded of the first glimpse of NEW YORK, when it is first seen from the distance.

We flew right over the heart of the city, which surprised us by its modern appearance. So different from anything we had previous seen in China. The airport, to the West of the city was paved with macadam and concrete and was peppered with small bomb craters, most of which had radiating lines from the craters caused by scoring of the surface by bomb fragments.

The operations office was in a modern concrete building, showing little evidence of damage. We got some native, charcoal burning trucks on which are TAT equipment and baggage were loaded. The equipment was stored in a warehouse and we boarded two trucks which took us into town. Just outside of the airfield we saw our first Japanese. They were in uniform, but unarmed. We understood that they had their arms taken away from them just the previous day. They were short, stocky-built fellows.

As we drove East through the town toward the Navy YMCA, we were quite thrilled by the reception received. The Chinese, most of them anyhow, cheered us, waived hats and handkerchiefs, and clapped hands. We felt like conquering heroes.

Our first stop was at the International YMCA, where the Army billeting office is located. It is on Bubbling Well road, opposite the race track, and next to the Park Hotel. The sidewalk was roped off here, and armed G-I [*GI?*] guards were on duty there.

The billeting office expected us and had figured on quartering us at the Haig Court Apartments, but this place was still in Chinese hands, as they took it over from the Japs, and hadn't turned it over to the U.S. Army yet. So we were sent to the Navy YMCA instead. It is in charge of a Mr. Hansen, a Dane who spent considerable time in Jap concentration camps. He put the men up on cots in the gym, and found rooms for the officers.

Chap. Woods and I occupied a nice, room on the 3rd floor, one of Mr. Hansen's own rooms in his apartment. Big 3/4 beds with Simmons mattresses. Also shower and wash room, too. SHANGHAI really is a modern city.

We had supper at the Y too. Woody and I didn't go out to the city, but remain behind to write letters. Some of the O and EM, of course, had to go out and investigate immediately.

This chapter from diary pages 133-142

ENDNOTES

---

[1] Mary Ellen Condon-Rall, and Albert E. Cowdrey, *The Medical Department: Medical Service in the War against Japan* (United States Army, 1998), 313; Blanch Armfield, *Medical Department United States Army in World War II, Organization and Administration* (Department of the Army, 1963),542, 546.

[2] Condon-Rall and Cowdrey (1998), 311; George L. MacGarrigle, *Central Burma: 29 January–15 July 1945* (U.S. Army Center of Military History, 1996), 2-11; Charles F. Romanus and Riley Sutherland, *Time Runs Out in CBI* (1959), 28-39; David Hogan, Jr. W. "Chapter 5: Special operations in the China-Burma-India Theater." In: *U.S. Army Special Operations in World*

War II (Department of the Army, 1992), 99-132. Historical Division, *Merrill's Marauders: February-May 1944.* (United States Army, 1945)
[3] Ford, Daniel. *Flying Tigers: Claire Chennault and His American Volunteers, 1941–1942,* 2007; Romanus and Sutherland, *Time Runs Out in CBI* (1959), 24; Chennault, Claire Lee, *Way of a fighter* (G.P. Putnam's Sons, 1949).

Chapter 10: In and around Shanghai: Setting Up, Winding Down

<u>WEDNESDAY, SEPTEMBER 19, 1945</u>

Went to billeting again and up to the office, where Lt. Col. Hieble [*also spelled Hiehle*] and Lt. Simpson were waiting for me. We drove by car through the streets crowded by pedestrians, rickshaws and "Pedi-cabs," tricycles. The Haig Court Apartments are on Haig Road, just off Bubbling Well Road, near the west boundary of the International concession.

This building is a nice, modern 9-story apartment building, set well back of a large grassed area. There were Chinese guards on the place. There is a circular driveway in front of the main entrance, with a covered entrance. The main floor is up a flight of stairs. Basements and sub-basements are unpopular in SHANGHAI, due to its being just a few feet above sea level, and its frequent flooding during heavy rains.

The Japs had occupied the building since the middle of May, and had messed it up a lot. They had used it for a hospital. They broke quite a few windows, and damaged the marble stairs by dragging things down them. The place was filthy and full of fleas.

The Japs had run off with most of the tenant's furniture and had ruined a lot of the things left behind. They had done only one constructive thing, they had built about a dozen hot-water tubs in some of the servant's quarters, and had put three outside and built several dugouts and pillboxes.

The elevators were not running, so we had to walk up. On the top floor, the 9th, was the owner's penthouse, a beautifully paneled and designed apartment, with 5 bedrooms, all with separate baths, a library, living room, dining room and kitchen, and a five room servants apartment. This apartment will be for the officers and will give us the use of its nice living room for our recreation, card and reading room as well as library. Generally speaking, we will use the first floor for offices and dining rooms, 2nd and 3rd floors for EM quarters, and 4th, 5th, 6th, and 7th floors for wards. Nurses quarters and operating rooms are to be on the 8th floor.

I stayed around all the rest of the day, meeting the numerous people that came around for business purposes. The O and EM who had stayed at the Navy "Y" came in early in the afternoon, as well as the planeload of 24 which we had to leave behind when we left. Our men certainly were pleased with their new place, and the officers especially were happy about their new quarters.

Three Jap civilians came in during the morning with an inventory list, in Japanese. They were told to bring an English list back with them at 1500. The owners really shouted at them, and the little Japs were as meek as mice. I smiled to think of how tables were turned. I could readily picture the Elias brothers [*the apartment building owners*] cringing while the Japs were bellowing at them.

The Japs came back at 1600 and they, Lt. Zeit, a Chinese officer and the Elias brothers checked up on the inventory. What a bellowing there was, it was really laughable and one of the questions was, "Where are the boiler room tools and the lawnmowers that the Japanese navy stole from us?" Really, not a question, just a severe demand.

The inventory was necessary in order to let the Japs turn the property over to the Chinese, and they in turn to turn it over to the owners who would lease it to the U.S. Govt. Quite a rigmarole. Anyhow, the negotiations must have been more or less satisfactorily concluded, as the Chinese guard was removed, and our own guard took over.

Lt. Zeit was so pleased with the appearance of the place, and our prospects, that he invited me out to dinner. We took a pedicab to the Park hotel. Their 14th floor dining room is a credit to a nightclub and dining room in any stateside hotel. It had large plate-glass windows affording a grand view of the city.

We had a fine dinner of steak, French fries, green beans, etc. The room was quite lively, and, as we had expected there were quite a number of women, mostly blond, but not so young. In fact, they appear to be quite experienced, and a few were such bags, that only a drunk would think of picking them up.

WEDNESDAY, SEPTEMBER 19, 1945 [*sic*]

It's unknown why he had two Wednesdays with dates of September 19. No other days or dates were unaccounted for.

A busy day, hardly dared to leave the place. It's quite a job to get things started and to work out all the plans, but it's lots of fun, too.

We have no cooking facilities, so had to make arrangements to feed the men, especially as some were broke anyhow. Freddie Elias had the manager of the Paramount hotel and nightclub came over. He's a big, husky Chinese, well-liked by the whites, as he sent large quantities of food to the internees at their internment camp. We arranged to give our men breakfast and lunch at the Paramount, and they could sign checks there and have it taken from their pay later on, no real hardship, as we are all on the same kind of per-diem.

Had breakfast at the Paramount. They had tables arranged for us in the Maskee Room, a round nightclub room. We had the typical breakfast of 3 eggs, thinly sliced ham, bread and butter and coffee, not bad, but a long time in serving. Among the visitors we had were Lt. Col. Hieble and Lt. Simpson of the Surgeon's office. They of course, are vitally interested in our hospital. Several engineer officers came around to inspect the place, too. The officers are all out buying cameras, which are quite reasonable here. Brummett believes that they can be resold in the states at a good profit. Well, think I'll stay out of the camera business for a while at least.

I tried to find the Kiessler and Baden restaurant near here, at which Lorenz had eaten. It is supposed to serve good food and have a nice bakery attached to it. Also since it's German owned, and the owners were not interred, it's not very popular with the European population. I couldn't find the place, so took a pedi-cab to the Pacific Hotel, where I had a nice meal all by myself.

THURSDAY, SEPTEMBER 20, 1945

Went down to SOS HQ in the International YMCA where I reported to Col. Oliphant, the deputy commander. This time I traveled by automobile. We have one car assigned to us for the day time, and one for the night, as well as a truck.

Saw Col. Seedlock, CE [*Corps of Engineers*] and Lt. Col. Allen, both of whom I had met at 448 [*ferry crossing*] and at LIUCHOW, the time we were all flooded in there.

Back to the hospital with our plans. Had Chaplain Woods and Lt. Budziszewski take care of billeting and putting the men in their permanent quarters.

Had a full crew of coolies working here now, under supervision of Mr. William Cheng, the Elias brothers' factotum [*handyman*]. They are cleaning floors, walls and windows.

FRIDAY, SEPTEMBER 21, 1945

Stayed around most of the day, attending to all kinds of things. Several tenants have come in to look at their furniture. They are having trouble locating places to live, poor folks, and may have to stay out at the internment camps till they find a home here.

The EM have been moved up to their quarters on the IId floor and are making themselves at home there.

Col. Johnson, Chief Surgeon, here, came out today to look the place over and seemed to be quite pleased with things. It has been raining hard here, and the streets are flooded. One of the lowest spots is just in front of our compound. The rickshaws are having a field day, just like the cabs back home.

SATURDAY, SEPTEMBER 22, 1945

The setting up of the supply rooms, pharmacy and outpatient dispensary are going on rapidly. We're still handicapped by tenants' furniture in these rooms.

This morning I drove down to the surgeon's office, saw Lt. Col. Hiehle [*Hieble*] and Lt. Simpson there again, and also Watson, now a Lt. Col. Saw Capt. Sullivan who told me that the hospital equipment was on ships in the harbor, and would soon be unloaded. Col. Hiehle started the wheels rolling for the transfer of the rest of our unit to fly here from LULIANG.

Drove with Lt. Ostroff to the Wheelock bldg., let them off there and had the driver take me to the Bund. This is a long esplanade flanking the west bank of the WANGPOO River, and is a world-famous street. We turned left and soon crossed SOOCHOW creek and then followed the river to the docks.

There were a number of cruisers and destroyers on the river, and around the bend were a lot of Liberty and Victory freight ships. They were unloading their cargo of trucks and 10 in 1 Rations [*provided one meal for 10 men*]. We also saw 2 ambulances that had just been unloaded. Wonder if we will get them, 16 were expected.

There were numerous Japanese soldiers in the buildings near the docks, all looking very harmless. There were lots of junks and thousands of sampans on the WANGPOO River and [*the*] SOOCHOW Creek was clogged with them.

After lunch today, bought a nice 10" high silver pagoda, on a teakwood base and enclosed in a glass box for $6.00. Quite reasonable but very fragile. It will be tough to keep polished up, as it will get black in Pittsburgh very soon. For supper, Peterson, Browne and I were invited up to a Chinese family for supper (See letter).[1]

SUNDAY, SEPTEMBER 23, 1945

The chaplain held services in our hospital today, and also held services on the outside. It was nice to hear the church bells ringing from the tower of the German church this morning at 10:00 and 10:30. Guess they haven't taken their church away from them yet.

They have gotten one service elevator running now, so several of us moved up to our permanent quarters on the 9th floor. We had coolies do the carrying. It's nice to have a nice big closet for clothes again. I made up my bed, put away my bedding roll, took all my stuff out of my Val-Pac, duffel bag and a barrack bag, and put the linens and socks in drawers and hung up my winter clothes. Wish my footlocker were here, it's been lost ever since our trip of nearly a week ago. Even set up my British chair again.

Had supper with Zeit, Lorenz and Brummett at Kiessler and Baden's restaurant, where I had 5 or 6 little fancy cakes again.

MONDAY, SEPTEMBER 24, 1945

Saw Col. Johnson and Lt. Col. Hiehle [*Hieble*] at the billeting office at the foreign Y. Told Hieble about Lt. Col. *XXX10* taking our 58 good cots, so he suggested we see Gen. Kenmer about [*this*]. Saw his assistant instead, who told us to get the cots.

Col. Hiehle and I swapped cars, as he has an old jalopy, about ready to fall to pieces, while I have a nice Studebaker. He expected Col. Armstrong, China Theater Surgeon, to arrive today, and wanted to meet him in a nice car. Lorenz, who was with me, and I drove out to the airport. Here I ran across Col. *XXX10*. He's a big, rough looking man, with a big scar across the bridge of his nose. When I saw how tough he looked, I tackled him hard with these words. "Col., I've come to get back those cots you stole from me." He didn't like to be called a robber, and said that he needed those cots. They hadn't been specially marked anyhow. I told him that they were in a separate pile with my own stuff, and that I needed them for my men, too. He said we could get them the next day.

We drove from the airport to the Wheelock bldg., in which the surgeon's office is located now. None of the staff were in. We understood that some things had been hauled to the basement from the airfield. I was looking for my footlocker, and was happy in finding it here. Made arrangements to get it shipped to our hospital.

We went to NANKING Rd., one of the main thoroughfares, and did a lot of window shopping and looking in the stores. The nicest dept. store is Wing On's. They even had some cloisonné ware there.

We walked all the way down to the Park hotel. Near here is a good barbershop that I'll have to go to the next time I need a haircut.

I left Lorenz there, and went into a photo studio to have some pictures taken, 6 for $1.

Took a rickshaw up to Wing On's and bought a couple of cloisonné vases and plates. Very pretty ones, too.

Previously I had exchanged $5.00 into CBR (China Reserve Bank, actually Japanese invasion money). Got $159,000.00 for each dollar. What an inflation. Hear that the CRB is to be invalidated on Oct. 1st, so I guess everyone is trying to get rid of them. By the way, the CN is getting stronger, and is now 600 to 1. (I bought some in CHANYI at 2400 to 1, so have actually quadrupled my money. Wish I had bought more of it at the time.

Walked up to the Palace Hotel were Lorenz and I had lunch at noon. Met a Lt. SG, McVicar from Cleveland, Ohio, and a Lt. JG, Spalding from New York there. We had a scotch and soda. They had planned on going to the SUN YAT SEN restaurant, on Nanking Road and inviting me to go along. It was a Chinese-style place, where we had a wonderful meal of turtle soup, barbecued duck and fried rice. The meal only cost us $1.00 each, too, and we had plenty to eat.

Unpacked my footlocker on reaching the hospital. It was nice to get into it again, especially as it was unharmed and in good condition.

TUESDAY, SEPTEMBER 25, 1945

One year ago, I left Staunton, VA. It's been one year since I've seen my little boy. Bet he has grown plenty in that time.

This has been a quiet day. Col. Hieble dropped in this morning and I showed him our quarters in the penthouse.

Sent out a large crew of men to load our equipment on the dock. There wasn't any there, so they came back. I'm willing for our men to load our equipment, but don't want them to do stevedore work for other outfits.

WEDNESDAY, SEPTEMBER 26, 1945

A rainy day, cold this morning, warming up toward evening.

Col. Armstrong, China theater surgeon, dropped in today. He liked the place, and seemed to be quite pleased with my plans and organization. He spoke of future plans for hospitalization, and said that the 172nd Gen. Hosp., with a depleted force, might take over our installation, while the 96th, also depleted of its longer-servicemen, might go to Nanking and set up a hospital there. That's rather disquieting news. Think I'd sooner remain in SHANGHAI.

THURSDAY, SEPTEMBER 27, 1945

A rather quiet day. Water pipes are being put in the basement for our kitchen sinks, and we had the gas people over to plan for gas for cooking. We have started to move some stores into the basement for our kitchen. Col. Heible states that our supplies will not be unloaded for several days yet. I asked him about promotions, and he told me that they had a big promotion board meeting at CHUNG KING recently, and that it was one of the most mixed-up deals yet. I wanted my officers promoted, especially as I had heard that the 95th F. H. had received theirs.

On returning from supper tonight at the "Hungaria Club" (a gyp joint), was agreeably surprised to find that two truckloads of officers and men had arrived from LU LIANG by plane. They hadn't eaten yet, and had gone to the Paramount Club to eat. As soon as they arrive back, they will put up their cots temporarily for the night, and be assigned to their permanent quarters.

Another plane load called up at 2045, so I had Budz drive over to the restaurant of Kiessler and Baden, and make arrangements for them to eat there tonight. Also had him make arrangements for the next group, which was expected in the following morning. K and B can feed a hundred men.

At 2130 the last group came in. They were happy, and hungry as the first group was. We had them go directly to the restaurant. I went along and talked with the officers. All the promotions I had asked for had come in. Poor Lt. Wurtzeback wasn't on the list and was very much downhearted, until I told him that I had seen his and another officers name (Sandlin) on another list, then he perked up.

Also heard that we were authorized a combat star and its attendant 5 points, so that raises my points to 74. Not enough yet.

MacMillan later explains the point system and how many a person needed to be rotated back to the United States.

FRIDAY, SEPTEMBER 28, 1945

Was awakened at 0600 this morning by another truck load of O and EM arriving. They had flown most of the night and had landed at the SHANGHAI airport, before dawn. Now all but Hogan, O'Neill and about 22 men are absent.

Later in the morning Col. Armstrong, Col. Johnson and Lt. Col. Hieble came in with bad news. We are to leave this place in shape for the 172nd Gen. Hosp. and 10 officers, 10 nurses and 100 EM are to go to NANKING and set up a hospital. Later on a message came in from Col. Hieble to prepare to take along 9 Off., 10 nurses and 73 EM. It looks as if we are to set up just one platoon. The remainder of the men are to be reported superfluous.

Spent all evening with Lt. Ostroff and Sgt. Bauer, going over the list of all men, their ages, points and time in service, and from this got 73 names of EM to go to NANKING with the unit. The remainder of the men are mainly high point and can be expected to go home soon.

SATURDAY, SEPTEMBER 29, 1945

Heard early this morning that Hogan, O'Neill and 16 EM had arrived last night and stayed at the Navy YMCA and would be out soon. They arrived at about 1030, with the same jubilant shouts, on seeing the place, that the preceding group had given vent too. I welcome them to "MacMillan's mansion."

Was invited, along with Peterson and Browne by Mr. Ying, our Chinese friend who had invited us to his home previously, to attend a Chinese funeral. He met us at noon in front of the Sun Dept. store. It was the feast held on the 100th day of the deceased (See letter to Babs about it).

Our PX is open now, and serving beer, soft drinks and cigarettes. A PX is always a help with a group of men. The newly arrived O and EM are having a good time exploring SHANGHAI and buying things. Well, we deserve a break, after having been kicked around as we have.

SUNDAY, SEPTEMBER 30, 1945

Col. Armstrong dropped in today, after having visited NANKING. He thinks that the NANKING setting-up deal may be called off. That suits me, as I'll get home just that much sooner. He says that this is the 4th time that Gen. McClure has changed his mind about needing a hospital at NANKING.

In order to get doctors back to civilian life, they may even send them back by plane. Think I'd sooner go by boat. Bought Brummett's Ikaflex camera from him for $30.00. It's a reflecting type and I think I'll like it.

MONDAY, OCTOBER 1, 1945

Col. Hieble came over this morning and told me that Col. Tyner and 20 EM of the 172nd Gen. Hosp. were due here in a day or so as advance group for their hospital. Well, that makes sure that we won't set up here. Hope we don't go to NANKING, then we can be declared superfluous and go home.

This evening a group of 12 EM from the portable surgical hospital dropped in and were quartered on our 4th floor. Looks as if the place is filling up fast.

When shopping with Browne, Peterson and a few of our Chinese friendsour and bought a lot of stuff for Babbie. Afterwards, we took them to dinner at the Park Hotel. Despite the rain, we had a nice time all day.

TUESDAY, OCTOBER 2, 1945

Went out this morning to see Col. Seedlock and Col. Armstrong. Discovered that Col. Seedlock had just left, and was actually out to see me at the hospital. Met Lt. Col. Sparks of the motor pool at HQ.

This evening Maj. Gen. Weart and Col. Oliphant dropped out to the hospital. Gen. Weart asked me when the hospital would be ready to treat patients, and I replied, "As soon as we get in the equipment."

Sgt. Brojac met with the EM and discussed the plans for the forthcoming anniversary dinner. They didn't like the idea of a dinner but wanted a dance instead. I told Brojac that, if they wanted a dance afterwards, they could have one, but no funds would be left over for it. Capt. Sullivan, the medical supply officer dropped in this evening, and it appears that the field hospital equipment has come in and will be sent out, starting today.

At about 1600, seven truckloads of equipment arrived, mainly cots and mattresses. It looks as if we will actually set up our hospital, even if we don't get to operate it.

Ah, well, they change their minds around here twice a day anyhow.

WEDNESDAY, OCTOBER 3, 1945

This morning Col. Tyner, 5 other O and 15 EM of the 172nd G. H. arrived here. Col. Tyner is to take over the building and to set up a hospital. Lt. Col. Hieble was with them, and I heard him tell Col.

Tyner that he would be in charge. Well, that leaves me out and sets me free to go home soon. Hooray!

Had the billeting O show the new party to their quarters on the 8th floor. We'll keep our quarters here, I hope, until we're ready to leave by boat.

Saw Col. Armstrong, China theater surgeon this evening and had Hieble's word verified. The 96th F. H. is to be declared superfluous and to be sent home. I'm a free man for a while. The heck with Haig Court. I'll turn all my worries over to Col. Tyner.

Hear that many EM object to the anniversary dinner and that Sgt. Feldmesser is one of the ringleaders. He had better watch out, or he'll get into trouble. Was invited with Browne and Petersen, to a cocktail party and buffet luncheon (rather supper), at Mr. Minutti's, the architect for the Eliases. Had a good time there, and enjoyed it a lot.

THURSDAY, OCTOBER 4, 1945

Moved out of my nice office to another one, not as large or well situated, but facing South and a lot warmer, these cool days, than the old place. Left my desk there for Col. Tyner to use. He is never around, but seems to be out all the time, often in Col. Hieble's company. Well, let him, if anything comes up, it's his headache. I'm through being tied down to my desk with various visitors. Guess he won't have so many, as I have all the ground work laid all ready.

This noon Mrs. Scheel, manager's wife of Kiessler and Baden, talked to me about her fears of their being evicted by the Chinese and being put in a concentration camp. If this were to occur, she would not be able to feed the 120 O and EM that eat at her place. She seemed to be resigned to being evicted, but knew that it would inconvenience us. I told her I'd see what I could do about it.

So I drove downtown this evening to the Wheelock bldg, where I saw Col. Armstrong. He went out to check on what could be done, and came back and dictated a letter to the Chinese authorities, pleading clemency for them, as closing their place would [*disadvantage*] Am. troops.

Went shopping later in the morning and told Mrs. Scheel at noon what I had done, which pleased her a lot.

FRIDAY, OCTOBER 5, 1945

Went to Surgeon's, office again, with some additional information for their letter to the Chinese. This morning Capt.'s Browne, Nowell and Lorenz, our 3 lowest points M.O.'s, reported to Lt. Brill, at the Exchange building, for duty at the internment camp. Hope this doesn't keep them from coming with us. Later on in the day, they reported back, and mentioned that a portable surgical hospital was being organized to set up in FORMOSA for a period of from 4-6 months. They are afraid that they will be assigned. Hope not.

Brummett, Zeit and I went shopping again today, looking over Yates Road, having lunch at the Sun Ya restaurant, where we had cold baked duck, fried noodles and chicken soup. .

Later we went to Wing On Dept. store, where I did some shopping. Got some chopsticks there and a nice embroidered linen tablecloth. Cloisonné is scarce, as it is a PEIPING [*Beijing*] product, and none has come in for years. Bought a nice black lacquered box for $1.00. Very pretty, too.

SATURDAY, OCTOBER 6, 1945

Our first anniversary of the activation as a unit. One year ago at camp Barkeley, the 96 capital F. H. was set up from the 6 training group. This morning Col. Tyner, of the 172 and General Hospital dropped in and was given a roster of all O with less than 75 points and all EM with less than 60 points.

Lt. Col. Watson dropped in and confirmed that fact that Capt. Nowell was to be transferred to the portable surgical unit, headed for FORMOSA, and that it was probable that Capt. Browne will be sent along to, with the possibility that he [*would*] be the CO.

Capt. Lorenz will be transferred to the 172nd Gen. Hosp. to work in the orthopedic dept. Sorry to lose these officers, as well as laboratory technicians Gard and Schimazi. But, despite their disappointment and crying the blues, they are all low point, young men, who have been in the army less than 1/2 the time I put in.

Bought Babs two silk kimonos this evening, blue and very pretty, one printed silk, the other embroidered. We had 16 quarts of good Gibson's Rye whiskey from our medical supplies, when we turned our stuff over to the Chinese at KWEIYANG and TUSHAN. Damn if I was going to give them that good stateside stuff, so I had it boxed and locked up. This evening had it uncrated, the labels removed and taken to Kiessler and Baden's restaurant, where our banquet was scheduled to be held.

At 6:15 p.m. Lt. Col. Watson, Lt. Col. Young and Maj. Bye, all of the surgeon's office, dropped into my room, and they and about 1/2 of our officers whetted their appetites on a bottle of Schenley's Black Label, my one remaining bottle of India jungle ration.

When we arrived at the restaurant, the men were in fine fettle and really feeling good. Well, why not, 35 quarts of good whiskey distributed among 170 men is a good deal, and they certainly were warmed up to it. They were a cheerful, happy bunch, but not rowdy or misbehave, though many were weaving and quite a few were sick.

Lt. Ostroff was toastmaster, and did an excellent job, especially as he had little time to prepare for it, and his efforts were extemporaneous. He called on Col. Watson, who only said "Shanghai is a little better than Texas." I was called on and gave the men a short talk, in a humorous vein by starting out with "This occasion is another milestone" talks—back in the states they were an object of kidding. My talk was well received and enjoyed by all. The party broke up early everyone feeling well, probably too well. *XXX2*, as usual, had to be put to bed. In fact I dragged him down the hall. He didn't stay in bed long and soon was lying on the floor, out like a light. I covered him with a blanket and left him there. "Two Drinks" *XXX2* we call him now. One to make him drunk and the other to make him paralyzed.

SUNDAY OCTOBER 7, 1942

The morning after for many men. There were many butterflies in stomachs, and heads too big to get through doors. All say it was a grand party.

At noon today, Mrs. Scheel, manageress of Kiessler and Baden was in tears. It seems that a couple of naval officers had come to their apartment, above the restaurant, and demanded a couple of rooms from them. They paid a few dollars for rent, and threatened them with eviction, as the Scheel's were accused of being among the Nazi leaders in the country, which they are not.

When I heard about this, I told them that he could not force them to rent any rooms they didn't wish to rent, especially when the women with them were common prostitutes, and when the naval officers had no authority. I told Mrs. Scheel to call me when they came back.

About an hour later she came to the hospital and told me that they were a few blocks away. Lt. Budz and I went to that place and sure enough, the two officers and their women were in front of this place in a car. I called the officer, a Lt. S. G. [*Senior Grade*], out of the car and asked him to give an explanation of his actions. It seems that he is a Liaison officer attached to the Chinese and had access to their

200

files of Nazi sympathizers. When he chose to pick on the Scheel's, he made a bad guess. I'm not going to see the people, who feed over 100 of my O and EM, 3 times daily, imposed on by any officers, Americans or any other kind, in the very Nazi spirit that we have been fighting.

I got the officer's name and Budz and I went immediately to town to get the matter straightened out.

First we went to G-2, Intelligence, but they were all out. Then we saw the Provost Marshal, who got in touch with the Navy Shore Patrol. We went there and then were referred to Commander Strocker's apartment in the Palace Hotel. He's in charge and is a fine man, one of the smoothest articles I have seen for a long time. He took our complaint and said that it would be investigated. I fully believe he will, too, and I hope the Navy O receives severe punishment for his un-American act.

MONDAY, OCTOBER 8, 1945

A quiet day. Picked up a set of lounging pajamas for Babs. Blue brocade silk ones, too.

Saw an Army nurse in one of the stores. Bet those girls are really having the time of their lives. Well, guess I'm enjoying shopping too, and expect to go broke doing so also.

TUESDAY, OCTOBER 9, 1945

Today Capt. Lorenz, Maj. Bates, and Lts. Ostroff and Donley were transferred from the 96th F. H. to the 172nd Gen. Hosp. Our officer's list is gradually thinning out.

This morning we moved out of our nice penthouse quarters to the 2nd floor, where we took the East wing for our 13 remaining officers. It's not as nice here as it was on the 9th floor. We really liked it there.

WEDNESDAY, OCTOBER 10, 1945

The double 10th, the 34th anniversary of the founding of the Chinese republic. All stores are closed today and most of the native population of SHANGHAI has gone downtown to celebrate. We saw some of their famous dragons and took pictures of the parade.

#3 EM were transferred out to Maj. Christopher, the Sanitary Corps officer, to work for him in testing water. Every day someone else is picked off from our unit, it seems.

THURSDAY, OCTOBER 11, 1945

Picked up my notebook from Commander Strocker, the head of the Navy shore patrol. Saw the Provost Marshal about the curfew and learned that it had been set back to the regular time, midnight.

Dropped into the surgeon's office and they had nothing new to tell me. Brummett and I ate lunch at the MARS CAFE and did some shopping. I bought a real Chinese gown, padded that Babs can use as a dressing gown and a couple of tablecloths.

On arriving back at the hospital, we heard that all personnel on the 2nd floor would have to move up to the 5th. The EM will move first, and the O later, probably the day after tomorrow.

FRIDAY, OCTOBER 12, 1945

The EM started moving this morning. It seems as if our moving was horizontal at first, and is definitely vertical now. We sure do get kicked around.

Lt. Col. Watson, the executive officer, of the 172nd Gen. Hosp. came over this morning, in need of 30 EM, 2 MC and 2 MTC O, to fill in vacancies in his outfit. In addition to that, we are lending him Petersen, Wurtzebach and O'Neil, to help get their hospital started. All the rest of us are to be declared surplus and sent home.

Had a good stateside dinner at the American club at noon, steak and even a piece of pumpkin pie.

Saw Lt. Col. Hieble and Lt. Sampson at the Surgeon's Office. Here we heard that, instead of going by ship to the West Coast, we shall probably go by air to KUNMING, be processed there, and then be flown to BARRACKORE, INDIA and go by boat from CALCUTTA via the SUEZ CANAL, MEDITERRANEAN, and ATLANTIC OCEAN, landing either at Boston, New York, or Newport News. Well, one way or the other, it looks as if we'll be home soon. Don't mind encircling the globe at all. Got Babs a blue mandarin coat, very thickly embroidered, and 5 costume dolls.

SATURDAY, OCTOBER 13, 1945

My daddy's birthday today—a grand man—wish I were home to help him celebrate it.

Hagan and I went to Surgeon's office this morning. The "Saint Olaf" deal is on again, at least as far as their trying to send us on it. Saw Lt. Col Theissen and his assistant, Lt. Col. Steward, the embarkation officer at their rooms in the Metropole hotel. They don't even have an office yet. They said that they had no clearance for us yet, but were working on it. Had radioed Gen. MacArthur and Adm. Nimitz for permission to ship us, but had received no answer as yet. Hope it's given approval. They were also awaiting the arrival of certain forms that have to be filled out before we can leave. These forms were sent from Manila over a week ago, and should be here by now. Col. Stewart was leaving this evening by plane to CALCUTTA,

INDIA, to pick up additional forms and papers there. He is to return on the 18th, the ship to leave on the 20th with us aboard, we hope.

The Army personnel aboard are to be transferred to the 172nd Monday morning, the 15th.

We went to the A60 office after that and got the one and only directive in the China Theater on processing individuals and units leaving the China Theater. We borrowed it to take along with us to study over Sunday.

We also discovered that the ribbon awarded us by the Chinese gov't., had been rescinded. Why, nobody knows, I suppose the Army wants to put out its own. I did get a map, and the orders, by which McCain and I receive a combat star for the China offensive, by being in LIUCHOW before the war ended.

In the evening, Westerfield, Hagan, McAulliffe and I were invited to the Pei's for supper. I really was stuffed (see Babs letter).

SUNDAY, OCTOBER 14,1945

A lazy day, packed two boxes for Babs and had McCain nail them shut. About 3:00 p.m. a messenger came in with a package for me. A dozen big chrysanthemums and a nice, rich layer cake, from Mrs. Scheel, manageress of Kiessler and Baden's restaurant. It was a gift sent to me, as she said later on as a token of appreciation for what I had done. Guess it's on account of chasing out the Naval Lieutenant who tried to seize her apartment, as well as the business our outfit had given her.

MONDAY, OCTOBER 15, 1945

Went down to HQ in Wheelock bldg. again. Ran across Col. Theissen by chance. He had nothing new to offer, but suggested that we make all plans and preparations to go, just as if we had orders. This uncertainty in the army is really killing, but feel that it will come out all right and that we leave soon. Be back for Thanksgiving at that rate.

TUESDAY, OCTOBER 16, 1946

Heard rumor that the 172nd didn't need our men, and asked Col. Watson about it; he knew nothing to that effect.

Hagan, Brummett, McAuliffe and I went to Gen. Chan's place, where we hoped to get some Samurai swards, but he was busy in a conference, so we only waited a little while, and then left without seeing him.

Met Col. Armstrong at entrance to Wheelock bldg., and he told me that it wasn't settled yet about our going on the "Saint Olaf." Up in his office Lt. Simpson told us that the War Dept. had OK'd the travel of "protected" personnel on the hospital ship. We are, of course, protected by the Geneva Convention, but the dumb China Theater thinks that this term applies only to the crew of the ship, and the medical personnel aboard. This matter is to be cleared up today.

This morning at 0900, held a meeting with the EM, and had Maj. Remy and Lt. Budziszewski talk to them on our plans for leaving, and what we had to do before then.

Went to the Army PX in Hamilton House, where I bought a short-sleeved dressing gown for Babs, a maroon red brocade, with gold pictures woven into it. $21.00, pretty expensive, no bargain, but guaranteed pure silk, and very beautiful. Sent another box home, set of dishes and Cloisonné vases, etc.

WEDNESDAY, OCTOBER 17, 1945

What a day! We could get no transportation for a while this morning due to a strike of drivers, and then Lt. Pierson, who is to be transferred to us for return to the states came up and told me that Lt.

Simpson, surgeon's office, had called him up on phone and had said, "The 96th F.H. is not sailing on the "Saint Olaf." To say that we were disappointed was a mild understatement. It was really a terrific letdown.

After lunch, Hagen and I went downtown, where we saw Col. Theissen, the port and embarkation officer. He verified this, but stated that we were going on the "Annabelle Lykes," which was to leave on or about the first of November. Well, that was better news.

At the surgeon's office we had confirmation and amplification of the orders. The "Annabelle" would actually dock on the West coast even before the "St. Olaf" got there. It was a faster ship, and would make no stops at OKINAWA, and other spots, as the "Saint Olaf" was scheduled to do.

1800 passengers could be taken aboard, doubt if they'll have it full, but you never can tell. KUNMING is closing up soon, and Hump travel is to close on 1st of November.

We also got verification of the information, received about a month ago, that Med. Dept. Officers, who had been in before Pearl Harbor, were to be discharged. That suits me fine, as soon as my leave and refresher course are finished, I'll be discharged after nearly 5 years of service.

Hurray for "Annabelle," and to hell with "Saint Olaf !"

THURSDAY, OCTOBER 18, 1945

Was invited out to a Chinese friend's house. our Had a nice supper, and nearly too much, "Shan-Tin," a yellow rice wine.

FRIDAY, OCTOBER 19, 1945

Coming down with the flu. Aches and pains and a little fever.

SATURDAY, OCTOBER 20, 1945

We are to move to the "Cathy Mansion." I'm assigned a private room, #914, with bath and a big closet. And a big comfortable bed. The other officers will be 2 in a room, four in an apartment consisting of living room, bedroom and bath. They are to sleep on native made Chinese beds, with rice straw mattresses. Guess the old man rates the best.

SUNDAY, OCTOBER 21, 1945

The officers moved in today. Still felt grippy and stayed in my nice stateside bed all evening.

MONDAY, OCTOBER 22, 1945

The EM moved in to their new quarters today. Believe I feel a bit better today.

TUESDAY, OCTOBER 23, 1945

Feel fine again, not even weak from my illness. No further developments in our plans on moving.

WEDNESDAY, OCTOBER 24, 1945

All quiet in Shanghai.

THURSDAY, OCTOBER 25, 1946

Bought a Zeiss Ikon, plate back camera today, with a double extension bellow in it. It can be focused on an object only 10' away. With this I can take life-size pictures of the eye. It has a Tessarf 4.5 lens and a Compur shutter. Fine camera, and well worth the $20 I paid for it. Wow! I have 3 cameras now.

FRIDAY OCTOBER 26, 1945

Lt. Simpson says that the "Annabelle Lykes" is due in on the 3rd and should depart on the 9th. Hope that's true, as it's good news. The sooner we can leave, the better I'll like it.

Capt. Browne, who was transferred to the portable surgical hospital that went on the Formosa invasion, dropped in tonight. He flew over from Formosa with a patient. He says poor *XXX11* is getting jittery and psycho. Don't know why he should, except that he is one of those fellows who have been too sheltered all his life.

No entry for Saturday October 27, 1945

SUNDAY, OCTOBER 28, 1945

Had all the O and EM given vaccine, typhoid and influenza shots today. The two former in preparation for going home, McCain isn't feeling well today, probably flu.

MONDAY, OCTOBER 29, 1945

Things are really fouled up now. The latest dope is that only 60 point men, or higher are going home. That means that 80% of our O and EM will be yanked out of the 96th and that our ranks will be filled up with strangers. It seems that the unit will really not be declared surplus at that, but will merely be an administrative unit to take the high point men back to the states. Tomorrow we should get a definite answer from Lt. Col. Theissen, in the meantime, it makes me sore, even though I'll go on the "Annabelle Lykes" one way or the another.

TUESDAY, OCTOBER 30, 1945

Well, its o.k. today. The unit is going out as a whole, of which I'm really glad. Our orders were cut yesterday, and an amendment to allow all of us to go will be cut today.

Hagen and I went to the CTRS (China Theater Replacement Service) in the HANKOW area, were they are setting up the processing place for men to go home. Here Lt. Col. Shaw and Lt. Newell are getting things in order for travel back to the USA.

Things really popped today. Hagan, Budz and I met with Shaw, Newell and Lt. Hartberg, and got our final instructions. We picked up tags, customs clearance blanks, and the lists of separation and replacement center. We will have to work all night preparing stencils [*waxed sheets for making copies*] for this job. One set of stencils to be sent by courier pouch to Seattle, where we will dock. The "Annabelle" is to arrive on the 3rd and depart about the 7th.

THURSDAY, NOVEMBER 1, 1945

The 18 nurses and 4 newly assigned O moved in this morning. Had a meeting with all our O and Nurses and told them about our plans. Westerfield helped them make out their baggage and customs forms.

FRIDAY, NOVEMBER 2, 1945

Packed my footlocker, bedding roll and duffel bag today, and put on tags. They will be turned in tomorrow morning, for transportation to the ship.

All the O are really burned up. There isn't first-class space enough for them all, due to nurses and women repatriates, so they'll be quartered in the hold, with the EM. It looks as if I'll be the only O of the 96th to get first-class accommodation.

Lt. Col. Miles, a USS Mann shipmate, told me that he had to sign a waiver also, so it isn't only the 96th that is getting a raw deal. Day before yesterday one of the Pei boys brought me a beautiful flower designed cloisonné vases. He gave its mate to Peterson, I coveted this extra one, so saw Pete about it, and we tried to arrange a deal. A civilian refugee was there, and he suggested flipping a coin, the winner to have the pair of vases. I was really thrilled when I won. These vases are really beautiful.

SATURDAY, NOVEMBER 3, 1945

This morning all our baggage was taken down to the CTRS (China Theater Replacement Service) warehouse. I packed my vases in my field desk and sent the desk along, too. Hogan, Remy and I went to the CTRS bldg. on Midway Road and it looks as if it's all settled. Our work seems to be ended and we seem to have clearance. All we need now is the order to embark.

Bought Babs a Jade ring and some blue silk, for a dress or blouse. Had dinner with the Pie's again; very good, even ate some Shanghai crabs. They are in season in November and October.

SUNDAY, NOVEMBER 4, 1945

Had a pleasant day. Brummet and I walked along the BUNDI and the HANKOW area of the WANGPOO river, where we expect the "Annabelle Lykes" to dock tomorrow.

This evening, just before supper, Hogan came in with the news that Gen. King-Woods had really fouled things up. "Snafu and Tarfon" King-Woods, that's his name to me now. He wants us to drop out all our low-point men at this late stage of the game, and all the low point officers, too. He's crazy! It shows how there is absolutely no liaison between him and the general staff here at all. Hogan saw Col. Nicholas, G-I of theater, and we all hope this silly business will be straightened out by tomorrow morning. The general even wants our clerks, who are to be left behind, to do all this extra paperwork. By the good Lord Harry, I swear I'll never order them to touch even one paper. I'll raise so much hell with the general that he'll have to court-martial me. Things have gone just far enough.

MONDAY, NOVEMBER 5, 1945

Well, it seems as if Gen. Woods has definitely set a policy, at last. The men with less than 60 points, will have to be dropped out of the 96th, and put in the CRTS pool, and our organization filled up with high point Army Ground Force men. I'm to retain an adjutant, first Sgt., two clerks and three cooks. At least these extra, low point men will go with us. It's not quite as bad as it seemed yesterday.

All our officers and nurses are to return with us, as med and dental O have highest priority.

Hogan is having our clerks on the job all night, cutting stencils. I find now that I'm to report to Fort Knox, Ky. at the reception center there. Hope to get a 45 day furlough and then be reassigned to an army hospital doing a lot of Ophthalmology.

WEDNESDAY, NOVEMBER 7, 1945

Two of our clerks were busy all day, mimeographing the stencils for our unit.

It's a wonder–our plans have not been upset for a whole 24 hours. Think of that! Nobody seems to know anything about the ship yet, even if it will be in tomorrow, its scheduled arrival date.

THURSDAY, NOVEMBER 8, 1945

I felt quite sad when the men with less than 60 points were transferred out today at noon. 83 of them, mostly all good men. I really realized that our old outfit was broken up. Their places will be taken by Army Gr. F. [*ground force*] men, none of whom are Med. Dept. men, mainly sig. corps, infantry, etc.

FRIDAY, NOVEMBER 9, 1945

Rumors are thick this evening that the "Annabelle Lykes" has finally arrived. Guess it's true, high time it was here. We'll have to go down tomorrow morning and find out for sure and to check on our next step.

SATURDAY, NOVEMBER 10, 1945

This is it! At 1:30 a.m. was awakened by Hogan, O'Neill and Bauer, with the news that we were to embark at 1: 00 p. m. today on the *USS Hocking*. This is a Naval transport vessel, which had just come in from KOREA, where it had disembarked a load of Marines.

Our clerks work the rest of the night. The nurses were deleted, as there is no accommodation for them aboard.

I went down to CTRS HQ, where the final work was being done. Gen. King was reasonably certain of our leaving, but hadn't gotten the final word on it yet. However, we went right on with our plans.

7 trucks were ordered for 1100 and the men and officers were loaded on, and were on the road to the docks before noon. On our arrival at the dock, we saw that the "Hocking" hadn't arrived yet. CTRS officers were present and assured us that the ship was soon to be in.

At about 1:30, the "Hocking" came into sight. It was about 450 ft. long about 5000 tons. We embarked at about 3:30. Maj. Remy being the first one aboard.

All the officers were quartered in one big compartment, forward, on the port side, on the weather deck. Naval officers, passengers, also occupied the star board side.

To celebrate our last night in SHANGHAI, Brummet, Budz and I went to the Sun Ya restaurant, where we had fried noodles, chicken soup, sweet and sour pork, and barbecue duck.

SUNDAY, NOVEMBER 11, 1945

Armistice Day. We stayed aboard all day, organizing the troops aboard all day. As usual, I was senior medical O of troops aboard. The ship's surgeon, Commander Sparks is from Ashland, Ky., a general surgeon. I had O'Neil draw a roster of MO and EM to run the dispensary. 2 officers and 4 EM daily.

Rumor has it that we are to go to Guam, where we are to refuel and to deliver 10 general prisoners, and then to proceed without further stop to a West Coast port. We are to leave at 5:00 a. m. tomorrow.

MONDAY, NOVEMBER 12, 1945

Up early, but not early enough to see us cast off from the dock at SHANGHAI. Off at 0500, on the nose.

We finally saw the "Annabelle Lykes" tied up at a wharf about 5 miles below SHANGHAI she is a typical Liberty ship. I'm glad that we are aboard a Naval transport.

Before noon we were out of sight of the mainland, and the flat, offshore islands. By this time we were also out of the muddy, silt laden waters of the YANGTZE mouth, and in the clean, blue waters of the Pacific. We saw numbers of rocky islands of the "Barren Island" group. When we passed the last one, our course was changed to SE (150°) and we were headed directly to Guam.

It was about this time that our destroyer escort sighted a mine. The "Hocking" stopped, and we waited for our destroyer to dispose of the mine. We could see small geysers of water where the bullets were hitting the mine. It didn't explode, but must have been punctured and sunk. We had been warned that we would be passing through a mine field all afternoon.

It was quite cold all day, but warmed up nicely in the afternoon, and stayed warm that evening.

TUESDAY, NOVEMBER 13, 1945

A beautiful day, practically cloudless, and the sea quite smooth. It has been getting warmer all the time. That's better than the cold and foggy weather we had expected to experience if we took the great circle route, instead of our Guam jaunt.

Shortly after noon we cited KUMA SHIMA, one of the OKINAWA group (KYU KYUS). It was hardly discernible off the port quarters. It was still in sight at 1600.

This ends Macmillan's diary.

This chapter from diary pages 143-171

ENDNOTES

---

[1] The existence of this or other letters or photographs mentioned by MacMillan are unknown.

Epilog

Macmillan and his troops bore the hardship of convoying over dangerous road conditions and battling tropical diseases and unsanitary conditions. Although the 96th Field Hospital was never fully established, many of its original personnel were assigned to other hospitals and sanitation units in small towns to treat and prevent diseases among both American and Chinese troops and Chinese civilians.

Some historians suggest that the overall efforts of the Army Medical Service as a whole were successful. Kirk T. Mosley and Darrell G. McPherson propose that, "the relatively low sick rates of U.S. troops stationed in the midst of unbelievably bad conditions indicate" that the objectives to keep troops relatively healthy were met.[1]

The United States Army phased out activates in China, after the Japanese surrendered in September 1945. However, several units were relocated to Shanghai. This included the 96th Field Hospital. After several weeks, many of the unit's original personnel, including MacMillan, were sent home. The China Theater was closed April 30, 1946 almost four years after it was established.[2]

ENDNOTES

---

[1] Kirk T. Mosley and Darrell G. McPherson in *Army Medical Service. Preventive medicine in World War II. Volume VIII*, ed. John Boyd Coates, (Dept. of the Army, 1976), 657.
[2] *Ibid.*, 652-653.

Bibliography

General References

Cressman, Robert J. "Chapter 7: 1945," in *The Official Chronology of the U.S. Navy in World War II*. Annapolis, MD: Naval Institute Press, 2000. Internet address as of April 24, 2015. http://www.ibiblio.org/hyperwar/USN/USN-Chron/USN-Chron-1945.html.

Department of the Army. *AR 600-50. Standards of Conduct for Department of the Army Personnel. Headquarters*, Washington, DC: HQ DOA, January 1988. Internet address as of April 24, 2015. http://www.loc.gov/rr/frd/Military_Law/pdf/AR_600-50_01-28-1988.pdf.

"General W. A. Mann." *Dictionary of American Naval Fighting Ships*. Washington, DC: Department of the Navy, Naval History and Heritage Command, Navy Yard, n.d. Internet address as of April 24, 2015. http://www.history.navy.mil/research/histories/ship-histories/danfs/g/general-w-a-man.html.

Gettis, Erin. *Camp Anza. City of Riverside: Camp Anza/Arlanza 2006–2007, Certified Local Government Grant Historical Resources Inventory and Context Statement*. Riverside, CA: City of Riverside Planning Division, 2007. Internet address as of April 6, 2015. http://ohp.parks.ca.gov/pages/1054/files/camp%20anza%20final%20report.pdf.

Ilayperuma, Isurani, "Evaluation of Cephalic Indices: a Clue for Racial and Sex Diversity." *Int. J. Morphol*, 29:1 (2011):112-117. Internet address as of April 24, 2015. http://www.scielo.cl/pdf/ijmorphol/v29n1/art19.pdf.

"K-rations." Internet address as of April 24, 2014. http://en.wikipedia.org/wiki/K-ration.

Lary, Diana. *The Chinese People at War: Human Suffering and Social Transformation, 1937–1945*, Cambridge University Press 2010.

Lydenberg, Harry Miller. *Crossing the Line: Tales of the Ceremony during Four Centuries.* New York: New York Public Library, 1957. Internet address as of April 24, 2015. https://archive.org/details/crossinglinetale00lyde.

Majumder, Partha P. "People of India: Biological Diversity and Affinities." In *The Indian Human Heritage,* edited by D. Balasubramanian and N. Appaji Rao. Hyderguda, Hyderbad, India: University Press (India) Lt, 1998.

Myers, James M. "Camp Barkeley," *Handbook*, Denton, TX: Texas State Historical Association, n.d. Internet address as of April 24, 2015. http://www.tshaonline.org/handbook/online/articles/qbc02.

The Navy Department Library, "Chapter 7: Action against Submarines, Aircraft, Mines, Chemicals." In *War Instructions United States Navy 1944. Section I. Antisubmarine Measure.* Washington, DC: United States Navy 1944. Internet address as of April 24, 2015. http://www.history.navy.mil/research/library/online-reading-room/title-list-alphabetically/w/war-instructions-united-states-navy-1944/7-action-against-submarines-aircraft-mines-chemicals.html.

"Rationing: A Necessary but Hated Sacrifice." *Life on the home front: Oregon's Response to World War II.* Salem: Oregon State archive exhibit, 2008. Internet address as of April 24, 2015. http://arcweb.sos.state.or.us/pages/exhibits/ww2/services/ration.htm.

Rowland, Buford and William B. Boyd. *U.S. Navy Bureau of Ordnance in World War II: United States. Navy Dept.* Bureau of Ordnance, Department of the Navy, 1953-World War, 1939-1945. Hathitrust.org. Internet address as of April 24, 2015. http://catalog.hathitrust.org/Record/001623097.

Ruffner, Kevin Conley. "The Black Market in Postwar Berlin: Colonel Miller and an Army Scandal, Part 1." *Prologue Magazine.* Vol. 34, No. 3, Fall 2002. Internet address as of April 24, 2015. http://www.archives.gov/publications/prologue/2002/fall/berlin-black-market-1.html.

Stewart, Richard W. "Chap. 6: World War II: The War against Japan." *American Military History, Volume II. The United States Army in a Global Era 1917–2008. Second Edition.* Army Historical Series. Washington, DC: Center of Military History. United States Army, 2010. Internet version address as of April 24, 2015. http://www.history.army.mil/html/books/030/30-22/CMH_Pub_30-22.pdf.

United States Department of Transportation. "Appendix B. Military Convoy Movement Facts," *Coordinating Military Deployments on Roads and Highways: A Guide for State and Local Agencies.* Washington: Office of Transportation, 1985. Internet address as of April 24, 2015. http://ops.fhwa.dot.gov/publications/fhwahop05029/appendix_b.htm.

"US Legal Definitions." Internet address as of April 24, 2015. http://definitions.uslegal.com/b/black-market/

"USS General A. Mann (AP-112)." *Wikipedia.* Internet address as of March 19, 2015. http://en.wikipedia.org/wiki/USS_General_W._A._Mann_(AP-112)

Ziegler, Philip. *Mountbatten: The Official Biography.* London: Collins, 1985.

CBI Theater, Army Medical Services and Burma Road

Armfield, Blanche B. "Chapter XII: Medical Department in China, Burma, and India." In *Medical Department United States Army in World War II, Organization and Administration,* edited by John Boyd Coates. Washington, DC: Office of the Surgeon General, Department of the Army, 1963. Internet version address as of April 24, 2015. http://history.amedd.army.mil/booksdocs/wwii/orgadmin/DEFAULT.htm.

Buchanan, C. M. and John R. McDowell. *Stilwell Road: Story of the Ledo Lifeline.* Calcutta: Office of Public Relations, India-Burma Theater of Operations, USF in IBT, Advance Section, APO 689, in conjunction with the Information and Education Division, IBT, 1945-1955. Internet version address as of April 24, 2015. http://cbi-theater-2.home.comcast.net/~cbi-theater-2/lifeline/Ledo_Lifeline.html.

Chennault, Claire Lee. *Way of a fighter; the Memoirs of Claire Lee Chennault*, edited by Robert Hotz. New York, G.P: Putnam's Sons, 1949.

Condon-Rall, Mary Ellen and Albert E. Cowdrey. "Chapter IX: The China-Burma-India challenge." *The Medical Department, Medical Service in the War against Japan.* Washington, DC: Center of Military History, United States Army, 1998. Internet version address as of April 24, 2015. http://www.history.army.mil/html/books/010/10-24/CMH_Pub_10-24-1.pdf.

Ford, Daniel. *Flying Tigers: Claire Chennault and His American Volunteers, 1941–1942.* Rev. Edition. Washington, DC: Harper Collins-Smithsonian Books, 2007.

Graham, A. Stephens. "Chapter XIV: India-Burma and China Theaters." *Medical Department, United States Army, Surgery in World War II. Activities of Surgical Consultants, Vol.II.* edited by B. Noland Carter. Washington, DC: Office of the Surgeon General, Department of the Army, 1964. Internet version address as of April 24, 2015. http://history.amedd.army.mil/booksdocs/wwii/actvssurgconvol2/chapter14.htm.

Historical Division. *Merrill's Marauders: February-May 1944. American Forces in Action series.* Washington, DC: Center of Military History, United States Army, 1945. Internet version address as of April 24, 2015. http://www.history.army.mil/books/wwii/marauders/marauders-fw.htm.

Hogan, Jr. David, W. "Chapter 5: Special operations in the China-Burma-India Theater." In *U.S. Army Special Operations in World War II.* Washington, DC: Department of the Army, 1992. Internet version address as of April 2, 2015. http://www.history.army.mil/books/wwii/70-42/70-42c.htm

Hunter, Kenneth E. [compiled by Kenneth E. Hunter and Margaret E. Tackley, edited by Mary Ann Bacon]. In Kent Roberts Greenfield [General Editor]. *United States Army in World War II. Pictorial Record. The War against Japan.* Washington, DC: Office of the Chief of Military History, Department of the Army, 1952. Internet version address as of April 24, 2015. http://www.allworldwars.com/The-War-Against-Japan-Pictorial-Record.html.

MacGarrigle, George L. *Central Burma. The US Army Campaign of World War II.* Washington, DC: U.S. Army Center of Military History, 1996. Internet version address as of April 24, 2015. http://www.history.army.mil/brochures/centburma/centburma.htm.

Mosley, Kirk T. and Darrell G. McPherson. "Chapter XVII: China-Burma-India Theater." In *Army Medical Service. Preventive Medicine in World War II. Volume VIII,* edited by John Boyd Coates. Washington, DC: Office of the Surgeon General, Department of the Army, 1976. Internet version address as of April 24, 2015. http://history.amedd.army.mil/booksdocs/wwii/civilaffairs/chapter17.htm.

Neel, Spurgeon. "Chapter II: Health of the Command: Rates and Trends." In *Medical Support of the U.S. Army in Vietnam 1965-1970.* Washington, DC: Department of the Army, 1991. Internet version address as of April 24, 2015. http://www.history.army.mil/books/Vietnam/MedSpt/chpt2.htm.

Newell, Clayton R. *Burma, 1942. The US Army Campaigns of World War II.* Washington, DC: U.S. Army Center of Military History. n.d. Internet version address as of April 24, 2015. http://www.history.army.mil/brochures/burma42/burma42.htm.

Rehn, John W. "Chapter VII: China-Burma-India Theater." In *Military History.* Washington, DC: Office of the Surgeon General. Department of the Army, 1963. Internet version address as of April 24, 2015. http://history.amedd.army.mil/booksdocs/wwii/Malaria/chapterVII.htm.

Romanus, Charles F. and Riley Sunderland. *Stilwell's Mission to China. U.S. Army in World War II.* Washington, DC: Office of the Chief of Military History, Department of the Army, 1953. Internet version address as of April 10, 2015. http://www.history.army.mil/html/books/009/9-1/CMH_Pub_9-1.pdf.

Romanus, Charles F. and Riley Sunderland. *Stilwell's Command Problems. U.S. Army in World War II.* Washington, DC: Office of the Chief of Military History, Department of the Army, 1956. Internet version address as of April 24, 2015. http://www.history.army.mil/html/books/009/9-2/CMH_Pub_9-2.pdf.

Romanus, Charles F. and Riley Sunderland. *Time Runs Out in CBI. U.S. Army in World War II.* Washington, DC: Office of the Chief of Military History, Department of the Army, 1958. Internet version address as of April 24, 2015. http://www.history.army.mil/html/books/009/9-3/CMH_Pub_9-3.pdf.

Seagrave, Gordon S. *Burma Surgeon.* New York: W. W. Norton and Co., 1943.

Sherry, Mark D. *China Defensive 4 July 1942–4 May 1945. US Army Campaigns of World War II.* Washington, DC: U.S. Army Center of Military History, Department of the Army, 1996. Internet version address as of February 28, 2015. http://www.history.army.mil/html/books/072/72-38/CMH_Pub_72-38.pdf. Also found in Hathitrust.org.

Sinclair, William Boyd. "Book 5: Medics and Nurses." *Confusion beyond Imagination: China-Burma-India in World War II in a Series of 10 Books.* Coeur d'Alene, Idaho: Joe F. Whitley, 1989.

Stone, James E., ed. *Crisis Fleeting: Original Reports on Military Medicine in India and Burma In The Second World War.* Washington, DC: The Historical Unit, United States Army Medical Department, Office of the Surgeon General Department of the Army, 1969. Internet version address as of April 24, 2015.
http://history.amedd.army.mil/booksdocs/wwii/CrisisFleeting/

Further Reading

Anders, Leslie. *The Ledo Road.* Norman: University of Oklahoma Press, 1965.

Churchill, Edward D. *Surgeon to soldiers; diary and records of the Surgical Consultant, Allied Force Headquarters, World War II.* Philadelphia: Lippincott, 1972. Limited internet version address as of April 24, 2015. http://catalog.hathitrust.org/Record/001622499.

Goodman, Anthony. *None but the Brave: a novel of the surgeons of World War II.* Helena, MT: Deer Creek Publications Group, 2012.

Hunter, Charles Newton. *Galahad*. San Antonio: Naylor Publishing, 1963.

Jackson, Calvin G. *Diary of Col. Calvin G. Jackson, M.D.* Ada, OH: Ohio Northern University, 1992.

Latimer, John. *Burma: The Forgotten War*. London: John Murray, 2004.

Linner, John H. Normandy to Okinawa: A Navy Medical Officer's Diary and Overview of World War Two. Edina, MN: Beaver's Pond Press, 2007.

Ogburn, Charlton. The Marauders. New York: Harper, 1959.

Office of the Chief of Military History. Order of Battle of the United States Army Ground Forces in World War II. Pacific Theater of Operations. United States Army Forces China, Burma and India. Washington, DC: Department of the Army 1959. Address as of April 24, 2015. (USAF CBI). http://cbi-theater-10.home.comcast.net/~cbi-theater-10/cbi-history/cbi_history.html.

Peyton, Frank W. A Surgeon's Diary: 15th Evacuation Hospital: Experiences in World War II, North Africa -- Sicily – Italy. Lafayette, IN: F.W. Peyton, 1987.

Rush, Charles W. World War II Diary of an American Surgeon: Lt. Col. Walter H. Gerwig, Jr, Surgeon, US Army Medical Corps. Amazon.Com: Kindle, 2014.

Tuchman, Barbara. Stilwell and the American Experience in China, 1911-45. New York: Macmillan, 1970.

Webster, Donovan. The Burma Road: The Epic Story of the China-Burma-India Theater in World War II. New York: Farrar, Straus and Giroux, 2003.

Wolff, Luther H. Forward Surgeon: The diary of Luther H. Wolff, M.D., Mediterranean Theater, World War II, 1943-45. New York: Vantage Press, 1985.

Appendix A: Glossary of Military and Other Abbreviations

A2: Intelligence Directorate

A3: Operations and Planning Directorate

A4: Logistics Directorate

A5: Civil Affairs

A6: Communications Directorate

AA: Antiaircraft

AC: Aviation Corps

ANC: Army Nursing Corps

ASN: Army Service Number

ATC: Air Transport Command

Bn: Battalion

CE: Corps of Engineers

CIC: Counter Intelligence Core

CID: Criminal Investigation Division

CO: Commanding Officer, also written as Co.

COM-CAR: Combat Carrier or a large
cargo plane for transporting personnel
and material

DC: Dental Corps

DIB: Directory Information Base

DO: Duty Officer

DS: Detached Service

EM: Enlisted Men

FOF: Fraternal Order of Fuddy-Duddies
[a fun "secret society" created
on board the *USS Gen. a Mann* for the officers

G-1: Assistant Chief of Staff, Personnel

G-2: Assistant Chief of Staff, Intelligence

G-3: Assistant Chief of Staff, Operations and Plans

G-4: Assistant Chief of Staff, Logistics

G-5: Assistant Chief of Staff, Civil Affairs

G-6: Assistant Chief of Staff for Information Management

G. H.: General Hospital

Hawsers: A thick rope for mooring a boat

IB: Theater: India-Burma theater

IP: Initial Point

JADS: Judge Advocates Division

JG: Junior Grade (Navy)

KP: Kitchen Patrol

MAC: Medical Administrative Corps,
a branch of the Medical Service Corps in the Army Medical Service

Mess: Food services

MO: Medical Officer

MP: Military Police

MTS: Motor Transportation Service

OD: Officer of the Day

O and N: Officers and Nurses

Ord. Room: Orderly Room

OSS: Office of Strategic Services

POB: Planned Operating Base

POL: Petroleum, Oil, & Lubricants

RR: Railroad

S-2: Intelligence Officer

S-3: Operations and planning unit

S-4: Logistics

Shavedtail: 2nd Lt.

SG: Senior grade

SOP: Standard Operating Procedures

Station H. or S. H.: Station Hospital

TAT: Equipment needed by troops during movement

TOE or T/OE equipment prescribed equipment for operation of the unit

T/O: Table of organization

TC: Transit Coordinator

TP: Telephone

Appendix B: People Mentioned in Diary

(Most did not have first names; rank and duty were often missing)
G. H. = General Hospital **F.H.** = Field Hospital **S.H.** = Station Hospital

Name	Rank	Duty, Affiliation, Location
Abelson	Capt.	MC, Base Surgeon, Base Sect III, and at Advanced Section 1, Kweiyang, China
Alcam (Misspelling of Allen who was promoted to Lt. Col.?)	Maj.	Engineer at SOS campground at Liuchow
Allen	Lt. Col.	CE, engineer SOS campground, Liuchow; 448 ferry crossing; and Shanghai, China
Anderson	Capt.	Gen. Cranston's adjutant, SOS HQ Intermediate Base #2, Section 2. Chabua, India
Armstrong	Col.	China Theater Surgeon, SOS HQ, Kunming, China
Arslanian		96th Field Hospital
Avery	Capt.	CO race track convoy area, SOS HQ, China
Balcercak		Barber and saxophone player, 96th Field Hospital
Bates	Maj	MC, assigned to 96th F. H. in Sept. 1945
Bauer	Sgt	96th F. H.
Baumgartner		Macmillan's driver, 96th F. H., Kunming, China
Baumhorst	Lt.	Member 44th F. H., Mong Yu, Burma near Burma- China border [1]
Baurnhardt (or Barnhardt)		MC, 96th F. H.
Becker	Lt. Col.	Transportation base station "A" Kunming, China

Name	Rank	Duty, Affiliation, Location
Beckman		96th F. H.
Blanchard	Lt. Col.	Shanghai, China
Borland	Maj.	SOS HQ, Kunming, China
Bornemann (or Borneman)	Lt.	Chief Nurse, 96th F. H.
Bowen	Capt.	CO, convoy camp near MongYu, Burma at junction of Ledo-Burma Road
Brill	Lt.	Shanghai, China
Brinsmead [?]	Maj.	Adjutant, SOS HQ, China
Bromberg		96th F. H.
Bronson (or Brunsen)	Capt.	96th F. H.
Brown	Maj.	DC, SOS surgeon's office, Base Section III, Kweiyang, Guizhou, China
Browne	Capt.	MC, in charge of Sanitation in Dibrugarh, India, 96th Field
Brojac	Sgt.	96th F. H
Brummett	Capt.	96th F. H.
Budziszewski (Budz) (or Butziszewski)	Lt.	96th F. H.
Burbank	Col	SOS Base Section III, Kweiyang,
Bye	Capt. [Maj.]	Supply officer, Surgeon's office, SOS, Liuchow and surgeon's office, Shaignhai, China
Calkin	T3	96th F. H
Carlson		96th F. H. Assigned DS to 3rd QM Med. Depo
Carroll	Lt	MAC, account inspector, 96th F. H
Cavanaugh	Lt. Col.	Theater, Surgeon's Office, Kunming, China
Chen, William	Mr.	Handyman, Haig Court's hotel, Shanghai, China
Christian	Pvt.	96th F. H
Christopher	Maj	Sanitary corps, HQ, Shanghai, China

Name	Rank	Duty, Affiliation, Location
Claiborne		96th F. H., assigned DS to 3d QM Medical Depot between Tushan and Liuchow, China
Clemo		96th F. H
Clubb	Maj	Post Adjutant, Chandimari, near Calcutta, India
Cornwath		MD, Ship's Surgeon, *USS Gen.W. A Mann*
Cole	Lt.	Inspection Officer, Camp Anza, CA
Cole	Capt.	14th Air Force, at Camp Ground near Chabua, India
Cook		Jeep driver, 96th F. H
Cook	Col.	ORD. SOS HQ Intermediate Base #2, Section 2. Chabua, India
Cranston, Joseph A	Brig. Gen	CO, Intermediate Section, Assam, India, OS [2]
Crawford	Col.	Theater Surgeon, Kunming, China
Davis	Lt.	Kunming, China
Delano	Col.	QM, 3d QM Medical Depot between Tushan and Liuchow, China
Dilts	Capt	Priorities and Travel Officer, airport base near Liulang, China
Donley	1Lt.	MAC, assigned to 96th F. H. September 1945
Dorsey		96th F. H
Dowing	Sgt	Tow truck operator Member of 96th F. H.,
Down	T/4	Stenographer/typist, 96th F. H.
Downs	W O.	S-2, SOS HQ Intermediate Base #2, Section 2. Chabua, India
Driscoll	Lt. Col.	CO, 95th S.H Kunming, China
Driscoll	Mr.	CID, near Burma-China border
Duffy .	Capt	SOS HQ Kweiyang, China
Eckrote		96th F. H
Edquist	Lt.	Transportation, Base Sect. HQ, Kunming, China

Name	Rank	Duty, Affiliation, Location
Elias, Freddie and brother		Owners Haig Court Apartments, Shanghai, China
Eliot	Lt. Col.	96th F. H
Eyler .	Capt.	Top Movement Assistant, Calcutta, India
Farmer	Col.	Transportation, Kweiyang China
Feldmesser	Sgt.	96th F. H.
Ferris	Capt.	CID, near Burma-China border
Fleiger .	Lt	QM, 3d QM Medical Depot, convoy camp between Tushan and Liuchow
Fry	Lt. Col.	Acting CO, 18th S. H, Chandimari near Calcutta. India
Fulton	Lt.	Burma Road engineer's camp at 410 km. between Tushan and Liuchow
Gard		Lab. tech. 96th F.H.
Garland	Maj.	Surgeon, SOS HQ, Kunming, China
Goodman		96th F. H.
Hagan	Lt.	S-3, 65th QM Depot Company, Chabua, India
Hagan	Capt.	MC, 96th F. H.
Hansen	Mr.	Danish, former Japanese POW in charge of Navy YMCA, Shanghai, China
Harris		96th F. H
Hartberg	Lt.	Embarkation, Shanghai, China
Heisler	Maj	QMC, SOS HQ Intermediate Base #2, Section 2. Chabua, India
Henderson	Lt.	Construction lineman, convoy camp between Tushan and Liuchow
Hewitt	Maj.	S-4, SOS HQ, Kunming, China
Hieble (also spelled Hiehle)	Lt. Col.	Surgeon's office, Shanghai, China
Hogan	Capt.	96th F. H.
Holzberg	Lt.	JADS, member 96th F. H. and DS, Kweiyang, China

Name	Rank	Duty, Affiliation, Location
Hordison	Pvt.	96th F. H.
Howell	Pfc	96th F. H.
Howes	Maj.	Pilot, airbase near Luliang near Kunming, China
Inman	Capt.	96th F. H.
Ireland	Col.	SOS HQ Intermediate Base #2, Section 2. Chabua, India
Johnson	Col.	MC, Chief Surgeon, HQ Shanghai, China
Johnston	Lt. Col.	CO, 22nd F. H. through early July, Chanyi, China
Kagle	Maj.	Kunming, China
Kay, Sammy	Maj.	MC, 234th G. H. near Chabua, Assam
Keith	Maj	SOS HQ Intermediate Base #2, Section 2. Chabua, India
Kelso	Lt. Col.	QM, 3d QM Med. Depot between Tushan and Liuchow, China
Kenmer	Gen	Shanghai, China
Kiessler and Baden's (also spelled Kiessling)		Restaurant where 96th F. H. ate, Shanghai, China
Kilgore	Lt.	QMC, SOS HQ Intermediate Base #2, Section 2. Chabua, Assam, India
King-Woods	Gen.	Shanghai, China
Koble	Capt.	SOS, Liuchow
Kwa, Chung	Dr.	Engineer, SOS campground at Liuchow
Lamber	Maj.	MC, 96th F. H.
Lamson		Chaplain, SOS HQ Liuchow, China
Langer	Maj	S-4, SOS HQ Intermediate Base #2, Section 2. Chabua, India
Lecesse		96th F. H.
Lee (or Yee?)	Lt.	Luliang, Airfield, China
Lenert	Capt.	MC, Sanitary Watch Officer, 96th F. H. on *USS Gen. W. A. Mann*

233

Name	Rank	Duty, Affiliation, Location
Lorenz		MC, 96th F. H.
Longworth		96th F. H.
Maguire, Paul	Capt. USNR	Captain, *USS Gen. W. A. Mann*
Margison	Capt.	Convoy commander, 96th F. H. near Assam, India
Marshall	Lt. Col.	SOS Surgeon, SOS HQ Intermediate Base #2, Section 2. Chabua, India
McAndrews	Capt.	MC, 20th Evacuation Hospital, Myitkyina, Burma
McAuliffe	Capt	MC (?), acting Catholic Chaplain 96th F. H. Conducted 1945 Easter Mass
McCain (Mac)		Macmillan's orderly, 96th F. H
McCandless	Maj.	In charge of a Chinese convoy, convoy camp between Tushan and Liuchow
McCarthy, "Charlie"	Lt.	On airplane from Liuchow to Kweiyang.
McClure	Gen.	Shanghai, China
McCrary	Maj	Motor Dispersal, Chabua, Assam, India
McNair	Lt. Col.	96th F. H.
McVicar	Lt.SG [1Lt] USNR	Shanghai, China
Meyer, Rudy	Col.	142nd General Hospital, Calcutta, India area
Miles, Roy	Lt. Col.	*USS G. A. Mann shipmate*; also met him in Shanghai and returned to USA with him on *USS Hocking*
Minutti	Mr.	Architect for the Eliase brothers, Shanghai.
Monks (or Monk)	Maj.	SOS HQ Intermediate Base #2, Section 2. Chabua, India
Morris	Maj.	CID, near Chabua, Assam, India
Morris	Lt. Col.	SOS HQ Intermediate Base #2, Section 2. Chabua, India

Name	Rank	Duty, Affiliation, Location
Moyer	Lt	in charge of debarkation at Siliguri, India
Mungas, Peter	Pfc.	96th F. H.
Napelli	T/5	96th F. H.
Nicholas	Col.	G-I of theater, Shanghai, China
Nowell		MC, 96th F. H
Oliver	Maj.	Transportation, Base Sect. HQ, Kunming, China
O'Neil, Eddy	Lt.	In charge of Mess, 96th F. H. in Dibrugarh, India,
Oliphant	Col.	CO, Base Section, III, Kweiyang, China; also Dep. CO, SOS HQ, located in International YMCA, in Shanghai, China
Olsen	Sgt.	96th F. H.; DS at 119th Ordinance Depot near Makum, Assam, India
Ostroff	Lt.	96th F. H.
Owens	Col.	234th General Hospital, near Chauba, Assam, India
Pearl	Capt.	Changi, China
Pei		Shanghai, China
Pendelton		96th F. H.
Perry	Sgt.	96th F. H
Peterson (or Petersen)	Capt.	96th F. H
Phillips	Maj	CO.? Convoy camping area Chubua, Assam, India
Phillips	Capt.	Transportation, SOS HQ, Kunming, China
Pierson	Lt.	Transferred to 96th F. H. in Shanghai, China
Radcliffe	Lt. Col.	S-4, SOS HQ Intermediate Base #2, Section 2. Chabua, India

Name	Rank	Duty, Affiliation, Location
Ratliff, Frank	Lt. Col.	S-3, Operation Officer, SOS HQ Intermediate Base #2, Section 2, Chabua, India[3]
Reed	Maj.	95th F. H.
Reed	Mr.	Old British troop area, near Dibrughar, India
Remy	Capt.	MC, 95th F. H ; later Maj. Remy at 96th F. H., Shanghai, China
Ricamore	Lt. Col.	Executive Officer, Advanced Section 1, Kweiyang, China
Riordan, Leo A.	Capt.	Burma Road engineer, CO, convoy camp between Tushan and Liuchow
Rugheimer	Lt. Col.	Post CO of troops, Calcutta, India
Rutledge	Mr.	Police officer, old British troop area near Dibrugarh, India
Sandlin		MC, 96th F. H.
Sendori		96th F. H
Scheel	Mrs.	Manager's wife of Kiessler and Baden restaurant, Shanghai, China
Scott	Col.	CO, SOS HQ, Liuchow, China
Schimazi		Laboratory tech. 96th F.H
Schlaybach		Member, 96th F. H.
Schulz	Rev.	Chaplain, 95th F. H., first met on *USS Gen. W. A Mann*
Seedlock	Col.	CE, SOS HQ camp, Liuchow, China; 448 ferry crossing; Shanghai China
Shaw	Lt. Col.	Embarkation, Shanghai, China
Shepherd		ARC, SOS HQ Intermediate Base #2, Section 2. Chabua, India
Sherman	Capt.	Transportation, Base Section "A," Kunming China
Shoemaker	Lt.	Transportation, Chanyi, China
Simpson, Wm. H.	Lt. Gen.	Chanyi, China[4]

Name	Rank	Duty, Affiliation, Location
Simpson	Lt.	Surgeon's office, 95th S. H., Kunming, China: Surgeons office, Shanghai, China
Sleasura	Sgt.	?
Sloan	Maj.	SOS HQ Intermediate Base #2, Section 2. Chabua, India
Snow	Cdr.	USS *Gen. W. A. Mann*
Sopka	Capt.	Officer, at Chabua, India camp ground
Spalding	Lt. JG,	Shanghai, China
Sparks	Cdr.	Ship's surgeon, *USS Hocking*
Sparks	Lt. Col.	Motor pool, HQ Shanghai, China
Stalzberg (also spelled Stolzberg)	Lt.	MAC, in charge of water in Dibrugarh, India, 96th F. H.
Stellings	Col.	AC, CO., Airport base, Luliang, China
Steward	Lt. Col.	Assistant to Col Thiessen, embarkation officer, Shanghai, China
Stewart	Maj.	Dental Surgeon, SOS, Kunming, China
Strocker	Cdr.	CO, Navy shore patrol, Shanghai, China
Sullivan	Capt.	Medical supply officer, 96th F. H.
Sweeney, Kate		ANC, 96th F. H.
Sweazy		96th F. H.
Stotzberg		96th F. H.
Taylor	Lt. Col.	10th Airborne, Liuchow, China
Theissen	Lt. Col.	Embarkation officer, Shanghai, China
Thomas	Maj.	Surgeon, SOS HQ, Kunming, China
Verder	Lt. Col.	14th Air Force, camp ground near Chabua, India
Wallace	Lt. Col.	MC, Surgeon, Intermediate Base #2, Calcutta, India

Name	Rank	Duty, Affiliation, Location
Watson	Maj. [Lt. Col.]	MC, Inspection officer, camp Swift and at SOS, Kunming, China; executive officer, 172nd G. H. Shanghai, China
Wedemeyer, Albert	Gen.	Chanyi, China
Weart	Maj. Gen	HQ Shanghai, China
Wei	Dr.	President of Shantung University, transported him from Yunnanyi to Kunming, China
Welty	Lt. Col	Executive Officer, British compound camp, Dibrugarh, Assam, India near Chabua
Westerfelt	Capt.	96th F. H
Weyrick	Col.	G-3, Airport base, Luliang, near Kunming China
Williams	Maj.	C. E., SOS HQ Intermediate Base #2, Section 2. ChabuaIndia
Woods, Marion	Maj.	Protestant Chaplain, 96th F. H.
Woolamb	Maj.	British officer, British compound camp near Dibrugarh and Chabua, Assam, India
Workizer		Officer, 96th F. H.
Wurtzebach (or Wurzetebeck)	Lt.	96th F. H.
Yee	Maj.	CO., 22nd F. H. Chanyi, Yunnan, China
Ying	Mr.	Chinese friend in Shanghai, China
Young	Lt. Col.	96th F. H.; Surgeon's Office Shanghai, China
Zanotta (or Zonatto)	Lt.	SOS HQ, Intermediate Base #2, Section 2. Cahaba, Assam, India
Zeit	Lt	Billeting, Shanghai, China

ENDNOTES

---

[1] This hospital was located at Dr. Gordon Seagrave's original hospital before Japanese occupation.

[2] Kirk T. Mosley and Darrell G. McPherson in *Army Medical Service. Preventive medicine in World War II. Volume VIII*, ed. John Boyd Coates, (Dept. of the Army, 1976), 640.

[3] Brief Army bio of Ratliff. Internet address as of Feb. 3, 2015 http://digital.libraries.ou.edu/sooner/articles/p19-22_1946v19n3_OCR.pdf..

[4] Charles F. Romanus and Riley Sutherland, *Time Runs out in CBI* (Department of the Army, 1959), 383-384.

Appendix C. Military Units Mentioned in Diary

F.H = Field Hospital G.H. = General Hospital S.H. = Station Hospital

7th Tank Battalion, Chinese Truck Convoy, near Panshien
14th Air Force, at Camp Ground near Chabua, India
18th F. H., Calcutta, India
20th Evacuation Hospital, Myitkyina, Burma
20th G. H. near Shingbwiyang, Burma
22nd F. H., near Chanyi [*Zhanyi, near Qujing*]
27th F. H., Kweiyang, China
44th F. H., located at the site of one of Dr. Gordon Seagrave's hospitals
  before Japanese occupation of Mong Yu, Burma near the Burma-China
  border on the Ledo-Burma Road.
49th Portable Surgical Hospital, Tushan, China
65th QM Depot Co. # 5 serial which was taken out of MacMillan's convoy
  June 28, 1945
95th F. H. traveled on *USS G. A. Mann* to Calcutta with the 96th F. H. and
  intermittently interacted and used men and matériel from the 96th F. H.
95th S. H., Kunming, China. From fall 1943 until its departure in the
  summer of 1945, the 95th served as the only large army hospital unit in
  China.
142nd G. H., Calcutta, India area. This hospital was a relay station for men
  enroute back to the states who had been POWs. The POW's
  built bridges and railroads from Thailand to Burma under the Japanese.
172nd G. H., Kunming, China. Sections of it were scattered over India and
  Burma when it arrived in early 1945 in Kunming. This hospital eventually
  replaced the buildings formally occupied by the 95th station hospital in
  Kunming. In the fall of 1945, after the Japanese surrendered, the 172nd
  moved to Shanghai occupying the Former Haig Court, Apartments, after
  the 96th F. H. had set it up.[1]
234th G. H., near Chabua, Assam, India
259th. S. H., Kweiyang, China
494th AA outfit, located near Chabua, Assam, India and the 96th's campsite.

ENDNOTES

---

[1] William Boyd Sinclair. *Confusion beyond Imagination: China-Burma-India in World War II in a Series of 10 Books*, p 145 and Chapter 10, diary.

Appendix D. Biographical Timeline of Col. Karl D. MacMillan, MC, USAR

(11 August 1904 - 19 December 1994)[1]

Date	Activity
11 Aug 1904	Born in Sydney, NS, Canada
21 April 1915	Immigrated with family to the United States
1919-1925 (aprox.)	Early ham radio operator, track and field in high school and college
22 May 1922	Graduated, Wilkinsburg High School, Wilkinsburg, PA with honors
Spring 1926	BS, University of Pittsburgh
Spring 1929	MD, University of Pittsburgh Medical School
6 June 1929	Commissioned 1Lt. United States Army Reserve, Medical Corps Officer
1929-1932?	Ear Eye Nose Throat (EENT) residency at University of Pittsburgh through USAR program
27 July 1930	Changed last name to MacMillan (his mother's maiden name) from Kutchka
Mid-1930s?	Promoted to Capt.
1932-1941	Private EENT practice, Highland Building, East Liberty, Pittsburgh, PA
23 June 1937	Married Barbara McCurdy in Sydney, NS.
7 June 1941	Son, Donald Alexander MacMillan, born in Pittsburgh, PA
16 July 1941	Called up for active duty military service
30 Aug 1941	Eye specialist, U. S. Army Eye Dispensary, Washington, DC
15 June 1942	Promoted to Major
1 July 1942	Ophthalmologist, General Dispensary, Washington, DC
16 January 1943	Student, Medical Field Service School Officer Candidate Class. Carlisle Barracks, PA
16 March 1943	Graduated from Medical Field Service School Carlisle Barracks, PA

Date	Activity
17 March 1943	Eye specialist, Woodrow Wilson General Hospital and Walter Reed Hospital, Washington, DC
1944?	Promoted to Lt. Col.
23 September 1944	Appointed Commander, of proposed 96th Field Hospital, CBI
6 October 1944	96th Field Hospital, CBI, officially established at Camp Barkley, TX
11 December 1944	Assigned to Camp Barkley, TX. Hospital Administration Training at the Medical Administrative Officer Candidate School
27 Jan 1945	Left camp Barkley, TX for Camp Anza, Ca
6 FEBRUARY THRU 12	**NOVEMBER 1945 MACMILLAN'S DIARY**
6 Feb 1945	Arrived Wilmington, CA, POL staging area for transport across Pacific to India
7 February 1945	Left for India on the *General W. A. Mann.*
15 February 1945	Crossed equator
10 March 1945	Arrived Bombay, India
14 March 1945	Arrived Calcutta, India
21 June 1945	Arrived Ledo, India
1 July 1945	Arrived Myitkyina, Burma
5 July 1945	Arrived Wanting, China near Burma-China border
10 July 1945	Arrived Kunming, China
9 August 1945	Arrived Liuchow, China
18 September 1945	Arrived Shanghai, China
12 November 1945	Left Shanghai on *USS Hocking* for San Francisco
8 December 1945	Student, Officer Training, Valley Forge Army Hospital, PA
10 August 1946	Released from Active Duty
1946-September 1950	Private ophthalmology practice, Pittsburgh, PA Active in Army Reserve Resided: Oakmont, (Pittsburgh suburb), PA
1948-1950?	President, Reserve Officer Association

Date	Activity
9 March 1950	Promoted to Col
5 August 1950	Called up for active duty service, Korean War
24 August 1950	CO, 371st Convalescent Center, Fr. Lewis, WA
4 September 1950	CO, Madigan General Hospital, Fr. Lewis, WA
24 October 1951	CO, Nara Station Hospital, Nara, Japan
27 November 1951	Chief, EENT Service, Osaka Army Hospital, Osaka, Japan
1 June 1952	CO, 8169th Army hospital, Camp Zama, Japan
23 April 1954	Awarded Legion of Merit
10 May 1954	Chief, EENT Section, 9963d Training Unit, Valley Forge Army Hospital, Phoenixville, PA
1 July 1959	Sailed to France with family
7 July 1959	CO, 34th General Hospital Orleans, France
27 August 1962	CO, and Post Surgeon, US Army Hospital, Ft. Jackson, SC
1962 (approx.)	Resided: Lakeshore Dr., Columbia, SC
31 August 1964	Retired from active service from the Army
31 August 1964	Awarded, Army Commendation Award
1984 (approx.) to death	Resided: Plantation Estates, Mathews, NC Hobbies: Golfing, photography
19 December 1994	Died, Mathews, Mecklenburg County, NC at age 90

ENDNOTES

---

[1] Biographical information from National Personnel Records Center, National Archives, Saint Louis, MO; family records; and news clippings from *Pittsburgh Post Gazette.*

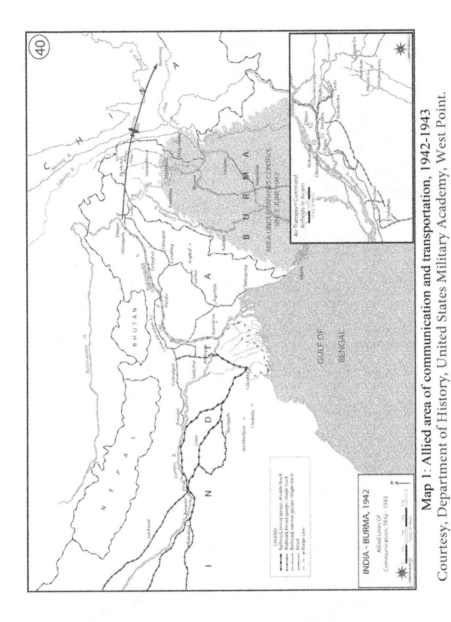

Map 1: Allied area of communication and transportation, 1942-1943
Courtesy, Department of History, United States Military Academy, West Point.

Map 1: Allied Lines of Communication

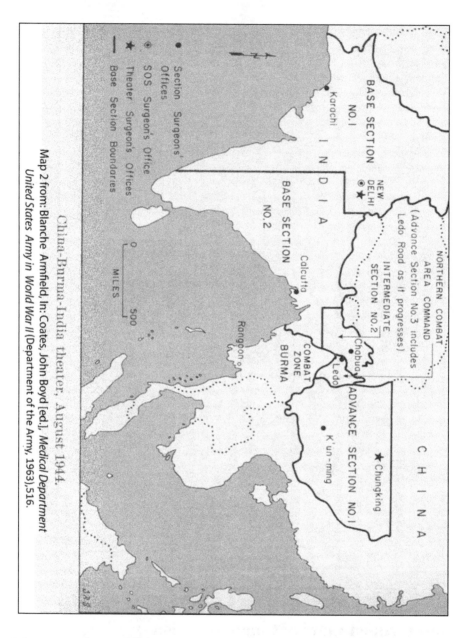

China-Burma-India theater, August 1944.
Map 2 from: Blanche Armfield, In: Coates, John Boyd [ed.], *Medical Department United States Army in World War II* (Department of the Army, 1963),516.

Map 2: Medical Command Offices C-B-I Theater

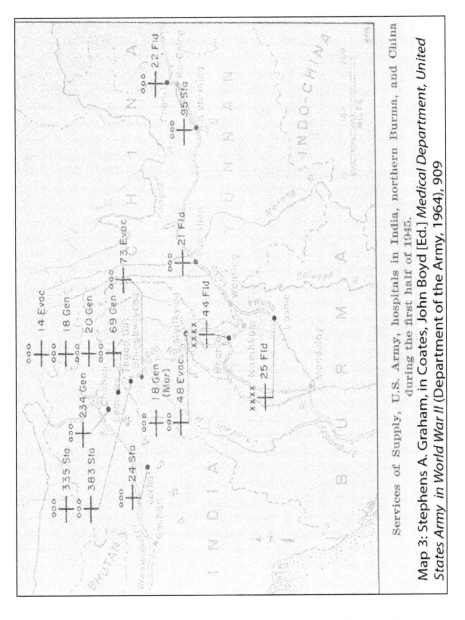

Services of Supply, U.S. Army, hospitals in India, northern Burma, and China during the first half of 1945.

Map 3: Stephens A. Graham, in Coates, John Boyd [Ed.] *Medical Department, United States Army in World War II* (Department of the Army, 1964), 909

Map 3: Service of Supply Locations in the C-B-I Theater

249

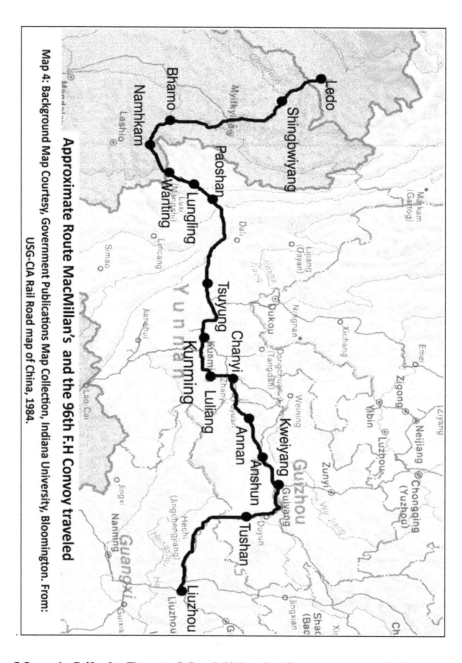

Map 4: Likely Route MacMillan's Convoy traveled

Index